THE BRITISH WILDLIFE YEAR

Other titles by the author

A Patch Made in Heaven

THE BRITISH WILDLIFE YEAR

DOMINIC COUZENS

HIGH LIFE HIGHLAND	
3800 15 0036629 3	
Askews & Holts	Oct-2015
508.41	£18.99

ROBERT HALE • LONDON

ISBN 978-0-7198-1185-2

Robert Hale Limited
Clerkenwell House
Clerkenwell Green
London EC1R 0HT

www.halebooks.com

A catalogue record for this book is available from the British Library

10 9 8 7 6 5 4 3 2 1

Designed by Dave Jones
Printed in India

Dedicated to three friends who passed away in 2014

Ron Kettle, treasured mentor

Richard Hanson, who introduced me to my future wife

Chris Parnell, fellow birder on the same local patch

CONTENTS

Introduction 9

January 11

February 26

March 40

April 57

May 79

June 101

July 123

August 145

September 165

October 182

November 200

December 217

Additional useful contacts 234

Further reading 235

Picture credits 235

Index 236

INTRODUCTION

This book is a celebration of Britain's wildlife through the seasons. It follows a typical year and, week by week, describes what is about and what can be seen by most people with a little time to look. If you want to know when the blackbird in your garden is laying its eggs, when an orange-tip butterfly is most likely to be flying and what is particularly worth looking out for in the third week of August, this is the book for you. It covers a whole range of wildlife, trees and flowers, farming and landscape, in the manner of a diary describing the changing countryside.

This book seeks to be different to others of its ilk. Firstly, it attempts to describe, where possible, what is going on with more precision than usual – noting what week, rather than what month, something is likely to happen. This includes such well-measured happenings as mammals giving birth and butterflies or moths hatching out. Naturally, there will be some variation from year to year, but using average timings helps us to appreciate what might be going on.

Another big difference from other such wildlife books is that there is an emphasis on what might be happening *locally* each week of the year. Other books are full of details about what exciting events might be happening in far-flung corners of Britain, but on the whole I have tried to select events that most people can see relatively locally. So, for example, I recommend looking out for bees pollinating flowers, enjoying the antics of birds on garden feeders, searching out daffodils and watching moths coming to lights – these sorts of encounters are preferred to kayaking for basking sharks and going to Shetland to seek out orcas. Inevitably, there are some more exotic recommendations, but generally I have tried to put the spotlight on what is well within reach for most people in Britain.

Just as the countryside exhibits appreciable changes from month to month, so do the lives of its inhabitants. On the whole, animals show specific seasons for breeding, moulting, hibernating and so on. This book gives monthly 'diaries' for a small range of common and popular animals: hedgehogs, badgers, grey squirrels, blue tits and common frogs.

This book also covers the whole spread of British habitats, from the seashore to upland moorland and everything in between. There is a section on the wildlife highlights for nine core British habitats for every month of the year, so that if you wish to know what to look for on the seashore in November, or by a river in February, you will get some idea. These sections are not exhaustive, but at least ensure that everywhere is covered in the book every month.

There are about 63,000 non-microscopic species of animals and plants on the British list, including the worms, algae, snails, flies and so on. Of necessity, therefore, any book like this can only give a sketchy idea of what inhabits every pore, every nook and cranny of Britain. Naturally, I have selected mostly the groups, such as birds, mammals, insects and plants that people generally come across, and make no apology for this. There is some information on reptiles, amphibians, fish, some molluscs and non-flowering plants, though perhaps not enough to satisfy their respective fans. Many of these branches of natural history are delightful cul-de-sacs of enthusiasm and learning which deserve a visit, even by a casual wildlife watcher. I hope readers of this book will follow some unexpected paths.

As I write this introduction, snow is on the ground here in southern England and the birds are flocking to the feeders. In just a few weeks, however, the picture will be so different – with verdant hedgerows and humming insects – that it could almost come from a different country. So, while many parts of the world have much more variety to their wildlife than us, we have the advantage of a wider range of settings in which to see it. That's part of the joy of living in Britain. I hope this books act as a companion to the wildly changing seasons and landscapes in all parts of our islands.

There is a word to describe the study of how wildlife changes through the seasons, and it is 'phenology'. Phenology describes the specifics of our annual life cycle – from the first flowering blackthorn to the last strains of song from a mistle thrush. In Britain the beating heart of phenology resides at the Woodland Trust. They maintain the Nature's Calendar website and undertake country-wide surveys of a variety of animals and plants in which anybody can take part. If you enjoy spotting the first catkins and the first leaf fall, let them know (www.woodlandtrust.org.uk).

DOMINIC COUZENS
Dorset

JANUARY

Birds such as blue tits start singing in December, and by the end of January there will be an appreciable chorus

INTRODUCTION

The New Year is not an entirely false concept in the natural world, except that it comes a week or two late. The winter solstice marks the shortest day of the year on 21–3 December, and the increasing daylight is a giant organic trigger for all kinds of natural systems: bird song, plant-flowering, leaf-budding. All are affected by temperature, but their primary driver is the length of the day, so it is a new start indeed.

That said, the countryside often looks dormant around this time. The trees are bare, the frosty air doesn't throb with flying insects, the vegetation is rough around the edges and bird song is subdued. However, the latter increases considerably as the month goes on, until by the end there is an appreciable dawn chorus. And a surprising number of invertebrates are still active. Honey bees don't hibernate, ant colonies are still busy, and within the soil it is almost business as usual. Dig down deep enough and the commonly found worms, beetle larvae, centipedes and so on are still around. The same applies to tree-boring invertebrates.

Many invertebrates do, however, avoid the winter in various ways. Ladybirds become torpid and may 'hibernate' indoors, as do some adult butterflies. Many other invertebrates simply pass the winter in a non-moving lifecycle stage such as an egg or pupa. Snails may plug the opening of their shells with mucus.

Although many well-known bird characters migrate to Africa, just as many species arrive from the continent to spend the winter here, so there is always something interesting going on for the birder. As for mammals, a small number hibernate – bats, dormice and hedgehogs – while others keep a very low profile, including shrews, badgers and weasels. Most, though, are still around, and several are in the middle of their breeding season, including squirrels, foxes and **wild boar**.

Weather-wise it is generally cool, wet and windy. Temperatures across England have an average minimum of 1.3°C, with only February being colder; in Scotland January is the coldest month, with an average low of -0.2°C. (The coldest air temperature ever recorded in the UK was -27.2°C in Scotland in 1982.) It is often very wet; indeed, in Scotland it is the wettest month of the year, while in England and Wales it isn't as bad as December.

In northern Scotland and the Pennines there is usually a covering of snowfall throughout the month. Storms whisking in polar air quite often bring blizzard-like conditions to the Highlands. The rest of the country only experiences snow intermittently, but long periods of below-freezing temperatures have a significant impact on wildlife, including birds and small mammals. In settled conditions with high pressure, frost and fog can be widespread.

HEDGEHOG DIARY: In January hedgehogs should be hibernating in a nest made of leaves, lodged under a thick bush, a log, a pile of brushwood or sometimes the floor of a shed. The nest is about 50 cm in diameter. These spiny characters are among very few British mammals that actually hibernate – that is, true hibernation, in which the body temperature falls drastically (in this case from 35°C to 10°C) along with a reduction in other bodily functions, including heart and breathing rate. Hibernation saves energy at a time when there is little food about to keep the animal going.

BADGER DIARY: It's a quiet start to the year for badgers. They spend much of their time underground in the sett, especially when it is frosty outside, and can be difficult to see.

GREY SQUIRREL DIARY: The calendar year starts off with a bang for squirrels, because this is their peak breeding season. Watch out for courtship chases, in which individuals will race along the ground and among the branches, often spiralling around tree trunks. Over and over again, several males will chase a single receptive female, often for hours. In between the many rounds of a pursuit the males chatter loudly, flick their tails and may even slap the bark with their front paws. Just one male will win the right to mate – presumably the individual with the greatest stamina!

BLUE TIT DIARY: The beginning of the year is tough for blue tits; the days are pitifully short and the abundant crops of autumn are in decline. Individuals bicker at bird feeders, or travel further afield, for example, to reed beds. Yet curiously, those individuals still surviving show a surprising amount of breeding activity. Males sing with vigour on mild days, and pairs – especially those that bred last year – are spending more time together.

COMMON FROG DIARY: For most of the month frogs are tucked up in their hibernation sites, either close to the water under a rock, or sometimes in mud at the bottom of a pond (they survive by taking oxygen in through the skin). Towards the end of the month, however, if it is mild, some adults will emerge early.

MONTHLY HIGHLIGHTS: GARDEN

Whatever the weather, nothing stops the gradual increase in the babble of bird song during January. I myself have heard a **great tit** singing when it was -12°C outside and there were several inches of snow on the ground, the songster boldly defying the weather. And, apart from the inevitable push of the shoots of snowdrops, crocuses and daffodils through the frosty soil, nothing is quite so subversive to the grip of winter, each wild voice defiant.

The great tit may sing even before December is over, but the main flush of song is towards January's end. The phrase is easy to identify, a cheerful repeating of two notes: 'Teach-er, teach-er, teach-er.' The chiming sound is slightly strained but invariably cheerful. One moment a great tit will be singing from a treetop, the next it will be down at the hanging feeders, bullying and harrying.

Blue tits are equally tough characters, but they may not start singing until the very last days of the month. **Coal tits**, which have a similar song to the great tit, but less rasping and sweeter, only get going in February.

Another song you are almost certain to hear is that of the **song thrush**. Much is made of this bird's decline in gardens over the last forty years, and while this is undoubtedly real it does not mean that the bird is rare. Far from it – most suburban areas should host a pair or two of these attractive spotty-breasted birds. The thrush is perhaps overlooked because of its retiring habits and because it tends to sing both early in the year and early in the day, when fewer people are tuned in. But its voice can dominate a late winter morning. Listen for loud, strident phrases delivered at a relaxed pace with a perfect broadcaster's enunciation, and above all recognize that each phrase is repeated several times.

In the words of Robert Browning's *Home Thoughts from Abroad*:

*That's the wise thrush; he sings each phrase
    thrice over,
Lest you should think he never could recapture
The first fine careless rapture!*

In more prosaic terms: if you hear a loud song you can't identify in early spring, it's most probably that of a song thrush.

Try to keep listening day after day, because you are certain to pick up other voices. The **dunnock**, for example, is not a well-known singer, but it is a very common garden bird that tends to start up in mid-January. At some time in your garden you will almost certainly have heard its sweet but limited, somewhat cyclical phrase, which sounds a little like the squeaky wheels of a moving supermarket trolley, but recognizing it is never easy.

Quite naturally, January is not a month when you are going to drool over the variety of flowers, but spare a thought for tough weeds that dare to creep into the untidy corners of your lawn or flower bed. A few **daisies** and **dandelions** will be growing strong, as will **common chickweed** and **petty spurge**.

January isn't a great month for flying insects, either, but some of the species that hibernate might be tempted out on a mild day. I myself have seen a **brimstone butterfly** in the first week of January, an incongruous sight among the bare branches and deserted borders.

On mild nights, there is a small selection of macro-moths that a dedicated trapper might catch. These include **red-green carpet**, **autumn green carpet**, **tissue**, **winter moth**, **pale brindled beauty**, **early moth**, **brindled ochre**, **tawny pinion**, **pale pinion**, **grey shoulder-knot**, **red sword-grass**, **sword-grass**, **satellite**, **orange upperwing**, **chestnut**, **dark chestnut**, **dotted chestnut**, **angle shades**, **oak nycteoline**, **silver Y**, **herald**, **buttoned snout** and **Bloxworth snout**.

The spring usher flies between January and March. In fact, only the male flies; the female is entirely wingless.

MONTHLY HIGHLIGHTS: WOODLAND

If there is anywhere you can pretend it is spring at this time of year, it would have to be woodland. Not many of the flowers will be open, but the shoots of snowdrops will appear, if not a few early flowers, and the green leaves of such plants as **dog's mercury**

In many areas, hazel catkins are the first unequivocal sign of spring.

will already be growing strong. However, the most encouraging sign could be the flowers of **hazel**. This small tree is a pioneer in many ways, having been second only to the birch in colonizing our islands after the last Ice Age. Metaphorically, it is defying ice and snow again, sending out its hanging 'lamb's tail' catkins of delicate green. You cannot see them without feeling glad and excited.

There are a few other plants about. The rare **stinking hellebore** flowers for the first time. If you had to survive in a January woodland it wouldn't be easy, but at least you might find some **oyster mushroom** and **velvet shank**, two fungi to keep you alive.

MONTHLY HIGHLIGHTS: FARMLAND

On the farm, dairy cattle are housed indoors while beef cattle are typically kept in open barns with copious barley straw bedding.

Lapwings feed on worms and other soil creatures. Snow and sharp frosts may cause them to evacuate their wintering sites in search of somewhere warmer and damper.

Most flocks of sheep will do fine outside, even in harsh conditions, if they are fed with supplementary food such as bales of hay or sugar beet. Supplementary food and bedding is also given to pigs.

A hard frost can be useful in January, because it will allow the farmer to spread slurry. Meanwhile, early ploughing will be useful for getting the soil ready for spring-sown cereal crops.

It might seem very surprising, but on mild January days it is possible to hear **skylarks** singing. Many people associate skylarks so much with the summer that they think larks migrate away, but instead they tend to gather in quiet flocks, feeding on the ground and keeping their heads down. At night they roost in the open, in small depressions in the field.

On the other hand, if the weather is cold, many farmland birds may be forced away, making emergency escape movements. Skylarks and thrushes will evacuate in flocks and both **lapwings** and **golden plovers** will make their way to estuaries to escape the frost, ice and snow.

In January thrushes such as **redwing**, **fieldfare** and song thrush may undertake short movements (usually less than 20 km) to find food, meaning that flocks or high numbers can appear in fields literally over-night.

MONTHLY HIGHLIGHTS: SCRUB AND THICKET

Wispy **traveller's joy** may be a dominant feature of the lowlands on chalky soil.

Magpies often start to build their nest on fine January days, bringing in sticks to make their large, domed construction. Those that begin construction (or refurbishment) so early are usually settled pairs that live in their territory all year. They begin early and progress in leisurely fashion, and as a result they construct a top-class nest in comparison to birds that begin later.

MONTHLY HIGHLIGHTS: GRASSLAND AND ROADSIDES

Grassland and verges look messy and tired in January. Apart from grass, there are remnants of last year's plants, such as the proud stems of **teasel**. Look out for the leaves of **silverweed**, still obvious in places. A few typical weeds are always in bloom, and include **groundsel**, **common field speedwell** and **grey field speedwell**.

It is a poor season for chalk grassland. However, look out for the leaves of **carline thistle**, which always look dead even when they are alive.

A road trip in January will almost always bring view of **rabbits**, and **brown hares** are just as hardy – the bare fields and paucity of vegetation can make these browsers easier to spot than usual. In the mornings and afternoons look out for **roe** and **fallow deer** grazing in fields.

MONTHLY HIGHLIGHTS: HEATHLAND, MOORLAND AND UPLAND

Gorse is in flower, but not much else. The scene is often dominated by ubiquitous **purple moor-grass** and, in wet areas, by colourful *Sphagnum* mosses.

None of the habitats in this section is very hospitable in winter. On heathland, however, look for the smart **stonechat**, which still hangs on making a meagre living among the heather and gorse. It is a partial migrant, with most upland and moorland birds moving to the coast or southward for the winter.

Up on moors the **red grouse** scratches a living by eating the shoots and other parts of heather. Red grouse are in flocks at the moment, and you might well flush some out as you walk the fells and hillsides in upland districts.

MONTHLY HIGHLIGHTS: RIVERS

January is not a bad time to look for **otter** and **American mink**. If you are really lucky, **polecats** have a habit of hunting by rivers, too, but even many avid mammal-watchers have never set eyes on this species.

On the whole, fish will be in the deeper stretches of water. Even species that don't appear to be migratory will often make movements to suitable overwintering waters. And they won't just be in deep water, they will be sluggish, too. Anglers look forward to better times ahead.

The pike looks fearsome and it is, eating a wide range of prey including smaller fish, ducklings, newts, frogs, small mammals – and even its own kind. Now is the main 'pike season' for anglers.

Having said that, January is a month for catching **pike**.

Bird-wise, kingfishers should be in evidence on slow rivers and **dippers** and **grey wagtails** on fast-flowing rivers. Also, look for **wrens**, which appreciate the dense riparian vegetation.

MONTHLY HIGHLIGHTS: LAKES, PONDS AND FRESHWATER MARSHES

Occasionally, **great crested grebes** lay eggs in January, if it is mild. On the other hand, if there are periods of frost and snow, birds such as **grey herons**, **moorhens** and **coots** may be displaced from smaller bodies of water and crowd into lakes or reservoirs.

There is one bird singing in the reed beds, albeit a localized one. The **Cetti's warbler** can sing at any time of year, but January sees an increase in levels. The song is loud and explosive, rather like a cut-price nightingale, but the phrases end quickly.

Bitterns may also start making their remarkable 'booming' sounds in January, usually from very large reed beds. The sound is similar to a person blowing over the top of an open beer-bottle. Males establish their territories by sound, and each male's 'boom' is slightly different to those of its peers. If you listen carefully, you may be able to discern the 'boom' of different bitterns.

MONTHLY HIGHLIGHTS: COAST AND ESTUARY

Perhaps surprisingly, several seabirds are already at their colonies at this time of year. Most noticeably, **guillemots** have

WEEK ONE Chasing Wild Geese

One of the many excesses of Christmas tends to be too much of the indoors. This trip helps you to get out, get your cheeks rosy and your fingers chilled and, with luck, experience one of the very best sights and sounds that Britain has to offer.

Your target today will be geese, but these are not the farmyard kind. Several different species breed in the Arctic during the summer and migrate south in family parties. For their winter quarters they require somewhere cool and damp, somewhere that won't be too snowbound or ridden by hard frosts. Fitting that profile perfectly, our islands are a haven for geese, one of the best winter locations in the world. Incidentally, geese also need a food supply while they are here, but these grazers are hardly fussy: grass will do, or crop potatoes and other arable foodstuffs. Again, we have these in abundance.

The other requirement that wild geese have is a safe, sheltered place to go to sleep at night, and this means the calm waters of an estuary, a quiet coastline or a large inland marsh or lake. If the countryside offers both, the geese will come and stay between October and March. Places to look for them are listed on page 22.

The idea of this expedition isn't, however, to see wild geese as much as to experience them, and to do this you are aiming to catch them at a particular point of their day. Every dawn, geese fly from their roosting sites (e.g. a lake or coast) to their feeding sites (inland on fields); and then at dusk they do the reverse. In both cases, large flocks can often be seen flying between one and the other. This is a magnificent sight. The birds often rise high (except for brent geese), and they invariably fly in formation, in Vs or Ws, and any number of other combinations. It would be a little fanciful to say that they write messages in the sky, but actually it isn't far off the mark. And, of course, owing to their time of flight, if you catch them on a sunny day they often move against the red sky of twilight. It is a spine-tingling sight, and for a moment you can forget the raw cold nipping at your fingers.

If that was all that there was to it, a wild goose-chase would be satisfying enough. However, there is also the matter of the sound of wild voices. To keep together, geese call. If it's a small flock, the noises are high-pitched and tinny; in larger numbers, the sound is more musical; when huge numbers fly over, there is an impressive roar. The precise sounds vary between species. My favourites are the **pink-footed geese** and **white-fronted geese**, which mix together nasal 'ang-ang' and musical, excited 'wick-wick' calls. Whichever species you hear, they always sound excited, and incredibly wild.

Goose commuting doesn't last long, just half an hour or so of twilight. The memories of large numbers of wild geese passing over in formation, however, will stay with you for a lot longer.

Wild geese, like these greylag geese, spend the day foraging on fields or meadows, but retreat to large bodies of water at night. Witnessing their commuting is a highlight of British wildlife watching.

returned after a brief time at sea after breeding and moulting, and some will already be in breeding plumage. **Northern fulmars** hardly ever leave the vicinity of their nest-sites and can be seen in January wheeling effortlessly around the cliff-tops. **Cormorants** and **shags** might also have returned to the vicinity of the breeding areas; the former are already acquiring white thigh colouring, and the shags their crests.

There will also be some birds present at **gannet** colonies, as there are in every month except December. These large seabirds will otherwise be patrolling the shallow seas of the Continental shelf, and can be seen at any time. They are often blown within sight of land by onshore winds.

Brent goose numbers reach a peak on most British estuaries in January and, often grazing alongside them, so do those of **wigeon**. They often feed on **eel-grass**, one of the few marine flowering plants in the world. Estuaries teem with birds throughout the winter, as do many other parts of the coast.

It's pretty much business as usual on the foreshore. Most of the usual rock-pool creatures are around just as much in January as they are in August. It's just that you get colder looking for them!

WEEK TWO A Conservation Task

The New Year is a time of resolutions, so how about this one? At one stage this year, join in a conservation task. To keep the resolution, you only need do it once, which could mean as little as a couple of hours in 365 days. On the other hand, it could open up all sorts of new avenues to explore and enjoy.

What is a conservation task? The idea is to volunteer yourself for practical work on a nature reserve or open space. All over the country reserves tend to require more practical management than the paid wardens can undertake by themselves, or even with contractors. Many nature reserves, therefore, encourage a network of volunteers to help with various activities, such as rooting out saplings and scrub, mending fences, digging ditches, filling paths and tracks, and so on. A good example is on southern heathlands, where encroachment by trees effectively destroys the habitat over time. Without management of such habitats, biodiversity would suffer.

You may or may not enjoy weeding or bush-bashing, but this is just one example among hundreds of supervised tasks. All of them benefit the environment, though, and they also benefit the volunteer; physical work outside, often in the company of like-minded people, is the usual recipe. On your average task there is a notable mixture of ages, backgrounds and temperaments.

You don't need any qualifications to be a conservation volunteer, but you might find yourself acquiring qualifications as a result: many organizations, including the National Trust and the National Trust for Scotland, run courses to teach skills to volunteers. You might discover an unexpected aptitude for dry-stone walling, for example, and for young people, in particular, volunteering can put a great deal of meat on a CV. Indeed, at present very few people will enter the professional conservation organizations without having done some appropriate volunteering first.

However, for the purposes of this diary, whatever your age and time of life, simply choose to do some voluntary work for conservation – or at least enquire about it. True, January is not the ideal month for working outside, but if you can tolerate it in the frost or damp, you are probably cut out for it.

A good source for information on volunteering is http://www.tcv.org.uk.

Everyone should make the effort to see a large starling roost; it is one of the great wonders of British wildlife. Many of the birds involved will be immigrants from other parts of Europe and Russia.

Great sites for geese:

- Solway Firth, Cumbria/Dumfries and Galloway
- Slimbridge, Gloucestershire
- North Norfolk
- Longstone Harbour, Hampshire
- Islay, Argyll and Bute
- Northumberland coast
- Montrose basin, Angus
- Loch Leven, Portland and Kinross
- Loch of Strathberg, Aberdeenshire

WEEKLY HIGHLIGHTS: WEEK ONE

- First **red squirrel** pregnancies
- **Mistle thrush** can usually be heard singing from now into the spring

WEEKLY HIGHLIGHTS: WEEK TWO

- First buds and leaves of elder appear
- First hazel catkins are usually recorded
- Female foxes enter oestrus, so this is the peak time for mating
- Nuthatch starts singing
- **Green woodpecker** starts singing (listen out for the usual 'yaffle' sound but note it going down the scale)

WEEK THREE Starling Roost

In autumn and winter, starlings gather together at night to roost communally. In some places roosts can hold large numbers: frequently thousands, sometimes tens or hundreds of thousands. Many people have seen these spectacular roosts on TV, as the birds wheel about in the sky and paint living movable pictures against the setting sun, like a giant amoeba, or like bees, or whatever the excitable presenter likes to describe. It just so happens that now, in late January, is one of the best times to watch roosts, as numbers will be high. And, contrary to what you might expect, there is probably a roost not far from you that you can witness yourself. Ask somebody from your local bird club or Wildlife Trust.

Quite why starlings gather together in large murmurations isn't fully understood. It could be to reduce an individual's chance of predation (statistically, you're less likely to be singled out in a larger flock), to keep warm in a micro-climate, or perhaps as a sort of information exchange. Part of the charm of experiencing the roost is that it is still something of a mystery. Nobody knows why the birds often perform the spectacular aerial displays before they bed down, although it is thought to be a form of advertisement – 'come and join us'.

Once you have a location sorted out, all you have to do is get there half an hour before sunset and wait (beware that the birds sometimes switch location without warning). It will be a trickle at first, with small flocks coming in from all directions, sometimes from up to 50 km away. However, these flocks quickly coalesce into larger groups, which fly to and fro over the reedbed, building or patch of scrub, or wherever the roost is sited. As they fly over, you will notice that the birds don't call; the only sound is the rushing of their wings.

At their own instigation, the starlings may or may not take part in their famous weaving flights prior to settling down. It seems to depend partly upon the weather, with clear sunny conditions apparently favoured. If they do, you are truly in for a treat, without doubt one of the great wildlife spectacles of Britain, if not the world. The sky-dance doesn't go on for long, just a few minutes at most, and the darkness soon ushers the birds towards their night-time perch. Only when they settle does the murmur of bird conversation begin, as the birds chatter, sing and call. For some time they jostle and bicker, the noise rising and falling. Like teenage girls on a sleep-over, they seem to get little sleep, and the chatter goes on all night, long after the grateful human audience has slipped away.

If you are keen to witness one of the famous large flocks, here is a list of some prime locations: Ham Wall, Somerset (the largest, millions of birds); Brighton Pier, East Sussex; Gretna Green in Dumfries and Galloway; Aberystwyth Pier in Ceredigion; Newport Wetlands, Newport; Snape, Suffolk; Slimbridge, Gloucestershire; Saltholme, Middlesbrough; Blackpool Pier, Lancashire; and Fen Drayton Lakes, Cambridgeshire.

WEEK FOUR Birds on a Feeder

This week, make time to watch the birds on your garden feeder. Or, for a change, why not visit a nature reserve with a feeder (and there are many) to see some different characters? Either way, it should be a compelling experience. The very familiarity of feeders often masks what superb wildlife viewing they can provide, some of the best the country has to offer.

The comings and goings on a feeder – the tits fleeing when a larger, more powerful bird, such as a nuthatch, **greenfinch** or even a parakeet turns up, or the bullying of coal tits by many other birds – are sometimes compared to a soap opera. This description reflects the drama, but it neglects one thing; this is real life. If a feeding blue tit is displaced by a great tit, the consequences are real. Birds that are bullied at a bird table may slip down the hierarchy, become unable even to make the briefest visit, and then they starve. In cold weather, the stakes are further raised. January days are very short, and if a bird struggles at a bird feeder its very survival will be jeopardized.

No bird-table drama brings this home like a **sparrowhawk** attack. The apparent peace of the garden, with birds 'taking turns' at the feeder, is shattered when this predator appears out of nowhere, grabs a meal and disappears. The bird population is one fewer, and the speed and finality can be shocking. Enthusiasts often find this upsetting, and with good reason. It brings a cold dose of reality into the entertainment provided by other birds. Of course, from the sparrowhawk's point of view, a bird feeder is simply a reliable, rich food source, just as the nuts and scraps are a reliable, rich food source for tits and finches. If it's any consolation, a marauding sparrowhawk is actually a sign of a healthy garden bird population.

And where else are you going to see a real-life hunt and strike – a fox leaping on a vole, a **stoat** taking a rabbit, a **peregrine** striking a pigeon, perhaps? These wildlife documentary moments aren't easy to come by.

Late January is a good time to watch the bird feeders, because as food supplies such as berries and seeds run out in the woodland, so the number and variety of visitors to gardens increases towards the end of winter. So, in addition to the usual blue tits and great tits, you might find more coal tits and greenfinches coming in, spiced up if you're lucky with rarer visitors such as **bramblings** or **redpolls**. If the weather is particularly cold and frosty, the effect will be magnified, and you might also find redwings and fieldfares on the lawn if you leave out apples or other fruits.

Feeding birds these days is easy, if expensive. There is much fun to be had in trying to attract different birds with the many commercially available mixes. Recently, there has been a revolution in bird-feeding, with specialist mixes designed to cater for everything from **goldfinches** to **blackcaps**. It is a perfect way to interact positively with wild creatures.

This week in the year also coincides with the Big Garden Birdwatch, a citizen science project run by the RSPB. It has been running on the last weekend in January for more than thirty years, and is the largest wildlife survey in the world. All you do is spend an hour watching the birds in your garden (or local park) and recording the highest number of each species recorded at any one time during the hour. Send in the results to the RSPB and you will be contributing to our knowledge of bird population trends. There is also a Big Schools Birdwatch, which is a class activity of an hour's birdwatching for children. Visit www.rspb.org.uk for details.

WEEKLY HIGHLIGHTS: WEEK THREE

- **Winter aconite** begins to flower in gardens, roadsides and churchyards – often the first bloom of the year
- Many great tits now in full song
- Dunnock begins singing in earnest
- Male brown hares come on heat for the first time this year, and will remain so until about August
- Mountain hares complete their autumn moult and should now look almost pure white

WEEKLY HIGHLIGHTS: WEEK FOUR

- The first **goat willow** ('**pussy willow**') catkins appear
- **Water vole** males become virile and breeding begins
- The first rabbit pregnancies of the year occur, and many more will follow!
- Peak numbers of Russian white-fronted geese are recorded on their English wintering grounds
- The first curlews may return to their breeding grounds

FEBRUARY

Rooks are among the earliest British birds to start breeding

INTRODUCTION

February is the last official month of winter, but the season can go out with a bang. In England and Wales it is the coldest month of the year, with average minimum daytime temperatures of 1.1°C; in Scotland the average is -0.1°C, fractionally milder than January. The chilly nature of the month is partly explained by the fact that the Atlantic Ocean is at its coldest after the autumn and winter, so the effect is especially marked in coastal areas. On the other hand, other aspects of climate calm down in February compared with the rest of winter; it is usually drier and less windy. Snow is routine in Scotland and in parts of northern and eastern England.

February is often grim because the winter seems to drag on. However, anyone who spends time outside can hardly miss the fact that days are getting longer. Sunrise is approximately an hour earlier at the end of the month than at the beginning, and sunset is about an hour later. February is a proper winter month, but from time to time it seems unintentionally to lift its cloak so you can see the spring enticingly underneath.

Aside from admiring the usual snow-drops and crocuses, therefore, there are plenty of subtle springtime signs. The level of bird song may dramatically increase, in terms of individuals and species, especially at dawn. A few trees may start flowering up in their canopy, barely noticed; they include **wych elm**, aspen and alder. On farmland and moorland waders may begin setting up territory, infrequently at first. The pace of life for badgers is hot, albeit hidden in darkness. And the occasional bumblebee may make an appearance, along with a spring sprinkling of moths and butterflies.

It isn't much, and February can be bleak. But there is visible and audible proof out there that it won't last.

HEDGEHOG DIARY: Hedgehogs are still hibernating in February, but they will periodically wake up at any time during the winter and might even stroll around, especially if it is exceptionally mild. Some animals may be displaced by flooding or disturbance and, if so, are in deep trouble. Even the healthiest animals have burned deep into their winter fat reserves by now.

BADGER DIARY: This is an exciting month for badgers. Most females give birth at this time of the year and, strangely, the month also sees plenty of courtship. The anomaly is that, regardless of when mating occurs, which may be at any time of year, the fertilized egg only implants in a female badger's uterus in December, with the subsequent short gestation culminating in late winter births. The cubs are born deep in the sett and won't appear above ground until April or May. However, just after giving birth the females become irresistible to the boars, who will make loud purring and 'whickering' noises as they fuss over them. The excitement can be heard from a considerable distance on still nights.

GREY SQUIRREL DIARY: Some mating chases continue (see January), but most females are already pregnant. Their attention will turn to building a drey for their litter, usually a slightly larger construction than the usual nest. By month's end, some females have already given birth.

BLUE TIT DIARY: The old adage about birds needing to be paired up by Valentine's Day has some truth to it; most blue tits do indeed have partners by month's end, and if they don't they will need to sort this out quickly. Having spent much time in the last few months joining flocks during the day, males are now focused on staying put, singing to defend their territories. Listen for a silvery, high-pitched trill. It is also well worth looking out for the blue tit's display, although it is subtle: a bird will simply fly more or less horizontally from one branch to another, but with an exaggerated, moth-like flight with super-fast, whirring wing-beats.

COMMON FROG DIARY: During February most of the frog population emerges from hibernation and, without much of a pause for breath, begins to breed. From the second week there might already be a chorus of quiet croaks, as males compete for attention from females.

MONTHLY HIGHLIGHTS: GARDEN

Flowers adorn the garden in the form of snowdrops, crocuses, forsythia and magnolias. They are a comfort to those desperate for spring.

February is an excellent month for garden visitors to the bird table. The supply of seeds or nuts in the wider countryside has been dwindling since the autumn, so birds such as **siskins**, **bullfinches** and redpolls may visit stations where they have been absent previously.

As mentioned last month, the garden is surprisingly full of bird song at this time of year, although the chorus can be dampened by particularly harsh spells of weather. In February, two common garden birds, which have hitherto been silent except for a few speculative, under-the-breath ramblings, begin to perform in earnest. One of these is the **chaffinch**, a species that has such a simple phrase that you can actually tell when the performer is out of practice and needs to polish up. To our ears the male simply repeats a single, zestful, chattering, accelerating phrase, which ends in a flourish. This is repeated over and over again, until by March and April it can be heard hundreds of times a day.

The other major singer that starts in February is the much-loved blackbird. True, it will sometimes sing quietly in January or even December, especially during the twilight, but in terms of being heard with enough power to fill a neighbourhood, February is the time. The song is gorgeous.

The Hebrew character is a very common moth well known to those who run light-traps in the garden. It is as much a sign of spring as a swallow or cuckoo.

It has longer phrases that that of the song thrush, with very little repetition, and when in full voice the song is fulsomely tuneful, indeed artful. It also has a tone that could almost be called reassuring, such is its effortless delivery. As far as this writer is concerned, I would prefer an evening of blackbird song even to that of a nightingale.

Not many butterflies are on the wing, but on mild days some may be aroused from hibernation, far more often than in January. Likely candidates include the gaudy and much-loved trio of **red admiral**, **small tortoiseshell** and **peacock**. Owing to the fact that gardens are good places for spring flowers, this makes them the most likely places to see these insects.

Meanwhile, the only consolation for moth trappers is that February is marginally better than January or December. Those that are usually recorded in February but not January include **small eggar**, **small brindled beauty**, **spring usher** and **dotted border**.

MONTHLY HIGHLIGHTS: WOODLAND

Some woods are carpeted by snowdrops, but even in their absence the woodland floor is not the same. Look out for violets, celandines, **wood sorrel**, dog's mercury and the arrow-shaped leaves of **lords-and-ladies**.

The gradual increase in bird song witnessed in gardens and in the wider countryside is every bit as pronounced in woodland, and as a bonus there is often a wider variety. And one sound that is more misunderstood than many is the sharp 'drumming' noise of the **great spotted woodpecker**. Easily heard echoing through the bare branches, the brief drum-roll is often thought to be the sound made when the bird is pecking at wood to get food. Not a bit of it! In common with the more musical bird sounds currently broadcasting, this is actually a form of advertisement. The bird selects a special piece of bark for its sonorous quality, and simply raps its bill against it with the deliberate intention of making a sound – just as a drummer does in a concert. No damage is done to the tree and no food is procured, but the woodpecker makes a territorial point to its peers and any potential mate. Of course, woodpeckers do make a noise when they are trying to pick through wood, but then it is a fitful tapping sound, often quite soft and not of broadcast quality.

Crossbills may begin to breed in spruce woods. They feed their young entirely on regurgitated seeds.

Sweet violets begin to flower, the earliest of various species of violet. They are easily distinguished by their strong, sweet scent, lacking in all the other species, such as **dog violets** (the epithet 'dog' tends to mean 'worthless', compared to a useful relative). The oil of sweet violets is still used in perfumery and has been since the time of the Ancient Greeks. In the Middle Ages the flowers were spread over floors as a form of deodorant. One of the compounds in the flowers, ionine, temporarily desensitizes the nostrils.

Dog's mercury could already be carpeting the woodland floor, but far more conspicuously with its oval, slightly toothed leaves than with its nettle-like spikes of yellow-green flowers. It is mainly found in ancient woodland and old hedgerows, but can dominate the woodland floor. It is quite poisonous (the epithet 'dog' was given by the ancients to dangerous as well as useless plants).

MONTHLY HIGHLIGHTS: FARMLAND

Quiet days in January or February are excellent for undertaking general farm maintenance, including repairing fences and overhauling farm vehicles.

Some flocks of sheep will lamb in January or February. This may happen outside, in which case the lambs and ewe are quickly housed, or the ewe may be brought in for a pregnancy scan first.

If you see a tractor working the fields, mid- to late February is usually considered to be the prime time for drilling spring cereals such as barley and wheat.

Some lapwings return to their breeding fields this month, and may even be seen displaying on mild days.

Gulls are often around in full force. If there is a tractor working the land, it will probably attract a contingent mainly drawn from two species, the **black-headed gull** and the **common gull**.

Meanwhile, **lesser black-backed gulls** begin to migrate overland towards their breeding sites, and can be seen flying over farmland in small flocks.

MONTHLY HIGHLIGHTS: SCRUB AND THICKET

There is a paucity of fruits available at this time of the year. However, **crab apples** are long-lasting even when fallen, and birds will mop up those that remain during February.

Wych elm comes into flower. This is a common hedgerow tree with small reddish-purple flowers very closely attached to the twigs. The diminutive but numerous blooms give the tree a reddish hue. This is the only species of elm that regularly reaches maturity in Britain.

MONTHLY HIGHLIGHTS: GRASSLAND AND ROADSIDES

Mistletoe comes into flower, although it is difficult to see the small yellow blooms high in the deciduous trees (usually limes, hawthorns, poplars, maples and willows) on which it leads a semi-parasitic life. It is probably easiest to see from the road than anywhere else, usually inhabiting lines of trees along field edges, or individual trees in the open. The white fruits enable the seeds to be spread when eaten by birds, especially mistle thrushes.

Although grasslands often look dead at this time of the year, they still play host to high densities of small mammals, notably the **field vole** (which doesn't hibernate and pretty much eats grass all year), but also **bank voles**, **wood mice** and shrews, plus rats in some places. These small mammals are much sought after by several predatory birds, including kestrels. In the evening, both the **short-eared owl** and, especially, the **barn owl**, can easily be seen hunting over fields with their low, wavering flight. In winter they will often come out well before sunset.

MONTHLY HIGHLIGHTS: HEATHLAND, MOORLAND AND UPLAND

Spring comes slowly to all three of these habitats, and it truthfully isn't much different to January.

In the uplands, however, there is one major special that begins flowering in late

February, the **purple saxifrage**. It forms low dense mats of attractive purple blooms on cliffs and rock ledges.

Bank voles are common prey species of many raptors, such as barn owls, especially throughout the hungry winter months.

MONTHLY HIGHLIGHTS: RIVERS

Several riverine fish spawn for the first time in February. This includes the well-known pike. The females move to well-vegetated waters, where several males gather and compete for attention. If things go badly, the female may eat one or more of her suitors; pike have a reputation for cannibalism.

Other fish spawning for the first time now include the dace. An early start allows the juveniles to take advantage of the spring flush of food in rivers. Dace are found in clean, swiftly-flowing rivers.

MONTHLY HIGHLIGHTS: LAKES, PONDS AND FRESHWATER MARSHES

Alder may come into flower towards the end of the month, producing small male catkins that are profuse and deep reddish, giving an unmistakable tint to the tree. The small woody cones produced last year are still present, too, giving alder its characteristic dense appearance.

Grey herons are very active at the moment. They are early breeders and are now earnestly nest-building, usually

Lakes can be chilly places to look for winter wildlife, but are surprisingly busy, even this early in the year.

constructing large stick nests high in trees close to the water.

This month **Bewick's swans** from Arctic Russia will begin to leave Britain on a long journey east and north, stopping off for many weeks en route.

MONTHLY HIGHLIGHTS: COAST AND ESTUARY

February is an excellent month to see various species of seaducks (**eiders**, **common** and **velvet scoters**, **red-breasted mergansers**

etc.) offshore, almost anywhere in Britain. They often gather in large flocks, and males may display to any passing females.

Some **ringed plovers** are already on territory on beaches and will perform short flight-displays. Many hundreds, on the other hand, will be sharing the estuarine mud with a range of other wintering waders.

Making a contrast to the tired and faded colours of the coast, **alexanders** provides a breath of fresh green. It begins flowering next month (it's like a yellow form of **cow parsley**) but has already

WEEK ONE Snowdrop Displays

The end of winter can drag, and if truth be told the snowdrop is not really a spring flower, but a 'promise of spring' flower. Sometimes, when the grip of cold seems particularly reluctant to relent as the weeks go by, we need these plants to remind us that warmer times are inevitable. Fitted with a protective sheath that shields the flower tips as they pierce the frosty or snow-ridden ground, these plants force their way into the late winter air: one of their country nicknames is 'snow piercer'. And it's true that they do indeed mark the first piercing of winter's blanket over the countryside.

Snowdrops, and the promise they bring, are widely celebrated, and this particular week usually marks the start of the admiration. Snowdrop festivals crop up everywhere from Dorset to Scotland, in places where large numbers dot the lawns, woodlands and riverbanks in their characteristic unruly manner, scattered and undisciplined. It is well worth going to such festivals, just to get the inevitable lift of the spirits. Most people would confess that snowdrops are not particularly impressive, either close up or in large clumps. Members of the onion family, they are hardly tall, nod downwards, are subtly rather than glaringly white and have a green V-mark on the petals (tepals). But none of this matters; the charm of snowdrops is what they represent.

The start of the snowdrop season coincides with the Catholic festival of Candelmas. The white of the plants is symbolic of purity. Not surprisingly, many of the best clumps can be found near monasteries, churches and other ecclesiastical buildings. Botanical records began rather late for this species, which suggests that, as a native plant, it was once probably quite uncommon and restricted to the south or west of England. However, a long history of planting has now made it a common sight in every corner of the land.

The National Trust's top ten snowdrop displays are at: Stourhead, Wiltshire; Anglesey Abbey, Cambridgeshire; Nymans, West Sussex; Dunham Massey, Cheshire; Kingston Lacy, Dorset; Belton, Lincolnshire; Fountains Abbey, Yorkshire; Attingham Park, Shropshire; Chirk Castle, Shropshire; and The Agory, County Armagh.

grown vigorous leaves that you are likely to see. On cliffs, the tasty, fleshy leaves of **rock samphire** are also growing. On beaches, the prickly leaves of **sea holly** are still obvious.

February marks the end of the oyster season. Why not visit the coast to enjoy this and similar foods such as winkles and mussels? If the fancy takes you, various seaweeds, such as kelp, are edible all year.

WEEK TWO White Mountain Hares

You might not be impressed with the idea of looking for white rabbits. After all, they could be in the pet shop, or even in your own hutch at home. But white hares – those are quite different. The search for them will, hopefully, take you to a Wonderland.

Neither rabbits nor brown hares are native to Britain, having been introduced from Spain and Holland respectively. That leaves the **mountain hare** as the only indigenous member of the British rabbit family. And although this distinction is intriguing enough, the real reason to look for one at this time of the year is to appreciate its remarkable colour changes.

And also, let's face it – unless we are going skiing or following extreme sports, what else might bring us into the high country in February? The mountain hare occurs above 300 m in the Peak District, the Isle of Man and throughout much of the Scottish Highlands, invariably in tough terrain subject to some brutal winter weather. Few other animals survive here, and it isn't the place for a gentle wander – at least, not far from the safety of a road or cottage. But if you do come up here looking for mountain hares, you will probably be on your own in the stark, bleak scenery, something out of a Brontë family novel. If the hares take you out of your comfort zone, it will be worth it.

British mountain hares are adapted to this harsh environment, subsisting on a diet of heather and grass which, let's be honest, is hardly difficult to find on these open mountains and moors. The diet obviously makes

WEEKLY HIGHLIGHTS: WEEK ONE

- First budburst of hawthorn is recorded
- Male moles begin to seek out females by building extra tunnels
- In good years, migrant **clouded yellows** may be seen on the wing
- First **red-throated divers** arrive to take up territory on small Scottish lochs
- Wren begins singing in earnest
- Skylarks begin singing

WEEKLY HIGHLIGHTS: WEEK TWO

- First leaves of hawthorn are recorded
- First queen wasps are seen
- First small tortoiseshells are typically seen
- First peacock butterflies are typically seen
- First **comma** butterflies are seen
- On average, this is the week that you are likely to hear the first blackbird singing

them tough because, unlike the relatively weedy rabbits of lowland UK, mountain hares don't even live in burrows. They make sheltered 'forms' under heather, similar to the forms of brown hares in grassy patches on the edges of fields, and as often as not they simply ride out whatever the weather throws at them. In the daytime they actually seek out snow patches in which to rest.

The reason for seeking out snow isn't to look tough, but to blend in: the coat of the mountain hare varies through the seasons, and at this time of the year it is pure white, except for the black of the tips of the ears. After a summer (May to September) when the coat is grey-brown with a distinctive bluish under-fur, the animal begins to moult in October. At first it is grey-brown with white blobs, ideal to blend it with patchy snow,

but by December it is fully white. By March it becomes patchy again, to coincide with melting snow.

So one reason that you should look for mountain hares in February is that they are at their vivid washing-powder-white best, regardless of the weather. If the hills are covered by snow, you will see them at their best; if there is no snow, the animals will look almost comically obvious. In Scotland this can make them dangerously clear to their arch-enemy, the **golden eagle**.

Another reason is that, regardless of their fearsome habitat, the mountain hares have already started breeding, so if you find them, they might be frisky as well as obvious. Even up here, spring is not so far away.

🌿 Great spotted woodpeckers begin drumming in earnest

🌿 On average, this is the week when the first official summer visitor appears in Britain. The wheatear winters in East Africa and the last birds can be seen in November. But here they are, back again

WEEK THREE Finding Red Squirrels

There are two species of squirrel in Britain, **grey squirrel** and red squirrel. The red is the native mammal and the grey a relatively recent introduction from North America. These days everybody feels protective towards red squirrels and wants to conserve them, while the grey is seen as the aggressive 'tree rat' responsible for the demise of the smaller, and much better-looking red squirrel. This is a somewhat black-and-white view of the situation, since the reality is that grey squirrels have simply taken advantage of a decline in their relatives, rather than forcing them out as such. But there is no doubt that the red squirrel is on the retreat and could disappear from many places.

Whatever the rights and wrongs of the situation, this week's suggestion is to get yourself to a place where you can see and watch a red squirrel. If you've never set eyes on one before, be assured that these little beauties are really very different indeed to the greys. They might look quite similar in books, but in the wild they are entirely distinct. They are lighter in body and a considerably warmer shade of chestnut brown, which is not patchy – on the grey squirrels there are reddish patches on the mealy grey fur. The most prominent difference, though, is in the red squirrel's funky ear-tufts, which contrast noticeably with the grey's rounded ears. You get the impression the red squirrel has just been to the hairdresser and its mum might not approve.

These ear-tufts are at their best in the winter, and have disappeared by mid-summer.

Red squirrels are found in Scotland, parts of northern England (Cumbria, Northumberland) and a few islands, including Anglesey and the Isle of Wight, and they tend (although this isn't a rule) to be found in conifer forests.

But how do you see one? By far the best way is to cheat and find a nut-feeder where they come regularly. Almost anywhere the red squirrels occur someone will be feeding them, and they take advantage of the easy food in their droves, making it possible to see several at once.

If you prefer a wilder experience, be assured that they are still quite easy to find, especially now that many females are pregnant and will be having their first litters of the year. They will be feeding up, while for the footloose males it is business as usual. If you visit a wood on a still day, listen for movements in the trees (often high up) or for the sound of cones falling (this noise could also come from crossbills). Red squirrels in the winter are usually at their most active in late morning, rather than early.

Many people say that red squirrels are more arboreal than greys and, while this is certainly the impression you get, they do spend plenty of time on the ground, too, so don't entirely confine your watching to the canopy. As you watch the distant branches you could miss that squirrel at your feet!

There are simply times when red squirrels are elusive and, if it is cold and windy, they can also be difficult to find. But here's an informative tale that I can tell you. A few years ago I went with my family to Brownsea Island in Dorset to see the squirrels. It didn't go well. It felt as though we checked every tree on the island, and after two or three hours we had seen precisely nothing. Somewhat dispirited, we decanted to the island's café to consider our next move. As we sat down at an outside table a red squirrel ran literally between our chairs and climbed up to the nut feeder in the café window, where it soon began chewing contentedly.

That's the sort of mammal watching I like!

The native red squirrel is said to spend more time in the treetops than the grey squirrel. The red squirrel is certainly smaller and slimmer and would probably beat its grey cousin on an assault course.

Places to see red squirrels:

- Brownsea Island, Dorset
- Formby, Merseyside
- Isle of Wight, Hampshire
- Newborough Warren, Anglesey
- Glenborrowdale, Highland

WEEKLY HIGHLIGHTS: WEEK THREE

- Average first flowering of **lesser celandine** in southern England (specifically 21 February)
- Coltsfoot flowers for the first time
- Earliest grey heron eggs
- Earliest **wood pigeon** eggs
- Earliest raven eggs
- Chaffinch begins singing
- First toad migration (2014)
- First red squirrel babies of the year are born

WEEK FOUR Visiting a Rookery

Are you getting tired of the winter and waiting for spring to arrive? If so, what you need to do is visit a rookery. In the noisy colonies of this sociable member of the crow family, spring is already swinging. The air is filled with raucous calling, there is more building going on than in an upmarket estate, and, like crowded neighbourhoods everywhere, tension is high. If you need to go somewhere lively, check out the treetops.

The **rook** is a common and widespread bird. Its nesting colonies are in tall trees within easy reach of fields, and can be spotted from a considerable distance at this time of the year, before the leaves hide them. Rooks commonly nest in villages and in readily accessible places where it is easy to observe them, so this particular expedition should be easy to undertake. All you need is to find your rooks, bring a pair of binoculars and watch.

Before you pick your binoculars up, though, it is hard not to be aware of the noise. As members of the crow family, you expect rooks to caw. They do caw, and include almost every variation it is possible to have: loud caws, soft caws, angry caws, smooth caws and caws on different pitches. You will quickly become aware that, besides the usual deep-voiced sounds, there are frequent countertenor notes, as if the birds' voices were breaking. You will be astonished at the sheer variation in sound.

The sheer bustle and noise should lift your springtime spirits, but even if it doesn't, the sight of birds bringing nest material into the colony surely will – what clearer sign of the season do you need? There is a large turnover of twigs in a rookery, not least because neighbours pilfer them from each other – something you might

- First litters of rabbits are born
- Mountain hares begin to moult their white coats
- Roe deer begin rubbing their antlers clear of velvet
- Earliest ever officially accepted cuckoo (15 February 1945)
- Great crested grebes start to return to their breeding lakes
- Lesser black-backed gulls begin to return to their breeding sites (although they won't lay eggs until late April)
- First time blackbirds are seen nest-building

WEEKLY HIGHLIGHTS: WEEK FOUR

- First flowering of **blackthorn**.
- Aspen comes into flower. The male catkins hang down like lamb's tails from this tall tree, and are white and silky. They come out well before the leaves.
- In marshes, **osier** begins to flower

indeed witness. In a large rookery the birds may have to travel some distance to acquire new material, so it is common to see them coming in, twig held crosswise in the bill, as if they were just back from the DIY shop.

Being spring, there will also be much inter-action and posturing between birds, although it is often quite subtle. Assertive males droop their wings, spread and lift their tails and call loudly in triumphant style. Females on the nest ruffle their feathers and make winsome begging calls, similar to those of chicks, and the males do indeed feed them while they are incubating (eggs will be on the way in the next two weeks). You will almost certainly see pursuit-flights, when a bird tail-gates another in the air, often over some trivial quarrel. However long you watch, something will be happening, and you will be surprised how quickly the time passes as you observe this soap opera in the canopy.

So a visit to a rookery should provide a breath of springtime air, but why is it that these birds should be nesting so early? They are several weeks ahead of the majority of other bird species. The reason appears to be that because rooks feed their young on earthworms and grubs from the soil these are easier to reach in early spring when the ground is moist from the winter months, and there is less plant cover. In previous generations, farmers would also till most of their crops in the early spring, giving the rooks a bounteous supply of food in ploughed fields. This happens less often today, because many farmers use autumn-sown crops instead.

- First **common lizards** emerge from hibernation
- First **adders** emerge
- Brent geese begin to leave British estuaries, most going to feed up in Holland and Germany before their journey to the Arctic
- Some golden plovers return to their breeding territories on British moorlands
- First eggs of the **mallard** (on average)
- First teal may return north towards their breeding grounds
- **Woodlarks** begin to sing in earnest and perform their song-flights
- The first **tufted ducks** return to their breeding areas
- **Corn bunting** starts singing
- **Marsh tit** starts singing
- **Lesser spotted woodpecker** starts drumming in earnest
- Wood pigeon starts singing

MARCH

The remarkable Northern wheatear is often the first genuine summer visitor to arrive, and it is one of the last to leave in the autumn

INTRODUCTION

Officially, 1 March is the first day of spring, but the annual joke is invariably that it doesn't feel like it. In reality, average temperatures are warmer than January or February, but October and November tend to be warmer. In England, the average maximum daytime temperature is 9.8°C (6.9°C in Scotland, 8.6°C in Wales). The overall weather tends to be calm, cool and dry. The cool is mainly influenced by the Atlantic, which has lost all its heat during the long autumn and winter. This means that, even on sunny days the temperature often drops sharply

at night. Snow often lies in the hills of Scotland, northern England or North Wales during the month. Indeed, there has been an increasing trend recently for snowfall in the first half of March elsewhere in the UK. The spring equinox, when the day and the night are of approximately equal duration, occurs on or around 20 March.

As far as wildlife is concerned, March is in some ways a warm-up act for the spring. Some animals, such as frogs, are embracing the delights of the season to the fullest extent, but on the whole, while the dancers take up their positions, the music hasn't quite started. Most paired-up birds haven't started breeding yet, while a few butterflies are just getting going. Some mammals begin early broods, but their success is highly unpredictable. Queen bumblebees are building up their colonies slowly. Fish relocate to shallower waters ahead of spawning.

The sluggish build-up to spring results in one of the real glories of the season, something entirely lacking in many parts of the world. The surge in sunlight and moderate warmth encourages a multitude of flowers to spring up on the woodland floor. It's a brief opportunity afforded by the fact that trees take a while to come fully into leaf, and its very ephemeral nature adds to the appeal. There are only a few species concerned, but what a show they put on. From lesser celandines and **wood anemones** to **bluebells** later in the season, the woodland flowers carpet the leaf-litter, grabbing their time in the sun.

Away from woodland, it is also a great blossom month. A lot of this is down to the abundance of blackthorn, which is at its best, but the many garden blossoms, together with magnolias, give the early month a suitably floral flavour.

Another of March's delights is the arrival of the first bird migrants from Africa. It is but a trickle at first concerning a few species such as **chiffchaffs**, **sand martins**, wheatears and **little ringed plovers**. But the major influx is imminent.

HEDGEHOG DIARY: Most individuals emerge from hibernation in March, but if the weather is particularly cold they will delay. Some already emerged animals can, in theory, go back to sleep during a frosty spell. Their priority now is to replenish their much-depleted resources, so they are often very active. It's a good time to provide them with meals of dog or cat food in the garden.

BADGER DIARY: The cubs are protected and suckled by the sow deep in the sett. On average there are two cubs, but the range is between one and five. The cubs are kept especially warm by large amounts of bedding, which has been collected since the autumn. The cubs were born naked, blind and helpless, but by month's end they are basically small versions of the adults. Meanwhile, young breeding-age individuals may leave their social group to look for a mate elsewhere; they won't necessarily get a friendly reception if a dominant boar is already established.

GREY SQUIRREL DIARY: This is the peak month for the birth of spring litters in squirrels. On average there are three young (a range of one to seven), born blind and naked inside the breeding drey. In the first week the mother stays close by the young, rarely travelling more than 100 m away from the nest to feed. By month's end she will travel further, and the youngsters will have a sparse covering of fur. The males take no part in family life.

BLUE TIT DIARY: March is sometimes a difficult month for blue tits. Ever since September they have depended on plant

Grey squirrels are among the few British mammals to breed in winter, with mid-winter courtship chases and young in March or April.

matter for food, including nuts from trees and seeds from herbs, but all these are well depleted by now, with little new production. The birds switch diet to animal food, but this is not yet abundant – it is a good time to keep the garden feeders well stocked. All breeding birds will now have a territory and a mate. You might well see pairs inspecting nest-boxes, or holes in trees, even pecking at the edges, but breeding is not on the cards yet.

COMMON FROG DIARY: March is usually the big mating and spawning month for frogs. For a week or two the waters of ponds and lakes foam with amphibians shamelessly going about their business with abandon.

Males croak and jostle for access to females. Look out for mating pairs locked in the 'amplexus' embrace, in which males cling on to the back of a female so that, when she lays her eggs, he will be able to fertilize them by saturating them with sperm immediately as they come out. Individuals can remain in amplexus for some weeks and some die of exhaustion before successfully breeding. Clouds of spawn soon appear, usually in the shallowest parts of the pond. The eggs actually sink before floating again.

MONTHLY HIGHLIGHTS: GARDEN

There is plenty of new growth in the garden, not all of it entirely welcome. You might find some rogue dandelions growing on your lawn, but if so, the end of the month is a good time to pick the growing leaves to add to a salad, or even a sandwich. The leaves are bitter, but they are an extremely healthy addition to any diet as they are crammed full of vitamins.

If you're picking dandelions you might want to look around for common chickweed, also, with its tiny, white star-like flowers that look too small for the rest of the plant. An abundant and frequently cursed weed of flowerbeds, it should be more appreciated because both the leaves and stems are excellent to eat when young and fresh, for example, in a salad. Forager John Wright says that the taste is 'not unlike lettuce, but with a bit of freshly-mown cricket pitch thrown in'. Now you've got to try it!

Take a good look at any starlings that appear in the neighbourhood. In the sun they are looking fantastic at the moment, with brilliant iridescent plumage. Furthermore, at this time of year there is a subtle difference between the sexes: both have yellow bills, but the base of the male's is light blue and that of the female pink!

There are more flying insects around in the garden, not least bumblebees and butterflies such as the brimstone.

In addition, a stack of moths appear for the first time in March. These include **orange underwing**, **light orange underwing**, **March**

With its fresh but subtle green colouring, the brimstone butterfly seems to sum up March. Individuals can sometimes be seen flying as early as January, but most won't appear until now.

moth, **mottled grey**, **barred tooth-striped**, **brindled beauty**, **oak beauty**, **engrailed**, **red chestnut**, **pine beauty**, **small quaker**, **blossom underwing**, **lead-coloured drab**, **common quaker**, **clouded drab**, **twin-spotted quaker**, **Hebrew character** and **early grey**.

MONTHLY HIGHLIGHTS: WOODLAND

Last month there were a few brave blooms of wild flowers on the woodland floor. But the weeks of March are perfect for witnessing the steady progress of colour covering the ground, before the leaves come out and smother the floor in shade.

One of the first woodland plants to flower is the lesser celandine, a relative of buttercups but with heart-shaped leaves and sharply pointed petals, between seven and twelve in number. A much-loved plant, described by the famous botanist John Gilmour as having the colour of 'gleaming gold [that] challenges the pale sunshine that gave it birth', lesser celandine can carpet the ground in woodland. From its earliest flowering at the end of February, it has a grumpy reaction to poor weather, closing its blooms in the cold and rain. It flowers until May.

Following quickly on after lesser celandine is a close relative, a sort of deluxe version, taller and with pristine white blooms, some of which have a pink tinge. The leaves branch off two-thirds of the way up the stem. Wood anemone, occasionally called 'windflower', carpets the woodland floor in March and April, but only in certain places, usually ancient woodlands, of which it is a good indicator. Patches of this plant spread at a rate of 2 m every 100 years.

It isn't only ground plants that are flowering. Some trees are, too, including ash, although you need to look carefully to see the small blisters of purple blooms near the tips of the twigs.

Wood anemones flower strongly in March and April, and sometimes form large carpets in ancient woodland.

MONTHLY HIGHLIGHTS: FARMLAND

This is the height of the lambing season, and the sight of newborn lambs in the fields is a favourite with visitors to the countryside. On the other hand, it's an exhausting time for sheep farmers themselves: ewes and lambs can be high-maintenance.

Meanwhile, on arable farms, spring cereals such as wheat or barley are being top-dressed with manure and fertilizer. Potato fields are sprayed with liquid fertilizer, and oilseed rape crops may be treated with nitrogen.

The fields may be drilled with new crops such as sugar beet and peas.

Now is a good time to see the lively, giddy display of the lapwing, since most breeding birds are on territory, usually on farmland fields. These broad-winged birds perform a kind of air-dance, swooping up and down and tilting from side to side, with a carefree, out-of-control style. At the same time they make loud, yelping calls and their wings throb in flight. It's quite a performance.

MONTHLY HIGHLIGHTS: SCRUB AND THICKET

No matter how fierce the weather, the flowering of blackthorn in March is a sure sign that cold spells cannot last forever, and spring will win in the end. Indeed, freezing weather in March or April is sometimes colloquially described as a 'blackthorn winter'. This abundant shrub, with its long, sharp thorns, has the unusual distinction of sending out flowers before the leaves. And what blooms they are! Unimpressive perhaps on their own, being just 5–8 mm in diameter and with five white rounded petals – but collectively they can give the impression that a localized fall of snow has settled on the branches. The whitening of the blackthorn hedges across the colourless countryside of early March can be seen, and appreciated, even at great distance.

Look out for **long-tailed tits** this month, especially if you see them around thorny bushes such as gorse or bramble; they could be nest-building. Theirs is one of the most

Blackthorn is one of the earliest flowers to appear 'in bulk', so to speak. As such, it is a very important source of food for invertebrates which, in turn, attract migrant birds such as the willow warbler.

complex and impressive constructions of any British bird. Between now and egg-laying in April they need to collect literally thousands of pieces of lichen, moss, cobwebs and small feathers, all of which will be used to make the small but cosy domed nest among the thorny foliage. The nest takes three weeks to build, and the pair usually works only in the morning.

MONTHLY HIGHLIGHTS: GRASSLAND AND ROADSIDES

This habitat takes a long time to catch the spring mood, but on many a roadside **primroses** will begin to flower in earnest. In some parts of the country they may come out as early as December. The buttery-yellow blooms provide an uplifting display in quantity.

Another common yellow spring flower out now is **coltsfoot**. It looks like a low-growing type of daisy, except for its very substantial broad, reverse-heart-shaped leaves.

Those aren't the only flowers to colour the reluctant roadsides. The delightful **germander speedwell** also begins to flower this month, a glorious blue. The leaves of cow parsley also begin to appear.

MONTHLY HIGHLIGHTS: HEATHLAND, MOORLAND AND UPLAND

Adders emerge and often bask near hibernation sites. They are sluggish at this time of the year and often allow good views.

Meanwhile, on upland moors, most golden plovers have now returned to their breeding territories and will treat those who venture out on mild days to fabulous display-flights. The male rises up to a height that lets its white underwings shimmer, and delivers a very pure, mournful, forsaken-sounding advertising call of two repeated notes. These birds are handsome, with a smart jet-black breast and upperside with golden spangles on a dark background.

Ravens are early starters when it comes to breeding, typically having eggs by the beginning of the month. They, too, will engage in much aerial display at the moment, the breeding pair soaring together and performing aerobatics, including flying upside down. Listen, too, for their distinctive croaking calls.

In a few wild corners of Britain, including the Scottish Highlands and Snowdonia, **wild goats** are giving birth to their kids.

MONTHLY HIGHLIGHTS: RIVERS

March is a great month for seeing kingfishers, before too much vegetation has grown up beside the water. They will also be displaying; often this is nothing more than excited chases, but if you are fortunate, you might see a male landing beside the female and presenting her a fish.

But that's getting ahead of things. A good many people have never seen a kingfisher, or have only seen one or two in their lives. So how do you actually find one? It's simple enough. First of all, find a stretch of water where you know kingfishers occur. To do this you need a slow-flowing, reasonably broad river with raised mud banks somewhere nearby. You can simply ask a local, or better still, an angler, to confirm whether the birds are around. Then all you do is choose a vantage point where you can see right across (e.g. a bridge) and wait, because kingfishers are territorial and, if it's their patch, they will soon come past. Look for a small bird flying very low, just above the water surface. Also listen out for a loud whistle, rather like a sound some squeaky toys make when squeezed. Good luck!

Young salmon often hatch out in March. They take the form of 16-mm-long hatchlings with yolk sacs attached, and are known as alevins. They remain in the gravel until the end of the month.

By the riverside it's a good month for catkins and blossom. The various poplars send out colourful male catkins, shocking pink in **black poplar**, faded pink in **grey poplar**, well before their leaves come out. **Grey willow** and goat willow, common waterside plants, are also replete with their soft blooms, with that of the goat willow plusher and yellower. These come out before the leaves.

Another waterside plant you might spot now is the **butterbur**. It has capacious heart-shaped leaves and a large flowering spike, rather like an orchid, with a multitude of mauve flowers wrapped up in bracts. It often flowers well by polluted rivers.

MONTHLY HIGHLIGHTS: LAKES, PONDS AND FRESHWATER MARSHES

Towards the end of the month, on mild nights you might be able to hear a chorus of amphibians. **Common frogs** make a low purring and **common toads** a curious sore-throated squeak.

Marsh marigold flowers for the first time, a sort of sumptuous blonde among spring flowers. It has potently large yellow buttercup-like blooms with large dark-green leaves, growing in healthy-looking clumps.

Watch out for ducks flying this month. Birds will often spontaneously take off, circle a pond and land again. A closer look will usually reveal one female and several males – two, three and often more. If three birds, two males and a female, are involved, it's called a three-bird flight. The female initiates it and it is a way for the male to prove himself, by accompanying the female and 'protecting' her from the other suitor. There is often much mid-air quacking.

Ducks are much in evidence generally. Species such as **goldeneye** and **goosander** build up their numbers on lakes and rivers. Look out for the 'head-throw' display of the former, hurling the head backwards until it almost rests on the back.

All three species of British **newts**, the **smooth, palmate** and **great crested**, enter ponds and begin their courtship.

Some freshwater fish, such as perch, exhibit seasonal movements from deep to shallow water at this time of the year. They are often sluggish in the winter and move to shallower parts of a wetland in order to breed.

MONTHLY HIGHLIGHTS: COAST AND ESTUARY

A few coastal plants come into flower in March. **Sea buckthorn**, best known for its orange, *Pyracantha*-like berries, comes into flower, although you would be hard-pressed

to notice the small green flowers. The first **wild cabbage** may bloom late in the month, along with **Portland spurge**. **Thrift** begins to turn some cliff-tops pink, but it isn't at its best yet.

For the coastal forager, **sea kale** makes a welcome appearance this month. The shoots, which may stick straight up from the shingle, are excellent.

The bulk of our wintering brent geese leave Britain this month, while **bar-tailed godwits** set off for their moulting grounds on the Waddensee, off Holland/Germany. Many individual ducks, geese and waders follow suit.

In contrast, the first **sandwich terns**, returning from Africa, make an appearance this month.

Common gulls, abundant wintering birds throughout the country, begin to head back to their northern breeding grounds.

Contrary to folklore, brown hares don't only get frisky in March, but throughout the summer and autumn. However, early spring is a particularly good time to watch them.

WEEKLY HIGHLIGHTS: WEEK ONE

- First flowers of wood anemone
- First budburst of **silver birch**
- The first returning individual sand martins are usually seen this week. These slight-bodied birds are similar to swallows, but browner and with a shorter tail. They usually breed on riverbanks
- **Yellowhammer** starts singing
- **Goldcrest** starts singing
- Raven usual first clutches
- Russian white-fronted geese begin to leave Britain

WEEK ONE Boxing Hares

Everybody has heard of the phenomenon of boxing hares, when the animals go 'as mad as a March hare', chasing around with seemingly inexplicable abandon and assaulting one another. Actually witnessing the show is much more difficult. That isn't because it's a rare event; in fact, it can take place any time between February and October. The problem is that performances tend to be fleeting, and often take place at twilight or in the dark. And, of course, you need to find your hares first.

The brown hare isn't uncommon, but you don't stumble across it in the way that you do rabbits. Hares don't live in warrens, for a start, but individuals spread out over their habitat: grassland or arable land with cereals, dotted with patches of cover. Most of the time they feed quietly out in the middle of a field, while rabbits prefer the edges. The only way you are going to see hares is to find the right habitat and watch. You can often do this by driving around the countryside checking open fields, where hares will appear at large. If you live in a rural area, ask a local farmer.

Sooner or later, the hares in any part of the country will turn frisky. Part of the frenzied nature of hare breeding encounters is that the females are only in oestrus for about one day a month. All the local hares know this, and hopeful males make sure that they remain in close touch with potential mates. However, there is a hierarchy among males, with the older, larger males having preferential access to females; some, indeed, simply stand guard by a favoured female until she is ready. Males will chase and bite each other.

The famous boxing, though, in which hares actually cuff each other with their paws from a standing position, is surprisingly not male-to-male combat. It is female retribution. If an undesirable male shows unwelcome interest, or even if a desirable male tries to initiate sexual activity, either may find themselves boxed. This form of combat is really the culmination of long hours of excitement and chasing for the hares, and makes for a compelling piece of wildlife viewing.

As mentioned previously, chasing and boxing are by no means confined to the month of March, but there is a reason for having a look for them in March. Firstly, this is the first time most females will be fertile this year, with the accompanying thrill that this entails. And secondly, none of the arable crops will have grown up high enough to hide the raunchy behaviour. Though not strictly seasonal, this window of opportunity early in the year is a classic time to watch it.

Lean, fit, bursting with vitality? The common toad does not fit the mould of a migratory species, but it can be a keen traveller.

WEEKLY HIGHLIGHTS: WEEK TWO

- First budburst of alder
- First budburst of ash
- First budburst of **field maple**
- First leaves of **horse chestnut** are recorded
- First budburst of **rowan**
- First budburst of **sycamore**
- First flowering of **garlic mustard**
- Grey herons lay their first eggs
- **Slow worm** and **grass snake** first emergence from hibernation
- Common lizard mating chases (until end of April)
- Average first births of fox cubs

- First emerged **red-tailed bumblebee** is recorded
- Male minnows begin to acquire their brilliant emerald green breeding colours, with red underside
- First **small white** butterflies are seen
- Early pairs of red-throated divers on Scottish lochs and moors may lay their first eggs
- Shag lays first eggs
- Early rooks begin laying their clutches
- Greenfinch and goldfinch begin singing
- **Treecreeper** starts singing
- The first main arrival of chiffchaffs on southern coasts of England
- The first little ringed plovers are seen

WEEK TWO Frog and Toad Migration

This is typically the week that most common toads start their remarkable migration. Yes, you read it right – their *migration*. Toads might only be able to waddle and crawl (with the occasional feeble hop), but that doesn't limit their determination to travel.

In March, they are all at it, sometimes in large groups. It can be possible to watch them crawling en masse across the grass, or a road, or a garden lawn, all travelling in the same direction. In the course of an hour you might see up to 100 crossing a single road or path. As a migration goes it is slow, but on occasion it can be astonishing. It is one of those hidden wildlife events that most people simply never know is happening.

The reason that toads migrate is that they are really land animals that reproduce in the water. They make the pilgrimage to a pond once a year, in the spring, while for the rest of the time they hide away under rocks or other solid objects, often in completely dry habitats. The water they are aiming for is their 'home' pond, the one from which they themselves hatched. For reasons unknown, toads are very fussy about their breeding ponds (they occupy a ratio of just one to every five or six ponds occupied by frogs), so a toad migration is often along a well-worn path followed year on year. It is thought that the toads might be able to detect their specific pond by smell. Their hibernation sites may be as far as 2 km from their 'home' pond, so it must be a very strong pull that they are following.

In fact, on occasion you can witness the relentless, powerful urge that drives these animals on. Their paths – some of which in theory could have been used for centuries – are often blocked by obstacles such as walls, roads or tree stumps, yet these indomitable creatures somehow manage to overcome them. The toad version of mountaineering is grimly impressive.

A combination of time of year and weather conditions signals the start of the migration. The amphibians travel in the dark, usually after a run of mild nights, especially after rain. In a given area there tends to be a very short window of opportunity to observe a significant migration, since most animals in a colony travel within a few days of each other.

Toads are not the only amphibian to migrate; common frogs do, too, but their movements are rarely as impressive as toad movements because a proportion of male frogs remain at the bottom of ponds during the winter, negating the need to migrate. They often move earlier in the year than toads, sometimes by the end of January.

How might you witness such an event? Owing to its unpredictability and brevity, it isn't easy. You might see a large number of squashed amphibians along a length of road during the day as evidence that it has occurred. However, as with many aspects of British wildlife, you need to seek out experts and locals. The three websites below should be invaluable for further enquiries:

- www.toadwatch.org
- http://www.froglife.org/
- http://www.arc-trust.org/ (Amphibian and Reptile Conservation Trust)

WEEKLY HIGHLIGHTS: WEEK THREE

- First leaves of alder
- First buds and leaves of beech
- First leaves of larch
- First leaves of field maple
- First flowers of hawthorn are recorded
- First budburst and leaves of oak trees
- First leaves of rowan
- First leaves of birch
- First leaves of sycamore
- First blooms of **cuckoo-flower**
- Earliest eggs of **robin**
- Earliest eggs of song thrush
- **Canada geese** lay their first eggs
- First clutches of moorhen
- First clutches of coot
- **Meadow pipits** start singing and performing their song-flights

- First baby rabbits are weaned and may appear above ground for the first time
- First brown hare pregnancies
- First wood mouse litters are born
- Any **common shrews** that have survived the winter now become mature and will soon breed
- First litters of **pine marten** are born, usually in tree holes
- **Red deer** begin to shed their antlers (until towards the end of April)
- The spring flight of **holly blue** begins
- The first wintering knots begin to leave British estuaries
- The first **greylag geese** begin to leave Scotland to return north to their breeding grounds in Iceland

WEEK THREE Daffodils

Several of our spring flowers straddle the line between wildness and the familiarity of the garden. Snowdrops and bluebells are good examples, in which it is usually impossible to tell whether they have always grown in a location for thousands of years, or whether they have been introduced by people. Daffodils are different, however. **Garden daffodils** are almost invariably larger and taller than the native daffodil, and have thicker, fleshier leaves, so their origin is usually much more obvious. And, in contrast to the previous spring species, **wild daffodils** are a good deal rarer than their cultivated cousins. This month, I have two suggestions. Enjoy the many wonderful displays of garden daffodils, often at their best at this time of the year. But if you can, why not take a trip to see a display of wild daffodils as well?

Garden daffodils are marvellously reliable indicators of spring, right from the end of December when the shoots first appear out of the soil, to their height of flowering, usually in March. Their yellow is perfectly redolent of the season: bright and breezy, but not overconfident or strident. They are around long enough to mark the spring, yet at their best, with firm stems, flowers inclined rather than nodding, and with perfectly formed blooms, they are fickle and ephemeral. You can often see spring's march reflected in individuals within a single flowerbed, from those still bashfully opening to those with frayed edges to the trumpets, all within a few metres. Even well into April there are some about, still trumpeting spring, perhaps like the band still playing on the sinking ship.

Wild daffodils are native to Britain in a few places, but most of those we see these days are cultivated.

There was a time – long ago now, perhaps 300 years – when our own native wild daffodils were as abundant as their cultivars are today. The species has been subject to a very long decline, no doubt with multiple causes, including woodland clearance, farming intensification, increased soil drainage and, latterly, the removal of wild bulbs to grow in gardens. These days they are rare in south-east England, but much commoner in the north and west. Indeed, the Lake District is a stronghold, and it is still easy enough to follow in the footsteps of the poet Wordsworth as he marvelled at a display near Ullswater:

I wandered lonely as a cloud
That floats on high o'er vales and hills,
When all at once I saw a crowd,
A host of golden daffodils;
Beside the lake, beneath the trees,
Fluttering and dancing in the breeze.
Continuous as the stars that shine
and twinkle on the Milky Way,
They stretched in never-ending line
along the margin of a bay:
Ten thousand saw I at a glance,
tossing their heads in sprightly dance.
The waves beside them danced; but they
Out-did the sparkling waves in glee:
A poet could not but be gay,
in such a jocund company:
I gazed—and gazed—but little thought
what wealth the show to me had brought:

For oft, when on my couch I lie
In vacant or in pensive mood,
They flash upon that inward eye
Which is the bliss of solitude;
And then my heart with pleasure fills,
And dances with the daffodils.

Incidentally, this famous poem was inspired by a walk that Wordsworth took on 15 April 1805. These days that would be quite a late flowering date.

Happily, there are still a number of places where you can enjoy the 'host of golden daffodils'. These, plus some of the best garden daffodil displays, are listed below.

Note also that there is a Daffodil Society at http://thedaffodilsociety.com/.

Wild daffodils:

- Dymock, Gloucestershire
- Farndale, North Yorkshire
- Kempley 'Golden Triangle', Gloucestershire
- Ullswater, Cumbria
- Dunsford Nature Reserve, Devon
- George's Hayes, Staffordshire
- Oysters Coppice Nature Reserve, Wiltshire
- Betty Daw's Wood, Gloucestershire
- Stocking Springs Wood, Hertfordshire
- Coed y Bwl, Gwynnedd
- Llandefaelog Wood, Powys

WEEK FOUR Seeing Water Voles

Not so long ago it was a no-brainer to see a water vole. You went to a river in the countryside and, if you took a picnic on a warm day and spent a little time, you would have a good chance of coming across one. These chubby voles used to be called 'water rats', and of course were made famous by the novel *The Wind in the Willows* by Kenneth Grahame, published in 1908. Common and perhaps taken for granted, in that era the water vole wasn't the sort of animal you actually went out to find.

Times have changed and, perhaps surprisingly, the water vole suffered the largest population drop that has ever been measured for a British animal, a 94 per cent plunge between 1990 and 1999. The various causes included loss of habitat and predation by introduced American mink. These days the numbers have recovered slightly, aided greatly by reintroductions by various conservation groups.

Although water voles are active all year round (they don't hibernate), March is a very good month to see them. Some have already started breeding, so they are busy, while at the same time the waterside vegetation in their habitat will not yet have grown into the usual jungle of the late spring and summer, so they have fewer places to hide. Now that the weather is warmer (hopefully) these rodents will be less inclined to spend large amounts of time in their burrows, so they are out and about more.

Water voles are easily confused with rats, not because they are very similar, but because **common rats** sometimes live in rivers and marshes in exactly the same habitat, and swim around in a manner very like water voles. However, rats are much heftier than voles, with bigger ears and eyes, much more pointed faces and longer, snake-like tails. Water voles have stubby noses as well as small eyes; their small ears are rounded, barely sticking out. When you see water voles, they are often steadily swimming across the water, or alongside the bank, showing their head and back. They are also often seen on a riverbank, sitting on their haunches and holding a piece of grass or other vegetation in their forelimbs, in the manner of a squirrel.

Sometimes you find signs of the creatures you're looking for before you see what made them. Water voles make a system of burrows that open out onto the riverbank, some below the water line but others above. The holes tend to be small, only 4–8 cm in diameter, and there may be several of them all within a small stretch of riverbank. You might also see the animals' greenish droppings on rocks or mud, or even see piles of green clippings of water plant stems about 10 cm long.

What everybody really wants to see, though, is the water vole itself. Where present, these rodents are easy enough to see, although they can be shy and you might have to be patient.

The best method is simply to stand beside a river and wait for one to swim past – each animal only has a territory of about 50–100 m of riverbank. You can do this by day or night, although dusk is usually a good bet. Another tip is to ask around, because the animals are often active in the same exact spot for several days running. You can also listen for the plop of an animal jumping into the water, an intentional signal to warn other individuals that there is danger about.

On the whole, these charming rodents give good views when you do find them. They have a bustling, busy look to them, quite similar to their character in the book. And, like *The Wind in the Willows*, they are a link to a gentler, bygone age.

■ For more information see:
http://www.wildlifetrusts.org/species/water-vole

The water vole has comparatively small ears and a blunt muzzle in comparison with the brown rat, which often lives near water.

WEEKLY HIGHLIGHTS: WEEK FOUR

- **Tawny owl** first eggs
- Blackbird earliest eggs
- Cormorant first eggs
- Jay first eggs
- First **natterjack toads** come out of hibernation
- On average, this is the week when the first returning swallows are seen in the UK (27 March); their relative, the sand martin, arrives a fraction earlier (average 25 March)

- The first **willow warblers** arrive from Africa right on month's end
- On average, the first breeding blackcaps arrive this week
- The first **ring ouzels** appear, soon to make their way to the uplands to breed; the first birds appear in the northern isles by month's end
- **Reed buntings** begin singing
- **Sika deer** begin to drop their antlers

APRIL

Swallows typically arrive back in the first week of April, but the vanguard can be several weeks earlier

INTRODUCTION

It's the middle of spring and the epitome of spring. April is at last a respectably warm month, with an average maximum daytime temperature of 12.4°C in England and 9.3°C in Scotland. A statistic to gladden the heart is that the average sunshine in England leaps from an average of 107.6 hours in March to 155.2 hours in April, making it the fifth sunniest month of the year, outshining the whole of the autumn, and the same trend is apparent throughout the UK. April has a reputation for its showers, but it is, in fact, the second driest month of the year on average in England and Wales, behind May; in Scotland, it is slightly drier than both May and June. Frosts are now unusual in most of the country but, on the other hand, snow showers are not uncommon in the first week, and in Scotland snow can still be lying on the ground.

Britain's well-defined seasons ensure that, for the wildlife watcher, there is quite a sharp dividing line between sparse treats and an almost absurd glut, and April marks the beginning of the latter. At the beginning of March you can watch the arrival of spring with relative calm, day by day. By the end of April there is so much to see that it can be difficult to choose what to look for next.

In February and March the exciting drive towards spring is mainly coloured by plants, but in April birds steal the show. Not only is the dawn chorus already loud and diverse, but April also marks the main arrival of summer migrants – birds which are only with us to breed. The best known of these are swallows and cuckoos, but there are many more, about fifty in total, and the vast majority make first landfall this month. The passage of birds may go on from March until mid-June; all the birds are in their finery and many are singing. Incidentally, at much the same time there is also a movement uphill, as birds become more abundant on moors and mountains, having taken winter refuge not far away.

As far as resident breeding animals are concerned, reproduction is in full swing. Almost everything is displaying, laying eggs, having litters, and so on. The countryside is noisy and busy. People might go for peace, but nature shouts.

HEDGEHOG DIARY: April is a month, as was March, for getting into breeding condition by eating well and gaining weight. On the whole the mild conditions prevalent this month are ideal for this purpose, and some hedgehogs actually mate before month's end. It's about this time of year that hedgehogs sometimes get themselves into trouble by raiding the nests of ground-nesting birds for eggs.

BADGER DIARY: The cubs born in February are well grown now, although they are still feeding on the sow's milk. They spend much time exploring the sett and, on occasion, will go as far as the entrance without actually going outside. Meanwhile, the rest of the social group will often go on feeding trips together. This is a time when badgers, as carnivores, will sometimes eat the eggs and young of ground-nesting birds.

GREY SQUIRREL DIARY: Young squirrels in the breeding drey remain dependent on their mother, who suckles them and aggressively defends them from all kinds of intruders, including other squirrels. If the mother feels threatened she will actually move them to another nest, one by one, in her mouth. Nevertheless, on foraging trips she often spends considerable time away from the nest, even whole nights by month's end. Meanwhile, all the males need to worry about is the annual moult, exchanging the heavier winter coat for a light summer one.

BLUE TIT DIARY: Female blue tits spend the month preparing to lay eggs. To this end they feed voraciously, helped by regular deliveries of extra food from the male. The females eat a few small snails to obtain calcium for the eggshells. The weather in April is critical, because if it is bad, the female will be in poor condition for laying and the caterpillar abundance, on which blue tits depend, could be delayed. The male spends much of the month singing to keep the territorial boundaries intact, and repelling any unwanted advances of other males. It rarely works entirely; both sexes routinely copulate with others outside the pair bond.

One of the many glories of spring is the profusion of blossom in gardens, hedgerows and orchards – here is apple blossom.

COMMON FROG DIARY: Mating is still going on in places. But the frog's short and sweet breeding season is almost at an end, the spawn left alone to produce the next generation. Many worn-out adults remain in deep water for several weeks after mating, while nearby the tadpoles hatch two to three weeks after the eggs are laid. At first they are bunched together in swarms, but soon become more detached and secretive.

MONTHLY HIGHLIGHTS: GARDEN

Don't laugh, but this is actually a great time of the year to watch pigeons. I'm not talking about the dull things that they do, such as wandering over the lawn feeding on grain left out for 'more attractive' birds. No, this is about displays. Pigeon displays are engaging.

If you have **collared doves** in your neighbourhood, watch out for them suddenly launching at a steep angle into the air and then spiralling down with their wings and tail spread. Wood pigeons do something similar, but they fly upwards, flap their wings noisily and then suddenly stall, as if stunned, before gliding down in the same direction they started from. The idea of the display is to show off to mate and rivals alike. It's pigeon theatre, and well worth a look.

Tits will lay their eggs at the end of the month, and their song peaks. In many ways April is a better month for bird song than May, because as soon as the eggs appear, many males cease singing so much, or stop completely.

Butterflies will at last become commonplace in gardens. **Large white** and small white make their first appearances, mixing in with brimstone and, if you are fortunate, **orange-tip**.

Holly blue is common in gardens in April. It is a restless, powdery-blue butterfly that characteristically flies around the tops of hedges and around its food-plant, holly.

Look out for bats during the evenings. Although bats may fly on mild nights at

any time through the winter, they only now truly begin to emerge. By far the most likely species you are going to see over a garden is the **common pipistrelle**.

Even if you didn't know the name of this butterfly, you might guess that it is called the 'orange-tip'. This is a male; the female is easily confused with other white butterflies.

MONTHLY HIGHLIGHTS: WOODLAND

One of our finest native blossoms begins to bloom in early April. The **wild cherry** is a substantial tree, lifting its white blooms somewhat higher than the familiar ornamental species that line suburban streets. In common with other spring blossoms, however, it lasts for a pitifully short time, and the fallen petals will soon adorn the woodland floor. The blooms are white and arranged in stalked clusters, like pom-poms.

Less popular, but still bright and breezy, are the yellow-green clusters of blooms of the sycamore, often growing prolifically.

There are some new additions to the woodland floor. One of these is the ever-modest wood sorrel (called 'alleluia' in parts of Europe because of its appearance near Easter). The small, white flowers with rounded petals have lilac veins, and in the rain the flower-head nods down to protect the pollen. The leaves are clover-like, three heart-shapes joined in the middle, and they have a bitter, lemon-like taste (good in sandwiches). Wood sorrel

The wild garlic probably counts as the smelliest flower of spring, if not the showiest. It is possible to use the leaves in cookery.

forms smaller patches than many spring flowers, often in damp areas (and sometimes on limestone pavements).

April sees the appearance of the first member of a star-studded family that will grace the countryside through the summer. The **early purple orchid** emerges in woodland and coppice, often in the company of bluebells, and also on roadsides, chalk downs and hay-meadows, sometimes in great numbers. At the height of its blooming, at the end of April, it smells fragrant, but apparently becomes less and less pleasant as time moves on. The name 'orchid' – don't say I told you – actually means 'testicle', referring to the double-lobed roots of this plant.

A species in another very popular family, **common dog violet**, comes into flower in April on wooded banks, and spreads through woods and in churchyards. This is one of the most numerous of our violets and can be found almost anywhere. It is scentless, unlike the earlier flowering sweet violet (see page 29).

In many parts of the country, you can now tell what is growing on the woodland floor by using your nose alone. **Wild garlic** (or **ramsons**) is now in bloom and often forms large colonies to the exclusion of other plants. The leaves can be used as an alternative to table garlic.

Several less celebrated blooms are also now making their first appearance of the year. Lords-and-ladies, variously also known as **common arum**, **cuckoo-pint** or **parson-in-the-pulpit**, is undoubtedly one of the oddest. This very common plant has large, arrow-shaped waxy leaves, and a bizarre flower consisting of a cobra-like greenish hood or spathe, often tinged purple, housing a club-like structure, the spadix. The whole flower gives off the smell of decay to attract flies, which crawl down the spadix and are trapped inside the spathe by back-ward-pointing hairs; they thus pollinate the plant but sometimes die for their trouble. Remarkably, the plant also gives off a slight heat and the pollen a faint light.

The swallow is a classic sign of the advancing spring in Britain, and is the same in South Africa, where our birds go in winter. After their long journeys (13,000 km each way) they usually return to the exact same place where they nested last year.

On a very different note, births of wild boar litters peak in April. They are born in a purpose-built 'nest'. They will be suckled until the end of June.

MONTHLY HIGHLIGHTS: FARMLAND

April can be a delightful month, especially for livestock, with an abundance of new grass growth. This is the time that many beef and dairy cattle are finally unleashed outside after months of being housed indoors. In the north and in uplands, they might have to wait a little longer. Meanwhile, lambing usually finishes this month.

Crops will be sprayed from time to time with fertilizer and weed-killer. Fields that are used for grazing may also be treated with fertilizer to boost growth. New crops planted this month may include potatoes, peas and certain types of oil-seed rape.

In orchards, apples and cherries are flowering.

Things are already giddy with life when that definitive bird of summer, the swallow, arrives. Swallows occur in many habitats, but farmland is their stronghold, with many choosing barns for their nests. You are also most likely to see your first of the year flitting over fields.

MONTHLY HIGHLIGHTS: SCRUB AND THICKET

The early-flowering shrubs, such as blackthorn, are still thick with blossom. They act as a magnet for the ever-increasing insect fauna, with bees and hoverflies particularly frequent customers.

Adding some exotic purple to the scene, **honesty** comes into flower.

Any kind of scrub will attract willow warblers this month, either those passing through or those breeding – birch scrub in Scotland can be full of them. Listen out for a delightful, gentle, slightly descending scale

with a wistful air. It is very persistent and a reliable sign of spring, especially up in the Scottish Highlands.

A popular and loquacious singer, the whitethroat, arrives this month and fills the air with its scratchy song. It is like an adolescent busker, keen but musically hopeless. Blackcaps, mainly woodland birds, can be heard in scrub everywhere.

MONTHLY HIGHLIGHTS: GRASSLAND AND ROADSIDES

For most of the summer, grasslands and roadsides will be thick with the delicate, lacy white flowers of various members of the carrot family. The flowers are on stalks which join at a point, like an umbrella, and are known as umbels. The first of these to flower is the ubiquitous cow parsley. It literally dominates the roadsides and byways with its feathery white flower-heads.

Among a range of other plants, the following favourites come into flower: **greater stitchwort**, garlic mustard, **cowslip** and **field forget-me-not**.

Many plant species flower in April. Stunning purple **pasque flower** blooms in a few calcareous grasslands, while some hallowed fields play host to a multitude of **snake's-head fritillaries**. Cricklade in Wiltshire, Magdalene College, Oxford (where the plants have been known since 1785), Mottey Meadows in Staffordshire and Fox Meadow in Suffolk are good places to spot fritillaries. Mid-month is best.

The moth-like **grizzled skipper** begins to

The much-loved cowslip comes into flower in April, and is especially abundant on the chalk.

fly on southern chalk grasslands. Rival males sometimes indulge in agile aerial battles.

April is a very busy month for stoats. Not only is this the peak month for births, but females are in oestrus almost immediately after, and mating activity is also high. All in all, this is a good month to see them (Mount Grace Priory, North Yorkshire, is famous for its population).

MONTHLY HIGHLIGHTS: HEATHLAND, MOORLAND AND UPLAND

Adders are displaying this month, although you'd be lucky to see them in the act. Rival males compete for female attention by raising up their front end into the air and swaying. The winner is the one that keeps going the longest.

A characteristic tree of this habitat (and many others) is the silver birch, which this month begins to produce its 3–6 cm long hanging catkins, which are greenish in colour. The closely related **downy birch** has broader, greener catkins, and is often found in uplands. **Bog myrtle** comes into flower.

Natterjack toads begin to call from ponds on heathland (and also sand dune slacks). In chorus, the males make a loud 'churring' (a sort of full-throated rattle that sounds rather like a **nightjar** and may be heard a kilometre away).

Most pairs of red-throated divers return to their breeding habitat of moorland dotted with small lochs. You might hear these birds' evocative wailing sounds.

In upland bogs and wet heaths, smart **dunlins**, with their inky-black breast patches, arrive for the first time on their breeding grounds. The song is like a sharp blast on a referee's whistle.

Blackbird-like ring ouzels are now on territory, on moorland with features often including a stream and some short turf on which the birds can feed. Their song is haunting and melancholy, and a bit like a faltering, unconfident song thrush, and is a feature of land above 800 m in the west and north of Britain.

Wheatears have also arrived, and the smart males set up territories by rocks or dry-stone walls.

MONTHLY HIGHLIGHTS: RIVERS

Crack willow comes into flower, later than other species, and with the leaves, rather than before them. The pendulous flowers are much longer and more finger-like than the 'pussy willows', and paler. Crack willow is the most abundant riverside willow, often used to support banks.

Several river fish begin to spawn in April, including the diminutive **bleak**, which needs the water to reach 15°C. It lays eggs in very shallow water in swift-flowing rivers. The **grayling**, a much larger fish with a 'sail' for its dorsal fin, also spawns in spring (March to June) in water some 50 cm deep over gravel beds. The eggs are buried. Another fish that begins to spawn now is the **stone loach**, a small, secretive fish that lives under stones and dead wood. The **bullhead** ('miller's thumb') has a similar lifestyle.

April marks the beginning of the migration of **European eels** upriver. Having hatched out in the Atlantic Ocean, the eels have arrived offshore and now begin a laborious journey upriver, where they will live for some considerable time. The migration takes place at night around the time of a spring tide and full moon. In contrast to the famous upriver migration of salmon, eels are able to move overland if it is damp enough and can even climb walls if there is enough purchase for their smooth skin. Man-made obstructions can still be a problem, though.

Meanwhile, **three-spined sticklebacks** are far from secretive, often being found in shoals in the shallows of rivers, ditches and lakes. Now is the time that the males acquire green side colouration and a scarlet belly. They build nests of vegetation and perform a zigzag dance to attract females. Once the eggs are laid the male is a zealous parent, fanning the eggs and protecting the young when they hatch.

Meanwhile, the young salmon that hatched last month now leave the gravel and begin to feed. They are known as 'parr' and live in the upper reaches of rivers for a variable time, from just a year to as long as six years, before heading downstream and becoming 'smolts', usually in the late spring.

MONTHLY HIGHLIGHTS: LAKES, PONDS AND FRESHWATER MARSHES

Freshwater lakes in early spring are perfect places to watch swans, grebes, coots and other waterbirds displaying.

You might well find both frog and toad spawn this month, possibly even in the same pond, although toads are more likely to be found in ponds with a large fish population (their spawn isn't as edible). Frog spawn is found in round gelatinous clumps with up to 2,000 eggs, each with a black centre. Toad spawn is in strings wrapped around vegetation. The strings are double stranded, with alternate rows of black eggs, making a zigzag shape.

Meanwhile, natterjack toads are only just beginning their breeding season and, unlike that of most frogs and toads, it goes on for several months and the females may spawn more than once. Their spawn is a single string, found in ponds in sand dunes and heaths.

Many water-birds put on impressive displays in April, ranging from the serene to the downright aggressive. Look out for pairs of **mute swans** cosying up breast-to-breast and arching their necks; the shape of the necks makes a heart – how romantic!

Sheets of water can, on the other hand, be battlefields in April. Those cutesy mute swans can turn nasty in a moment, charging towards intruders and driving

Several moth species, including the pale pinion, first come out in the late autumn, before hibernating and then reappearing to breed in the spring.

them off with violent flaps of their formidable wings. The threat display with the neck feathers ruffled and the wings slightly open is known as 'busking'. You are also likely to see some aggression from coots. They often approach each other head-down – a common sight of anger in water-birds – and will attempt to chase an intruder off. If birds are well-matched, they will perform a floating equivalent of kick-boxing, raising up on their haunches and kicking with their outsize feet. Moorhens will also fight like this, but before physical skirmishes break out they will ruffle their bright white backsides in threat.

Arguably the most impressive water-bird displays of all are those of the great crested grebe. Males and females interchange their roles in a sort of ballet-dance on the water-surface. By far the most common display that you are likely to see is known, not inappropriately, as 'head-shaking'. The two members of the pair simply face each other and shake their heads, as if disagreeing, while simultaneously lowering and raising their necks; both make staccato, gruff calls while doing so.

If you are fortunate, you might witness the pinnacle of great crested grebe display. If you see the two birds diving simultaneously and coming up with weeds in their bills

– keep watching. Eventually they will swim quickly towards each other, meet breast-to-breast and rear up, their feet paddling wildly and foaming the water. As they do so, they both waggle their heads from side to side, all the time carrying weeds in their bills. It's great stuff!

April is a big month for freshwater fish, with a number of species spawning from now into the summer. The **rudd**, for example, lays its eggs on waterweed and, at the same time, the males acquire a brilliant blood red pigment on their ventral fins and tail. The rudd is a shoaling fish, including when spawning.

The handsomely striped perch is also spawning communally, laying bands of eggs around weed or rocks.

Feeding on a variety of fish, **ospreys** arrive their Scottish breeding grounds.

MONTHLY HIGHLIGHTS: COAST AND ESTUARY

Among the coastal flowers blooming now are sea buckthorn, **common scurvy-grass**, wild cabbage, alexanders, **suffocated clover**, **dune pansy**, Portland spurge, thrift, **sea mayweed** and **spring squill**.

Unexpectedly, bluebells often thrive on sea cliffs and islands, giving a splash of blue to more open habitats than we are used to seeing.

April is the last month it is wise to forage for shellfish, including mussels, cockles and razor shells, before the summer.

Whimbrels head north through Britain at the end of April and the beginning of May. They usually go by the coast but sometimes overland, too.

WEEKLY HIGHLIGHTS: WEEK ONE

- Average first leafing of hawthorn
- First blooms of wild cherry
- First rowan blossom
- **Carrion crow** first eggs
- Mistle thrush first eggs
- Peregrine first eggs
- **Linnet** starts singing
- First litters of water vole of the year
- First young brown hares (aka leverets) of the year are born
- Main arrival of swallows into the country, after their journey from South Africa
- First **common redstarts** arrive from Africa on the south coast
- First arrivals of **yellow wagtail**
- First arrivals of **tree pipit**
- First common toads leave ponds, having bred
- First orange-tips fly
- **Speckled wood** butterflies begin to emerge

WEEK ONE Bird of Prey Watch

Birds of prey catch the imagination like no others. Making a living by killing requires supreme flying skills, a battery of keen senses including eyesight and hearing, tip-top bodily heath and a degree of boldness and verve. Being at the top of the food chain means that, compared to other birds, the killers have smaller populations and are less frequently encountered. Add these things together and you have star quality.

Seeing raptors is not always easy, and that is why you need to take time, perhaps in the early spring, to visit a watchpoint for them. Not long ago, bird of prey watchpoints were kept secret, passed on only by word of mouth to trusted acquaintances, for fear of persecution of raptors by gamekeepers and egg-collectors. These days, though, many bird of prey populations are in recovery mode and both those problems have subsided, along with a boost in population following the removal of various organochlorides in farm products.

In recent years conservation organizations such as the RSPB have felt confident enough to set up special areas – some manned, others not – where you can watch such species as peregrines at the nest, or near the nest. The most famous of these are in the cities, such as London (National Gallery), Derby (Derby Cathedral) and, most recently, Sheffield (University building), but others are sprinkled around the country and are proliferating. One of the longest-standing reliable sites has been Symonds Yat Rock overlooking the River Wye in Gloucestershire/Herefordshire. Nearby, the New Fancy outlook in the Forest of Dean should help you add goshawk to your list of sightings, although you will typically need a telescope to see these. Even if little else is happening, buzzards will be about and you might hear them giving their complaining, mewing calls.

The spring is an excellent time to visit any watchpoint. You won't see young in the nest, but you might witness the birds displaying or catching food. Choose a fresh, sunny day with some wind, and arrive any time after about 10 a.m. If you visit a manned site (http://www.rspb.org.uk/discoverandenjoynature/seenature/events/) there will be somebody on-site to point the birds out and identify them. The more popular the site, the more help you will get.

Peregrines attract much attention, partly because seeing a kill has to be one of the great sights in all nature, unless you happen to be a pigeon, in which case it is overrated. The peregrine only eats birds, and it often hunts by a method known as 'stooping', basically a dive from a great height onto a bird, which is struck by the talons and often has its neck broken on impact. Peregrines are known to exceed 150 km/h in near-vertical stoops – a truly thrilling piece of raw nature. There is a puff of feathers and a quick death.

The buzzard is by far Britain's noisiest bird of prey. Its mewing calls are easy to hear through the spring and summer. Note the broad wings and short tail.

Exciting as they are, peregrines are not the only birds of prey that it is now possible to watch. You can see goshawks in the New Forest, for example, including by web-cam. There are reliable golden eagle and **white-tailed eagle** sites in the Highlands, and **marsh harriers** are easy to see, especially in East Anglia. For further details on watching **red kites**, see pages 210–12.

As it happens, you don't always have to visit a special area to see some spectacular action. On clear, sunny days in March and April, one of our commonest birds of prey, the sparrowhawk, will display over woodlands. The male, and sometimes the larger female too, will soar lazily upwards in a circle, often ruffling the feathers under the base of the tail to make them conspicuous. One or more birds will also give a shrill call. Sometimes they will be more active, closing their wings and diving down towards the woodland canopy, only to pull upwards at the last minute.

Early spring is also an excellent time to watch buzzards. They are pretty common these days, so it is easy to find some good action. The display involves a bird soaring over a wood to a good height, and then plummeting down with its wings folded, only for the bird to swoop upwards at the last moment using the momentum of its dive, thereby describing a broad U shape. This is occurring in a wood near you, in every corner of Britain.

Like buzzards, most birds of prey are on the up. Catch the mood and visit a site to enjoy them.

WEEK TWO Pond-Dipping

Children have hijacked the gentle art of pond-dipping. It should be part of every wildlife enthusiast's routine, but ask anybody about it, and they will invariably think about school and holiday activities for the young. Ponds, though, are fascinating for all ages, and they teach valuable ecological lessons as well as providing entertainment. So why not attend a session? You can always hitch on the back of a child that you know.

Pond-dipping is typically considered a summer activity, but spring is actually very good, too. You have a chance of seeing newts and sticklebacks in their finery in spring – newts have bold spots and orange bellies, while male three-spined sticklebacks have brilliant red undersides (these display colours will fade later). There will also be more frogs about and, of course, tadpoles.

Pond-dipping has an easy part and a difficult part. The easy part is catching something to look at. At almost any pond (or small river, for that matter) all you need to do is to sweep the net through the water at any depth, and you will catch something, large or small. The more difficult part is identifying it. There is an impressive diversity to pond and river life, so you need a book to help you through the maze of bugs, insect larvae, water fleas, snails, worms, beetles and small fish. If you attend a session run by a local Wildlife Trust or nature reserve, there will be somebody on hand to guide the process.

You will need a certain amount of cheap equipment for a successful session. The net can be a rank-cheap one bought at the sort of store you normally ignore; the wildlife won't know the difference. You'll also need some jars to observe what you have caught; jam-jars are fine, but white plastic tubs (such as those used for ice-cream or margarine) are particularly good for having a light background that shows up the captures. For each pond-dipping session, you will need several. Also useful is some kind of magnifying glass. You can buy special observation pots that have a lid fitted with a magnifying lens. If you attend an official session, there might even be a microscope provided for the many smaller inhabitants of the ponds.

One of the great lessons of pond-dipping is the demonstration of aquatic ecology. It is easy to find plant-eaters beside meat-eaters, and within a sweep you will catch predators and their prey at the same time. You can easily see relatively closely related creatures with completely different lifestyles. One of the peculiarities of the pond ecosystem is the predominance of fascinating bugs, by which I mean true bugs, or ***Hemiptera***. For example, there is the pond skater, which uses the surface tension of the water as its own skating rink, and slides across to catch terrestrial animals that are struggling on the water's surface. The backswimmer does something similar, but paddles on its back just below the surface to reach similar prey. On the other hand, the **water scorpion** and **water stick insect** have long breathing tubes at their rear ends to help them touch the surface while remaining within the weeds in wait for prey that they grab with their legs or pincers.

Another useful lesson taught by pond-dipping is metamorphosis. While everybody knows about butterflies and caterpillars, it is a revelation when you encounter dragonfly and damselfly larvae, as well as mayflies and others. The remarkable switch from an aquatic lifestyle to a terrestrial, even flying, lifestyle is in some ways more profound than the jump from inert pupa to dazzling butterfly.

As with all forms of wildlife watching, pond-dipping has its hall of fame consisting of those animals that everybody wants to see. In that category would be the water scorpion, water stick insect, **water spider**, **great diving beetle** and **great pond snail**, as well as any small fish. If you see any of these you will be doing very well indeed.

Pond-dipping invariably comes with safety warnings, of which 'Don't fall in' tends to be the most obvious. But please take care of the pond, also. Don't keep your captures in their pots for too long (perhaps ten minutes) and don't scoop the bottom of the pond with too much vigour. Pond systems are robust, but they can be damaged.

One more thing: when you've finished, don't forget to take the child that you have borrowed back home.

WEEKLY HIGHLIGHTS: WEEK TWO

- Average first leaves of ash
- First flowers of horse chestnut are recorded
- First flowers of oak come out
- First flowers of silver birch
- First flowering of **oxeye daisy**
- Long-tailed tit first eggs
- Lapwing first eggs
- First **herring gull** eggs
- **Jackdaw** first eggs
- First eggs of wood lark
- First orange-tip butterflies on the wing
- First flight of grizzled skipper (over southern chalk downland)
- Average date of first arrival of **house martin** (8 April)
- Look out for earliest swifts
- First nightingales arrive and can sometimes be heard in coastal scrub where they don't normally breed
- Average first arrival of **grasshopper warbler**
- White-fronted geese begin to leave Scotland on the first leg of their journey to breeding grounds in Greenland
- The last winter-visiting redwings and

Fallow deer are the only British deer with palm-shaped antlers, grown only by the males. The bone of antlers is the fastest-growing in the animal kingdom.

fieldfares are seen before they leave for the Continent
- Red squirrels start moulting
- First births of **wildcats** in Scotland; they will remain around their mother's den for at least a couple of months
- First births of stoat litters, between six and nine young in all, usually in an underground burrow vacated by a rabbit or rat
- First birth of weasel litters
- First main arrival of **common white-throats**
- First main arrival of **reed warblers**

WEEKLY HIGHLIGHTS: WEEK THREE

- First flowers of elder are recorded
- Primrose day (19 April)
- Song thrush first eggs
- Robin first eggs
- Starling first eggs
- First eggs of lesser black-backed gull in their dense colonies
- Great and lesser spotted woodpeckers stop drumming
- Early broods of red squirrels are weaned
- The last **hazel dormice** finally come out of hibernation

Bluebell displays might be very much part of the British spring, but on the continent and the rest of the world, sights like this are pretty rare.

- The first litters of bank voles are born
- Fallow deer bucks begin to shed their antlers, and the adults begin to moult into their spotty summer coats (if they have them)
- Grass snake mating balls
- Typical time for first cuckoo heard in UK (southern England)
- First large white butterflies are on the wing
- The first migrant **whinchats** appear, usually on the south soast
- The first **pied flycatchers** arrive from Africa
- First main arrival of **garden warblers**
- First main arrival of **sedge warblers**
- First arrival of **hobby**
- First arrival of **turtle dove**
- **Barnacle geese** begin to leave Britain for their Arctic breeding grounds
- The last pink-footed geese are seen in Scotland before they transfer to Iceland to breed

WEEK THREE Bluebell Woods

Not many people need extra encouragement to go to view bluebells. It should be part of everybody's spring calendar. The sight of a woodland floor covered by the electric blue of these members of the asparagus family, or even a cliff-top or open field similarly adorned, is simply too inspiring to miss.

Although bluebells are common almost everywhere in the UK, absent only from Orkney, Shetland and parts of the Western Isles, they are a famously British phenomenon. The species does occur abroad, from northern Spain to Germany, and it does form some impressive carpets directly across the Channel in France and Belgium. But the sheer abundance of bluebells in our country, and the effect they have on our countryside for a few glorious weeks in spring, is unique. It has been estimated that somewhere between 25 per cent and 50 per cent of all the word's wild bluebells occur on our islands.

We should appreciate them, and we do. Many poets and writers have eulogized about the carpets, especially those in woodland. Gerard Manley Hopkins wrote that, 'In the clough, through the light, they come in falls of sky-colour washing the brows and slacks of the ground with vein-blue'. Richard Mabey speaks of the bluebells under the beeches in the Chilterns, saying, 'with the filtered light dappling the trunks and the bluebells shifting in the breeze, ambling through the flowers is like walking underwater'. Anne Brontë, one of the famous literary sisters wrote that:

There is a silent eloquence
In every wild bluebell
That fills my softened heart with bliss
That words could never tell.

And who would argue? There is perhaps no other spring plant that induces the same blissful delight in the most perfect time of year. A bluebell walk induces a yearning for spring to go on forever, and it is a gentle tragedy when the last flowers finally wither.

For now, though, in the third week of April, the peak of flowering is upon us or lies in the near future. It's time to enjoy the bliss.

Good sites for bluebells:

- Ashridge Estate, Berkhamsted, Buckinghamshire
- Arlington, Sussex
- Skomer, Wales
- Hole Park, Rolvenden, Kent
- Blickling Hall, Norfolk
- Hackfall Wood, Ripon, Yorkshire
- Long Wood, Cheddar, Somerset
- Wood of Cree, Newton Stewart, Dumfries and Galloway

- Glen Finglas, Trossachs
- Winkworth Arboretum, Godalming, Surrey
- Coed Cefn, Abergavenny, Powys
- Gaer Fawr Wood, Powys
- Chrik Castle, Wrexham
- Hardcastle Crags, Hebden Bridge, West Yorkshire
- Trench Wood, Dunhampstead, Worcestershire
- Kew Gardens, London
- Speke Hall, Speke, Liverpool
- Clumber Park, Worksop, Nottinghamshire
- Bunny Old Wood, Nottinghamshire
- Garston Wood, Dorset
- Lanhydrock, Cornwall

WEEKLY HIGHLIGHTS: WEEK FOUR

- First flowering of several orchids: early-purple orchid (woodland, grassland, verges; widespread), **green-winged orchid** (old pastures, hay meadows, dunes; local, southern), **lady orchid** (open woodland on chalk; rare, mainly Kent) and **early spider orchid** (chalk and limestone grassland rare in southern England), plus **bird's-nest orchid** (deep shade in woods; widespread) and **common twayblade** (widespread and often common on grassland, hedgerows, open woods, dunes, quarries, limestone pavements)
- Blue tits and great tits begin to lay their clutches of eggs
- Magpie first eggs
- **Little owl** first eggs
- Chaffinch first eggs
- Dunnock first eggs
- Kingfisher first eggs
- Wood pigeon first eggs
- Grey wagtail first eggs
- Nuthatch first eggs
- Golden plover first eggs
- Stonechat first eggs
- Treecreeper first eggs
- Average first arrival of **spotted flycatcher**
- The first **lesser whitethroats** arrive in the south of Britain, to scrubby sites
- **Common sandpipers** begin to take up territories along streams and beside lochs
- Main arrival of house martins
- The first returning swifts are usually seen this week (23 April)
- Peak flight of orange-tip begins (to end of May)
- Peak flight of **green hairstreak** begins (to mid-June)
- Young fox cubs may appear above ground for the first time
- There is a strong passage of bar-tailed godwits, especially along the south coast of England

WEEK FOUR Hearing the Nightingale

The impact that the nightingale has had on English culture is astonishing. It's a small, brown, highly secretive bird that spends very little time here. It arrives in April, sings for just over a month, and then departs for Africa in August – a brief stay indeed. You wouldn't think that it would make much of an impact at all.

It does, of course, have a terrific song, but this is not the only reason that Keats and Coleridge raved about the nightingale in such rarefied language. To understand the appeal of the nightingale, you have to embrace its context: it sings at the height of spring, that most romantic of times, and it also sings at night, often alone in the darkness (it also sings by day, but then has competition from an already replete daytime chorus). The very fact that its notes fade away late in May, not to be repeated until next spring, make its performances still more precious. The nightingale chimes with the season, short but sweet.

If you do go to hear a nightingale this month, keep this in your mind because, empirically, the song is impressive rather than overwhelmingly sweet-sounding and musical; some motifs are harsh and rattling. To use a metaphor, the nightingale's song seems professional rather than emotional. The song is deliciously clear and rich, and it has a remarkable dynamic range, sometimes whispering, sometimes clamorous. Some phrases begin with accelerating, tragic, sobbing notes, but that is as weepy as it gets. In some ways, it's just too perfect.

But take a nightingale trip, because you need to hear the real thing. Like a pop concert, the vocal prowess is less important than the overall experience. You will probably be taken to a blackthorn thicket overrun with white blossom, or a coppice with an undercarpet of bluebells, and the air will be heavy with the scents of spring. The profusion of fresh green leaves on the trees and shrubs will still be new enough to thrill you. To set you up there will be warm-up acts from a range of common woodland birds, all of whom are expected to be overshadowed later. And, of course, for the added drama, darkness falls for the main act.

The first few phrases are the most exciting, especially if you have never heard a nightingale before. It can be a real spine-tingling moment when it is confirmed that, yes, you are really listening to Britain's most celebrated songbird.

It might have a famous song, but the nightingale is very much a small brown bird. It sings by day as well as by night, but only for a brief period in the spring. Birds heard at night outside this time are probably robins

MAY

No bird defines spring quite like the cuckoo, whose arrival in April or May is accompanied by its loud song and whose departure is swift and secretive

INTRODUCTION

It's warm, dry and one of the sunniest months of the year; what's not to like about May? In England, the average daytime maximum temperature is a balmy 15.8°C, while in Wales it is 14.5°C and in Scotland it is 12.8°C. Only the summer months and September are hotter. The average number of sunshine hours, 190.6, is second only to July, while the average rainfall is the lowest of the year throughout the UK: on average it only rains at all significantly on nine of the month's thirty-one days. Not surprisingly, severe weather events are very unusual

– that is, unless you count thunderstorms, which often make their first appearance of the year in this month.

As far as wildlife is concerned, May is April's big brother. Much of what goes on in April goes on even more in May. For many of us, May just cannot last long enough. All the animals are looking splendid in breeding dress, they are making noises and they are often so distracted that they are easy to see. You could do a book of wildlife highlights just for this one month.

The biggest differences from April are, perhaps, the greatly enhanced diversity of wildflowers and the increase in invertebrates.

In May the countryside everywhere seems to have been rinsed in fresh, vivid green.

While there are plenty of flowers around in April, May sees the beginning of the time when botanists will want to make pilgrimages to their favourite rarities such as orchids, limestone specialists and localized shrubs. The latter include some of the rarest plants in the world (see the scrub and thicket highlights for May on pages 85–6). For the next ten weeks or so, plant finders will be among the happiest of all of Britain's inhabitants.

Invertebrate lovers won't be far behind. May is one of the glut months, when species seemingly innumerable of flies, beetles, ants and bees come out and do their thing. In fact, Britain has about 4,000 species of beetles and 7,000 species of flies. They are not all out and about in May, but anybody

studying them has some giddy weeks ahead.

HEDGEHOG DIARY: This is the big month for hedgehog mating, and it is really worth witnessing if you possibly can. The process is hilariously noisy, bad-tempered and prone to disaster, as you can imagine with each animal having 5,000 sharp spines. Hedgehogs don't form pair bonds, so any female is fair game to any male. When the sexes meet, the male's advances are invariably rebuffed by the female, who makes loud snorting noises which may continue for many minutes. The commotion often attracts other males, who need to be repelled by the first male, a process that might take time and energy. The female often chooses to leave the scene as the males bicker, head-butting and barging each other. Eventually, after much fuss and perhaps several nights, the female finally relents, presses her body close to the ground and allows the male to mount. Awkwardly, he climbs aboard and holds on by biting the female's shoulder spines with his teeth. Copulation often goes wrong and doesn't always impregnate the female, yet hedgehogs have managed to survive over the millennia despite this.

BADGER DIARY: The process of weaning the cubs begins, although they still depend on milk. The cubs' adventures take them to the entrance of the sett and just beyond, but not usually very far. Most adults begin to moult, revealing a thinner summer coat. As in previous months, mating activity does not diminish, and May is a good time to see badgers mating – if the coupling is successful, implantation of the blastocyst will be delayed until late in the year.

GREY SQUIRREL DIARY: It's a key time of year, when the spring litters leave the nest and venture into the outside world. Early in the month they take their first steps away from the drey, nervously exploring in their mother's company. Very quickly, however, they gain confidence, and the members of the litter may play together on the branches nearby, learning the skills that they need for their arboreal life. Towards month's end they stop suckling and become independent.

Now they have much to learn about finding food and avoiding predators.

BLUE TIT DIARY: The month begins with the females completing their clutches, which range in number from eight to ten eggs. They are then incubated by the female only, while the male maintains the territorial borders by song. Incubation isn't constant, and the bird will often take short breaks to feed and stretch her legs. Towards the end of the month, after between thirteen to sixteen days, the eggs hatch. A time of extreme hard work for the adults has begun. At first the female broods and the male collects food, but soon both adults are hard at it, making up to 800 visits to the nest-hole a day between them. They bring in one small caterpillar each time, often eating larger caterpillars themselves. Obviously, the abundance of caterpillars is critical for the success of the brood.

COMMON FROG DIARY: Tadpoles undergo metamorphosis, gaining hind limbs first, then losing their external gills and shortening the tail, the latter appendage being the last thing to go. Meanwhile, many of the adults are no longer aquatic animals, but live instead in vegetation next to water.

MONTHLY HIGHLIGHTS: GARDEN

Pretty much all the usual garden birds will be breeding, including robins, tits, greenfinches, starlings and magpies. Early nests of blackbirds will release fledged young from the first week of May.

This muslin moth is a male; the female is white. It's a wonder they ever meet, because the male flies at night and the female by day.

The orange-tip is in many ways the definitive spring butterfly, rarely if ever being seen beyond June (unlike the brimstone, for example). This individual is perched on garlic mustard, one of the food plants of its caterpillars.

The chances are that, sometime during the month, the eggs laid by blue tits and great tits in the garden nest-box will hatch this month (often in the third week). This, therefore, will be a time of extreme hard work for the parents. The comings and goings to the nest-box, each time carrying a caterpillar, make compulsive garden viewing.

During the month house martins will arrive and set about refurbishing their mud nests made beneath the eaves of buildings. They collect mud on the edges of pools and may need 1,000 pellets to complete construction.

Swifts turn up in earnest and fly over gardens. They usually nest on tall buildings, everywhere from rural to urban areas.

Churches and other towers provide ideal high-rise crevices.

On a fine day gardens will be full of brimstone, large white and small white – subtle spring colours.

MONTHLY HIGHLIGHTS: WOODLAND

Oak leaf-burst is in mid-May. The brilliance of the green of an oak wood in spring has to be one of the joys of the season. The male flowers, easy to see now, are loose, drooping greenish catkins.

May is the peak month for seeing several butterflies, most notably the gorgeous orange-tip, the male of which looks like a white butterfly that has dipped its wings in

The main leaf-burst of oak trees occurs in mid-May, although the odd plant begins much earlier.

the juice of an ice lolly. Arguably, this is the only common butterfly with a flight period restricted to the spring, although it may occasionally be seen as late as July in Scotland. It prefers damp fields and meadows, laying its eggs on spring blooms such as the cuckoo-flower and garlic mustard.

Much rarer is the **wood white**, a butterfly of woodland rides characterized by its slow, lazy, low flight just above the ground. It is localized in central and southern England. Another of the less common woodland spring butterflies is the **Duke of Burgundy,** which looks like a fritillary but isn't. It is mainly confined to rides within ancient woodland, although it also occurs on chalk downland. Males are famously territorial and some of nature's most elegant and harmless-looking fights occur in Duke of Burgundy colonies.

May sees some new flowers enter the woodland scene, although in contrast to the early blooms, they are usually found in clumps along rides and edges, rather than in the deep woodland. One of the showiest is **bugle**, with its bolt-upright stems and hanging-decoration flowers, making it look distinctly like an orchid. Its flowers are a deep blue. Two other May favourites are the **yellow archangel**, an indicator of ancient woodland, and **lily-of-the-valley**, which particularly favours ash woods.

Oak woods in the west and north host special breeding birds, including pied flycatchers, redstarts and wood warblers.

Birds are obviously abundant in woodlands in May and many of them are widely distributed. However, some have particular attachments to various sorts of trees, not least three species of small insectivorous birds with a particular attachment to **sessile oak** woods in the west and north (although also occurring more broadly). These three are common redstart, pied flycatcher and **wood warbler**, the former two nesting in holes in trees and the last named on the ground. Pied flycatchers, in particular, can easily be encouraged to use nest-boxes and will neglect natural holes if boxes are available! This makes them easy to see, and also to attract to suitable gardens.

Of the three, the wood warbler is the easiest to detect by sound. Its main song is a loud shivering trill, like a spinning coin coming to rest, and it also delivers a confident series of 'pew' notes. This song contributes much to the spring chorus of these woodlands, but it quickly stops when the birds pair up. Catch it now.

MONTHLY HIGHLIGHTS: FARMLAND

The fields are lush with grass and cattle should be thriving. Lambing is over and it is a time for general sheep maintenance, including shearing, tail-cropping and ear-tagging. With all stock now outside, farmers may clean out the buildings used to house them.

Hawthorn is a plant that keeps on giving: insects thrive on its blossom; birds feast on its berries; and humans can eat both its berries and fresh green leaves – though not its seeds, which are toxic.

For dairy farmers, every day is a long one. The cows are milked twice a day, once at 5–6 a.m. and once at 3–4 p.m.; they obviously need to be brought inside for this purpose.

Meanwhile, crops should be growing well, and farmers will spend much time spraying cereals, potatoes, sugar beet and peas, and also muck-spreading. Many fields are now entirely yellow, the colour of flowering oil-seed rape.

May is an important silage month. Silage is fermented, and high-moisture-stored fodder fed to livestock. It is mown from grass or crop fields and either stored in silos or in bales, which are often wrapped in black plastic, to be used later in the year.

Oil-seed rape fields are much loved by small white butterflies. Linnets and other small birds may also breed in them.

MONTHLY HIGHLIGHTS: SCRUB AND THICKET

Some of our finest blossoms are at their best, not least – surprise, surprise – May blossom. May is an old name for hawthorn, and both this and its close relative **Midland hawthorn** adorn miles of hedgerow and scrub throughout the country, with their dense clusters of white (and sometimes pink) blooms. The blossom is richly fragrant, and you can also eat the fresh leaves straight from the tree.

Looking into reasons why you might be proud to be British, the word whitebeam or sorbus might not spring to mind. Nevertheless, it happens that we host a number of species of these shrubs, flowering in May and June, that occur nowhere else in the world. One, *Sorbus whiteana*, was only discovered in 2005, in the Avon Gorge, near Bristol. The Avon Gorge is a hotspot, with twenty species in all, but the Brecon Beacons and Wye Valley are also excellent. Several of these whitebeam species are highly endangered.

In complete contrast, **stinging nettles** will soon be in flower, but now is the best time to collect them for consumption, because the newly grown leaves are tender.

Green-veined whites are flying. They have a distinctive fluttery flight compared to the other whites. They need various types of lush vegetation and lay their eggs on plants such as garlic mustard.

The quintessential 'scrubby' bird is the common whitethroat, a small, very perky warbler that is extremely common almost everywhere. It has a very short, scratchy song that is delivered with such insistent frequency that it provides the definitive soundtrack to May hedgerows. This small bird sings from bush-tops or overhead wires, and the white throat is ruffled so that it looks as though it is covered in shaving foam. The bird also lifts into a song-flight, holding its position in the air unsteadily and rising and falling before returning to its sing-post.

Another classic scrubland bird is the linnet. For much of the year linnets are dowdy, brownish finches, but in summer the males, at least, show off a brilliant crimson breast and forehead. Look for them perched on the top of scrubby bushes such as bramble, gorse or blackthorn.

MONTHLY HIGHLIGHTS: GRASSLAND AND ROADSIDES

The horse chestnut is a common roadside tree, and in May it looks magnificent. The tall branches are festooned with candelabra-like flower-heads with up to forty white or deep pink flowers.

Buttercups are often at their best in May, and may dominate entire fields and hillsides.

A number of roadside favourites come out in May, including **red campion** and **sweet cicely**. The latter is a cow parsley lookalike, commonest in the north of England. The leaves have an aniseed flavour and can be used in cooking.

In the north, **bird's-eye primrose** and **Scottish primrose** come out, the former on carboniferous limestone in the Pennines and the latter on cliffs and calcareous grassland in Scotland. Both of these primulas are of almost indescribable purplish colours.

On chalk downland among the new flowers this month are **horseshoe vetch** and **wild thyme.**

The **dingy skipper** begins to fly, but hardly lights up grassland and heathland with its plain, moth-like colours. It spends most of its day basking on bare ground.

St George's mushroom is at its best now, very good to eat, in pasture and woodland edge.

MONTHLY HIGHLIGHTS: HEATHLAND, MOORLAND AND UPLAND

Down on southern heathlands it's a great time to look for sand lizards: warm days with hazy sunshine are best. They are most easily found in open patches among deep vegetation on south-facing slopes.

Nearby, this is the mating season for the very rare **smooth snake**.

A number of unusual plants come out in May on heaths and bogs, including **butterworts**. Their purple flowers are nothing special, but the leaves and other parts are covered with sticky glands, meaning that any insect landing on them is trapped, dies and is eventually absorbed.

Right now boggy parts of acid heath and grassland play host to one of the most distinctive of all members of the sedge family: the confusingly named **cottongrass**, which isn't a grass. There's no doubt about its resemblance to cotton, though, as the white inflorescences bob in the wind. It often grows in large patches. There are four species in Britain.

Patches of wet heathland and moorland will turn pink this month with the flowering of bog myrtle, a low-growing shrub with reddish stems that produces small catkins. However, the glory of this plant is its scent, which is resinous and balsamic, and may carry for some yards away from the clumps.

Now is a good time to look for the unobtrusive green hairstreak, which also occurs in woodland and chalk downland and

One of the loveliest of spring moths is the magnificent emperor moth, which is mainly found on heathland and moorland. The female releases a chemical scent (pheromone) that can attract males from several kilometres away.

requires patches of scrub among lower vegetation. It is the only British butterfly with a green underside and flies until the end of June.

On upland bogs, listen out for the strange buzzy bleating of the **snipe**, reaching its peak this month. The bird flies up into the air, drops steeply down and flexes the outermost tail-feathers away from the rest. The rush of air through the feathers makes a sound rather like a sheep. You can often hear this in the evening and at night.

The delightfully colourful **dotterel** returns to its breeding grounds on high plateaux in the Highlands. The female is more colourful than the male and, once she has laid eggs, leaves her mate to incubate them. Dotterels travel north in small groups called 'trips',

The ptarmigan breeds further north than any other bird species in the world. In Britain it is mainly confined to high Scottish plateaux.

and birders delight in spotting them when they stop for a break in the journey north.

On mountaintops, female **ptarmigan** moult from their white winter plumage to a beautifully cryptic greyish-brown scalloping. The males, however, remain white throughout the month, and stick out like a sore thumb.

They aren't the only white birds. Look out too for **snow buntings** in their smart black-and-white plumage. No small bird breeds closer to the Arctic than this one, and they are at home on bleak Scottish hills.

MONTHLY HIGHLIGHTS: RIVERS

Many common river fish will be spawning.

The **roach**, which also occurs in standing water, lays its eggs in shoals. The young require a good dose of warm summer weather to survive into the autumn. The **barbel** spawns in late May, laying its eggs in gravel, also in shoals.

May is a busy time for common sandpipers, which mainly breed along northern rivers and beside lakes and lochs. These small waders fly very low over the water with flickering wing-beats, and they constantly waggle their rear ends when walking. They are also noisy, uttering high-pitched, piccolo-like calls. Their first clutches hatch in May and the first chicks can be seen at the end of the month.

American mink usually have their litters in May, so the mother will be busy collecting food for her young.

MONTHLY HIGHLIGHTS: LAKES, PONDS AND FRESHWATER MARSHES

If you visit marshes with reed beds in May, listen out for the continuous, spirited songs of reed warblers and sedge warblers, which are at their noisiest at this time of year. Reed warblers are confined to stands of **common reed**, are often bunched together and build their nests over water. Their song consists of long phrases of chirping, irritable notes in a noticeable rhythm; the birds usually sing from below the reed-tops. Nearby, the closely related sedge warbler prefers to sing not from reed beds, but from interspersed bushes within a marsh, and it often perches well within view. Its song is less rhythmic and with harsher notes. As soon as they are paired, male sedge warblers stop singing, so the first half of May is best. Reed warblers carry on for longer.

Another slightly different sound you might hear in southern Britain is the duck-like quacking of **marsh frogs**.

One of the fish of slow or still water that is spawning now is the **bream**, a shoaling fish that needs both shallow water (for the young) and deep water (as refuges and silt-feeding areas for the adults). The **tench** requires the water to reach 18°C in order to spawn, which it does in densely weeded lakes and wetlands, sometimes now but often later in the summer.

Look for the delightful frayed blooms of **ragged robin** in waterlogged soil by marshes, in ditches and banks.

There's a dance going on at the bottom of ponds in spring, as male newts, sporting their best spring colours, dance in front of females and waft their scent towards them with flicks of their tails. All the newts – smooth, palmate and great crested – acquire bold patterns with black spots and anything between red and light orange on their bellies in a further effort to impress the opposite sex.

MONTHLY HIGHLIGHTS: COAST AND ESTUARY

Thrift is blooming at its best, a familiar pink backdrop to seabird colonies.

Breeding fulmars are often in low numbers in May because the females go off to sea to feed up prior to egg-laying.

The peak arrival of **great skuas** to Scottish islands and maritime moorland occurs early in the month, and they soon settle into defending their territory by all means necessary. Adults threaten by raising their heads to the sky and opening their wings in heraldic style.

The main season for otter cub births begins in the far north, in north-west Scotland and Shetland. In the rest of the country otters may breed in any month.

Salmon smolts enter estuaries this month

and begin a short process of adaptation to the marine environment. They then swim out to the deep sea and will remain there for any time between one to three years.

Estuaries can seem quite empty of birds in summer, but one bird at least will ensure that it isn't quiet. The **redshank** is a very irascible and incredibly noisy saltmarsh bird. If you don't find one, it will find you and complain.

WEEKLY HIGHLIGHTS: WEEK ONE

- First flowering of several orchids: **white helleborine** (woods, especially beech on chalk and limestone, southern England), **narrow-leaved helleborine** (open woodland on chalk or limestone; widespread but very local), **man orchid** (chalk and limestone grassland, verges; south-east England and Midlands, uncommon) and **fly orchid** (open woodland, fens; widespread but localized)
- Wren first eggs
- Meadow pipit first eggs
- Great spotted woodpecker first eggs
- Curlew first eggs
- Great skua first eggs
- Ring ouzel first eggs
- Chiffchaff lays its first clutch of eggs
- Kestrel first eggs
- Merlin first eggs
- **Storm petrels** arrive at their breeding colonies on offshore islands
- **Manx shearwaters** lay their single egg
- Peak flight of orange-tip
- Peak spring flight of brimstone begins (to third week of May)
- Peak spring flight of **brown argus** begins (to end of June)
- Peak spring flight of **small copper** begins (to second week of June)
- Peak spring flight of small white begins (to end of month)
- Peak spring flight of green-veined white begins (to end of month)
- Spring peak of **Adonis blue** begins (to end of June, chalk downland)
- First cuckoo heard (northern Scotland)
- First leverets (young brown hares) of the year become independent
- **Reeves' muntjac** (a deer) begins to shed its antlers and grow a new set

On 3 May 1915 the poem 'In Flanders Fields' was written by Lt-Col John McCrae. He wrote it upon the death of a friend at the Second Battle of Ypres in World War I. It would be a poignant day to see an early **common poppy** flowering.

In Flanders fields the poppies blow
Between the crosses, row on row,
That mark our place; and in the sky
The larks, still bravely singing, fly
Scarce heard amid the guns below.

We are the Dead. Short days ago
We lived, felt dawn, saw sunset glow,
Loved and were loved, and now we lie
In Flanders fields.

There is nothing quite like the colour of poppies. The poppy has been a common arable weed for thousands of years, and its actual origin is obscure.

WEEK ONE Dawn Chorus Walk

Bearing in mind that the dawn chorus is a natural phenomenon that happens throughout the spring every single morning and in every corner of the land, it is remarkable how many people have never actually heard it properly. It is also extraordinary that there should be an International Dawn Chorus Day in the first week of May, as if the dawn chorus itself were an annual event. But that only goes to show how much our society has lost touch with the natural world and its predictable cycles. Of course, sometimes we are woken by bird song and tolerate it through the foggy veil of sleep, and sometimes we are aware of the burst of bird song as we come, for example, to the end of a night shift. But few of us ever actually concentrate on it and give it our full attention. This is the week to put that right.

The best way to enjoy the dawn chorus is to join an organized trip where an expert will identify the birds and tell you what's going on. You can, of course, do it yourself, but this is one natural event that really does benefit from a commentary, even if you only do it once. You will also discover that, if you are joining a group of people, you will be far more alert than you would be on your own.

The dawn chorus is, strictly speaking, the pre-dawn chorus, so the surge of bird song will begin frighteningly early – at about 4.30 a.m., depending where in the country you are. However, in order to hear the birds singing during the transition from dark to light and to hear the authentic dawn chorus, you must be prepared to begin this early. Incidentally, if the forecast is for a windy morning, the birds won't be at their best.

The dawn chorus is the surge of song, typically performed by every individual singer of every species of songbird in the neighbourhood, in the twilight before sunrise. It is a short burst, usually lasting just twenty to thirty minutes at the most, although individual birds will carry on singing lustily all day. What makes the dawn chorus special is the remarkable number of simultaneous voices at its peak. It's almost like a wave of sound crashing over your ears, and it can be quite overwhelming when you are out there submerged in it. It is perfectly apt to liken

it to a rousing and spellbinding passage of music at a concert.

To many listeners, though, it is actually the build-up to the dawn chorus that is most enjoyable, since it is quite slow. Your experience will begin in complete darkness and your ears strain for the first voice. It is often a hooting owl, in fact, finishing its own night shift. If you are in an open area, the skylark really does live up to the phrase 'up with the lark' (often up before 4 a.m. where I do a walk each year). In woodland or a garden you are most likely to hear a robin first, or a blackbird. These species often hunt in shady leaf-litter, and have large eyes, perhaps meaning they are switched on to sing sooner than other birds.

Once the first voice has begun, others will be logged every few minutes, and it is fun to note down the succession of species. After the robin and blackbird, the song thrush is likely to be an early starter, along with the wren and wood pigeon. Several species are typically late risers: chiffchaffs and dunnocks, in my experience, are almost always among the last to start up. By 5 a.m. you should have accrued a list of twenty or so species. However, this is not a trip to try to learn bird-song identification. It is better just to enjoy the succession of species and the babbling peak of the chorus.

By the time it is light, the peak has passed. At this time of the year there will still be plenty of song, but your emphasis can shift to a well-earned cup of coffee. But before you go, it is worth contemplating what the dawn chorus actually means.

Why do birds have a short burst of voices in the twilight? Actually, nobody is entirely sure of the precise function. It is probably a roll-call of who is still alive after the night, an inadvertent advertising of free territories. In some species it is thought to be the morning proclamation by males (as a rule of thumb, only male birds sing) to assure the females that they are competent and healthy, and that the females should therefore not contemplate mating with somebody else. Dawn also happens to be a perfect time for song transmission: the clear air and lack of other activity means that a song is about twenty times more obvious than it would be in the middle of the day. It is also convenient to sing when it is dark and a bird cannot yet get down to feeding. But, these considerations aside, the dawn chorus is actually a quirk that we still don't fully understand.

Attending a dawn chorus:

- Check the listings of bird clubs, RSPB groups or your local Wildlife Trust. Some nature reserves run their own dawn chorus walks. There is bound to be an organized walk somewhere near you.

- For details on International Dawn Chorus Day see: http://idcd.info.

The blackcap is a noisy and spirited contributor to the dawn chorus, but is usually well down the order of earliest starters.

- Look out for first flowers of **dog rose**
- First flowering of orchids: **coralroot orchid** (alder and willow carr, beside lochs, dune slacks; mainly Scotland), **greater butterfly-orchid** (grassland, woods and sand dunes, on chalk and limestone; widespread) and **burnt orchid** (close-cropped chalk grassland; rare and scattered)
- Sparrowhawk first eggs
- Greenfinch first eggs
- **House sparrow** first eggs
- Wheatear first eggs
- First clutches of blackcap
- Common redstart first eggs
- Nightingales lay their first eggs
- Willow warbler first eggs
- Linnet first clutches
- Ringed plover first eggs
- First clutches of reed warblers
- Starling stops singing
- Births of summer brood red squirrels
- The last **edible dormice** finally emerge, bleary-eyed, from hibernation. Some have been there since late October!
- Main arrival of the spotted flycatcher, one of the last of the summer visitors to show up
- Peak arrival of common whitethroat
- First flight of dingy skipper (open sunny places, widespread but rare in Scotland)
- First flight of **chequered skipper** (rare, west of Scotland on damp grassland)
- The spring peak in large white butterflies occurs

The cuckoo is much easier to hear than to see – note how this bird is dropping its wings down in characteristic fashion.

- First flight of wood white begins (to beginning of July)
- Peak flight of green hairstreak begins
- Spring flight of **small blue** begins (to end of June, mainly on chalk or limestone grassland; localized)
- First brood **common blues** are flying (until the third week of June)
- Duke of Burgundy flies for the first time
- **Pearl-bordered fritillary** begins to fly for the first time
- **Wall butterfly** is on the wing for the first time
- First flight of **small heath** butterfly

WEEK TWO Hearing and Seeing a Cuckoo

This is the time of year when cuckoos are migrating north, singing as they go, so it's a great opportunity to catch up with them, even in places where they might not necessarily stay around. In recent years it has become harder and harder to encounter a cuckoo. The species declined by 49 per cent in the UK as a whole between 1995 and 2010, and in England by 63 per cent in the same period. Northern Scotland is now one of the best places to hear cuckoos dominating the spring atmosphere.

Nevertheless, all is not lost and the cuckoo is still widespread. So how do you encounter one and hear the wonderful, evocative sound, so far-carrying and easy to imitate? Part of the key is in the timing. As the old poem suggests, May is the very best month:

In April come he will,
In May he sings all day,
In June he changes his tune,
In July he prepares to fly,
In August go he must,
If he stay until September,
'Tis as much as the oldest man can remember.

In fact, though, now that the cuckoo is not so common, it is best to listen out at the beginning and the end of the day. The birds are particularly vocal at dawn and in the very early morning, and they will sometimes continue into the near darkness of evening. People can spend the whole day in the countryside and still fail to hear a cuckoo if they don't listen at these times.

Where should you listen out for them? On the whole, avoid large open agricultural fields. The edges of woodland, marshes, heaths and moors and coastal scrub are all worth trying. Cuckoos tend to avoid built-up areas.

Many people who have heard multiple cuckoos in the past confess that they have never seen one. There is a good reason for this because cuckoos are shy, and won't allow you to creep close to them when they are singing. Their song is also very far-carrying, so while you might be able to hear the bird, it might just appear as a dot in the distance. In fact, part of the trick is to recognize the bird in the air: it flies fast and low, with quick, regular wing-beats that characteristically never seem to rise above the back. As soon as you hear one cuckooing, wait for it to stop and then look out for the flying bird. Male cuckoos wander about over a wide area, so sooner or later the singing bird will be on the move.

If you're lucky you might see one perched. They often select dead parts of trees, or overhead wires on which to sit. It's often not the top of a tree or a shrub that they choose, but a side-branch. The bird is pigeon-sized with a long tail, and often hangs its wings down below its body, as if deliberately dishevelled like a delinquent youth.

- First flowering of orchids: **lesser twayblade** (moors and bogs; mainly northern), **lesser butterfly-orchid** (grassland, woods, heaths and moors; widespread, on more acidic soils than greater butterfly-orchid), **chalk fragrant orchid** (dry calcareous grassland; widespread), **heath fragrant orchid** (hill pastures, heaths, moors; widespread, but commonest in Scotland), marsh-fragrant orchid (fens, damp chalk grassland, meadows; widespread), **common spotted orchid** (common and widespread in many habitats), **early marsh orchid** (bogs, fens, marshes, dunes; widespread, but uncommon), **narrow-leaved marsh orchid** (fens, marshes and wet meadows; mainly East Anglia – scattered elsewhere) and **military orchid** (chalk grassland, woodland edge; very rare – just Oxfordshire, Buckinghamshire and Suffolk)
- Bullfinch first eggs
- Skylark first eggs
- **Pied wagtail** first eggs
- Lesser whitethroat first eggs
- Garden warbler first clutches laid
- First clutches of **oystercatchers**
- Main arrival of nightjars
- Mountain hares complete their moult and now look bluish
- First litters of common shrew are born
- First sika deer fawns are born
- First roe deer fawns are born
- First **Chinese water deer** fawns are born
- For anglers, this week often heralds the start of 'duffer's fortnight' (see pages 99–100)
- Peak time of the year for the spawning of minnow in rivers
- First appearance of dragonflies: **beautiful demoiselle, banded demoiselle**
- First flight of **swallowtails** in their fenland habitat
- First flight of rare **Glanville fritillary** (mainly Isle of Wight; cliffs)
- First **small pearl-bordered fritillaries**
- **Painted lady** butterflies usually make landfall in Britain for the first time. Numbers vary, with millions in some years and very few in others. Early ones are probably insects that hatched in North Africa and have travelled here direct
- On average, the eggs of blue tits and great tits hatch this week, although it does vary according to spring weather, with poor weather in April delaying things
- Mistle thrushes stop singing

The extraordinary red fox is one of the world's most adaptable mammals, living everywhere from the Arctic to hot deserts, taking in suburban Britain along the way.

WEEK THREE Watching Urban Foxes

Foxes can be seen easily enough throughout the year, but the height of spring is special, because that is when the cubs are most easily seen together. The youngsters first appear above ground in late April and by early June they have left the earth and will move about the neighbourhood, with litters splitting up. Therefore, May is the best time for watching fox family activity.

Actually finding an active earth can be difficult unless you are fortunate enough to have one in your own garden (gardens are very popular sites, and foxes often raise their young beneath sheds, for example). The best idea is to ask around the neighbourhood and see whether anyone has foxes; those who do often find them fascinating and may allow you to watch from a suitable vantage point. Wildlife clubs are also a good source of information. And, of course, foxes also use churchyards, patches of waste ground, communal gardens and other accessible places – they are remarkably adaptable.

If you intend to watch foxes at their best, visit the earth at dusk (or even dawn, if you are not disturbing anybody). During the long spring evenings they will often be visible well before it gets dark. If the foxes feel safe, they will make little effort to conceal themselves, especially the cubs, although for the first few evenings above ground they will be suitably cautious.

If all goes well, you should see both adults and cubs during a night vigil. For their part, the adults will spend most of the darkness collecting food and bringing it in. Urban foxes live in small groups consisting of a dominant male and female along with several young adults, and every one of these individuals will pitch in. So you might get three or four animals making deliveries on an average night. They bring in a wide variety of food: 'small birds, pets, pigeons, chickens, squirrels, hedgehogs, rats and vast numbers of meat bones', according to Stephen Harris, author of *Urban Foxes*. They also bring an assortment of play items for the cubs, including balls of all kinds, clothes and, a great favourite, shoes. Human footwear causes endless fascination for foxes of all ages, presumably because shoes and boots are smelly and a good size to chew.

The cubs lap it all up with charm and brio. They spend the evenings eating and playing. Much time is spent mock-fighting and chasing and, to be honest, they can cause havoc and destruction in a garden – flattening the lawn, wearing down plants and investigating everything. They chew plastic, dig, scatter plant pots and leave no item unturned. They will throw gloves or plant pots into the air and then jump on them, to practise their hunting skills. Nothing is wasted – except the garden itself, or the land next to the earth. After a few weeks they can catch some food for themselves, although it tends to be easy stuff: earthworms on rainy nights, beetles, ants and a few fledgling birds. They are comically bad at first, showing that hunting skills are complex and difficult to acquire.

When they first emerge, the young cubs look surprisingly different to the adults. Their fur is a dark chocolate-brown, their faces are much rounder, with a less pointed snout. This changes over the first few weeks that they emerge and they are soon simply smaller versions of their parents. Incidentally, most litters contain four or five cubs.

It isn't easy being an urban fox. Rather like many a city dweller, life for them is fast, short and full of action. It seems that many individuals only live about eighteen months, and the youngsters are the most vulnerable once they have left the care of the adults and their entourage. These moments in the spring, when all is carefree, are special and brief – rather like the season itself.

WEEKLY HIGHLIGHTS: WEEK FOUR

- First flowering of orchids: **lady's-slipper** (very rare; a few sites on limestone in the north of England), **heath spotted orchid** (heaths and moors on acid soils; widespread), **northern marsh orchid** (marshes, fens, meadows and dune slacks; northern half of UK) and **monkey orchid** (dry grassland and woodland edge; very rare, Oxfordshire and Kent)
- Goldfinch first eggs
- Yellowhammer first eggs
- Common whitethroat first eggs
- First eggs of sedge warbler
- Whinchat first eggs
- Lapwings begin to gather in flocks of hundreds, mainly on farmland, having finished breeding
- First **large skippers** appear
- First **marsh fritillaries** are on the wing (until second week of July), in grassland (including chalk and woodland clearings; localized)
- First births of polecat litters
- The first red deer fawns are born

WEEK FOUR Duffer's Fortnight: Trout and Mayflies

If you've never tried fishing but thought you might, and wondered how to do it, there is plenty of literature to help. But if you've ever wondered *when* to start, there's an unequivocal answer in this book – now.

This time of year is much beloved of anglers, especially those who prefer fly-fishing. The end of May and the beginning of June are affectionately known as 'duffer's fortnight', the time when just about anybody can catch a trout, even the rank beginner. It's not quite a case of throwing in a line and pulling something out, but it's as close as any fishing gets.

The reason that this fortnight is so blessed is that the fish are preoccupied with a bounteous time of plenty. They are dazzled by large hatchings of mayfly, and they drop their guard. The best time to catch distracted fish is typically in the mid- to late afternoon. At such times the river can seem to be covered with swarms of mayflies, from just above the surface to several metres above; the sight can be eye-catching and sometimes even remarkable, especially when the sunlight catches the semi-translucent wings of these fragile creatures.

In truth, duffer's fortnight is probably something of a fisherman's tale, because various mayfly hatchings occur at other times in the summer. Nevertheless, the late May and early June appearances of the insects are well worth seeing and understanding.

Mayflies themselves are famous for their short lives, although strictly speaking this is misleading. Some species live as nymphs for up to two years under the water's surface, so it is only the adult stages that are ephemeral. But how ephemeral they are – even if mayflies are not gobbled up by a fish, they may only live for a matter of hours, not even a day. And during this brief time they exhibit two winged stages. First to appear is a sub-adult that is dull in colour (it is called the 'dun' by anglers) and can barely fly, but it still shows the long body, lacy wings held together over the back and three long tails reminiscent of a mayfly. After some hours it moults into the full adult (the 'spinner'), a more colourful form.

The adult life may be short, but it is full of purpose. The years of living underwater as a nymph come to a crescendo. Once airborne, the adults have the task of dispersing, and above all meeting a member of the opposite sex. To achieve this, it makes sense for large numbers of mayfly – millions along a stretch of river – to emerge at the same time and join together into an enormous mating swarm (dominated by males – the females fly into it to get hitched), which is what excites fish and anglers alike. If the emergence was stretched out over a long period of time, this would reduce each individual's chances of finding a mate during its brief frolic.

Adult mayflies are almost embarrassingly functional in appearance. They have large wings for flying (even though they are weak in the air and are probably dispersed by more gusts of wind than under their own steam), the males have specially adapted eyes for looking upwards in the mating swarm, and the males also have elongated forelegs for holding the females during courtship. There is no place for anything like a gut, to allow them to feed, and this is why they succumb after such a short time. The females lay their eggs by dropping them into the water. Shortly afterwards, they drop dead on their dancefloor, the water's surface, and the spinners' span is spun.

Of course, as far as a trout is concerned, it matters not whether it eats a male or female mayfly, a dun or a spinner, catches it in mid-flight or in its death throes. It is a meal, all the same, part of a rare glut of food. It seems entirely reasonable that, in such a feeding frenzy, some of its caution is lost.

For the human observer, duffer's fortnight is a perfect combination of the very best of spring: sex, dancing, beauty and doom. And if the drama is played out on an idyllic sunny evening by a glinting river, so much the better.

JUNE

One of the few birds that sings well into the height of summer, the corn bunting has a short ditty, sounding like the jangling of keys, which it repeats hundreds of times a day.

INTRODUCTION

The Summer Solstice, when the sun is highest in the sky (the North Pole is tilted most towards the sun), occurs every year in June. The actual point usually occurs on 21 June, but sometimes on 20 June. This also corresponds to the most daylight in a twenty-four-hour period, although the precise amount varies according to latitude.

Despite the fact that the longest day is in June, this does not mean that the month is the hottest. The seas around Britain take longer to warm up than the land, so through the UK both July and August are hotter on average. In England the average maximum June temperature is 18.6°C, while in Scotland it is 14.9°C and Wales 16.8°C. You might also expect June to be the sunniest month of the year, but in England July is sunnier and in Scotland May is sunnier and there are fewer midges!

June for the wildlife watcher is Christmas in summer. It is the month that keeps on giving, delivering a deluge of wildflowers, grasses, invertebrates of all kinds, fish, pond life and almost everything else. And there's plenteous daylight, and generally fine weather, in which to enjoy the extravagance.

At large almost everything is producing. Plants outdo each other in blooms to pollinate; insects fly everywhere as if falling out of an overstocked cupboard; birds are busy with young; and small mammals scatter the ground with litters. Even animals that mate in autumn and winter, such as bats and foxes, are having young now because of a neat trick called delayed implantation – the fertilized embryo is only plugged during the spring.

The only dark cloud on June's horizon is the lack of a dark cloud on the horizon. Although rain can be a problem in June, a lack of rainfall actually affects more of our wildlife adversely. Dry conditions can be serious for a range of creatures, from squirrels to fish.

Other than that, June rocks. It's a huge outdoor wildlife party.

HEDGEHOG DIARY: June is the peak season for hedgehog litters; after the grubby flirtations of May, gestation only lasts for just over four weeks and the youngsters are born in high summer in a nest which is larger than the hibernaculum, and made of grass and leaves. Most litters contain four or five young; at birth they are pink and blind and their spines, not surprisingly, are covered with skin. They do appear almost immediately, however, but are white. The male plays no part in nurturing the youngsters, but the mother will sometimes move them to a different nest if disturbed.

BADGER DIARY: The cubs' supply of milk from the sow ceases by the end of the month and they must begin to find their own food.

They will now boldly leave the sett every night and join their mother on feeding trips. By the end of the month they will have toured the social group's territory several times over. Within the rest of the group mating behaviour will persist.

GREY SQUIRREL DIARY: The newly independent juveniles often remain together in sibling groups; they may not separate until the autumn. Both juveniles and adults build summer dreys, which are much lighter structures than the winter shelters. This is the time of year that the healthiest females become ready to breed again. There is a resurgence in courtship, although it is very easy to overlook up in the treetops.

BLUE TIT DIARY: Plenty of blue tit broods leave the nest at the end of May, but June is the month when you are most likely to notice them in the wider countryside. They are obvious because, more than almost any other British bird, blue tit youngsters are mass-produced. You see one, then another and another as the juveniles follow their parents around, beseeching them to feed them with persistently frothy calls. Fluffy to look at and with yellow cheeks, they roll off the production line with cheap plumage, which they will need to replace almost immediately.

COMMON FROG DIARY: This is the month when the young froglets usually complete their development from tadpoles. However, the timing depends on the temperature of the water, and can be delayed until the

Juvenile birds are often dishevelled and, in the case of robins, spotty as well. It will take quite a transformation to produce the immaculate, orange-breasted adult.

The gorgeous rosy footman is a moth of the south of Britain. Its caterpillar feeds on lichens.

autumn. The young are 12–15 mm long and tend to sit around on rocks beside the pond.

MONTHLY HIGHLIGHTS: GARDEN

The garden is glorious. Flower bling is everywhere, delighting eye and nose alike. Insects are everywhere, attracted by the blooms. You could spend an entire day in an averagely sized garden looking at small creatures and never get bored.

Take a look at your local starlings and you might wonder why so many seem to have gone brown? In fact, the brown versions are the young, looking very different from the adults, and June is the time when it is easiest to see them as they nag their parents for food on the lawn. The youngsters make

a very distinctive noise, a sort of explosive 'tscherr' that sounds a little like a fizzy drink escaping from a shaken bottle.

On warm, settled days – the sort when the barbecue calls siren-like to you from its corner of the garden – your outdoor supper may be interrupted by muffled squeals. Just as the light fades and the first midges bite, take a look up into the sky, where one of the garden's intriguing dramas is taking place. The squeals come from swifts, which spend most of the day circling above treetop height catching flying insects. In the evening at least some of these birds, mainly juveniles, wheel higher and higher into the sky and will actually spend the short night aloft, at an altitude of 1,000–2,000 m. They do so in small groups and evidently socialize beforehand, hence the screaming calls. It is now known that these birds sleep while flying, but they keep alert with one side of their brain and then the other, alternating between the two, resting and awake at the same time. Watch them as they rise higher and higher, eventually lost to view as they gain altitude and the light fades.

June is a great month for moths in the garden; it is possible to see a 100 species in a single night. Many will be attracted to night-flowering blooms such as **honeysuckle**, and the scent can carry for half a mile. Among the commonest current species are **heart and dart**, **small magpie** and **mother-of-pearl** (micro-moths), **garden carpet**, **common carpet** and **brimstone**.

Bats are feeding babies at the moment and living in small communes known as maternity roosts. Males are usually excluded and have their own roost sites. Poor weather can be a big problem.

MONTHLY HIGHLIGHTS: WOODLAND

One of the glories of the woodland edge in June is honeysuckle, which flowers from now until early September. It is possible to pluck the occasional tuberous flower and drink the nectar from the base, but it's really the overpowering sweet scent that is honeysuckle's glory. Samuel Pepys called honeysuckle 'the trumpet flower' that 'blows scent instead of wind'. The smell is most intense on soft June nights, and attracts moths and other insects in droves.

Welsh poppies flower in rocky, damp woodlands, mainly in Wales and south-west England.

Several trees are in flower at the moment, although they are quite easy to miss. One of these is holly, with small, four-petalled white flowers in inconspicuous clusters. Bushes are either male or female, and insects carry the pollen between the two.

One of the sights of June is male speckled wood butterflies in combat. It is a territorial conflict, although to our eyes it might look more like an aerial ballet choreographed within a shaft of sunlight. Sunny spots within a wood are jealously guarded by males on the lookout for females, who in turn are attracted to the basking spots. Females are welcomed, of course, but when a rival male enters an incumbent's patch, the two combatants buffet each other, spiralling gracefully upwards, lit up by the sun. The winner, evidently the last to pull out of the spiral, is almost always the one defending his territory.

Two uncommon butterflies are characteristic of woodland edges in June, the **small pearl-bordered fritillary** and the pearl-bordered fritillary. Both lay their eggs on violets, usually common dog violet. The pearl-bordered fritillary is the first to fly, often in early May, but June is a good month to catch up with it, especially in Scotland, where it favours south-facing woodland edges with a dense growth of bracken.

One of the very last migrant birds to arrive in Britain is the spotted flycatcher. Now is a good time to see one in the canopy, restlessly flitting into the air from a high perch, snapping up a large meal such as a bee, blowfly or butterfly. These birds used to nest commonly in gardens as well as woods, but have severely declined in recent years.

MONTHLY HIGHLIGHTS: FARMLAND

Cattle and sheep are grazing outside. Some sheep may be sheared in June rather than May.

On many farms, June sees the beginning of hay-making. Hay is cut grass or legumes that are dried and stored to be fed to animals as fodder later on in the year. Warm, dry days are obviously best. The hay is usually stored in bales.

June can be a feast for the ears, as well as for the eyes, and one of the best places to appreciate this is on farmland, especially where arable fields are separated by hedgerows. Here you can listen out for two very distinctive bird songs that are among the best-known and best-loved in Britain.

Everybody appreciates the skylark, immortalized in Ralph Vaughan Williams' 'The Lark Ascending'. In a sublime display, the bird rises from the ground, hovering with fast wing-beats, ascending steadily and all the time giving outpourings of shrill, rapid song. The song is characterized by its continuous nature, the notes carrying on, breathlessly, for minutes on end – they are like the continuous trickle of a mountain stream. The performance might include a few snatches of mimicry, but otherwise is composed of hurried, trilling notes. The lark may rise up to about 30 m, whereupon it will oscillate up and down for a few moments, before the bird begins to descend as steadily as it rose. Only for the last few metres does the singing stop and the bird plummet to earth. The nature of the song, plus the fact that skylark males often live in close proximity, means that, on a summer country walk in the right habitat, you can be serenaded by these birds for almost the whole day. Incidentally, despite the emotional connection of the song to spring, skylarks will sing in almost any month of the year.

Nearby, a quite different songster may be singing from the hedgerows. Its song is a repeated phrase often rendered 'A little bit of bread and no cheese'; aptly, it is also likened to a bird singing a sentence and then exhaling heavily at the end, as if out of breath. The song is not nearly as sweet on the ear as the skylark's, but with its dry, rattling quality it is equally evocative of warm summer days – a male yellowhammer may repeat its little ditty 5,000 times in a single day. The bird is a real 'looker', too, with a brilliant yellow head and upper breast.

A real highlight of this month is the flowering of common poppies in the fields, which continues to a lesser extent into July. As you look over the sea of scarlet flowers you are probably repeating an experience familiar to peoples from thousands of years ago. Poppies have been found associated with Neolithic earthworks, and it is probable that the association of this plant with broken-up soil is as old as agriculture itself. The actual origin of the plant is unknown.

Poppies often grow up after land has been disturbed, hence their association with war and turmoil. However, they are also common on field edges.

Ever since the Napoleonic Wars people have noticed how the upheaval of warfare, with its associated disturbance of the soil, has promoted the flowering of poppies, the seeds of which can remain viable for at least seventy years. The scarlet colour is readily symbolic of the shedding of blood. Vast numbers of poppies and other flowers sprung up after some of the grimmest battles of World War I, including Ypres and the Somme, leading eventually to the plant being taken up as a token of Remembrance Day.

MONTHLY HIGHLIGHTS: SCRUB AND THICKET

Good news – stinging nettles are beginning to flower!

June is the peak month for flowering **wild roses**, often found in abundance draped over hedgerows and roadside verges. The decorative blooms, which range from white to deep pink, are sweetly scented: that of the **burnet rose** has been described as a 'mix of honey, clotted cream and jasmine'. The commonest species is the dog rose, which can be any colour.

On chalky soils in particular, the **dogwood** shrubs will be loaded with their flat-topped clusters of creamy-white flowers, looking like umbels. They make a glorious contrast to the rich dark green of this shrub's leaves.

The definitive June blooms are those of wild roses. They come in colours ranging from white to deep red, and many smell heavenly. There are dozens of different species.

Do wild cucumbers grow in Britain? No, but there is a single representative of the cucumber family in the UK, and that's the **white bryony**. A very common climber, it has soft greenish-white flowers with delicate veins. But look: do not touch! The whole plant is extremely toxic.

Another toxic plant, **woody nightshade** also appears, with its exotic yellow and purple blooms.

MONTHLY HIGHLIGHTS: GRASSLAND AND ROADSIDES

One undoubted highlight of grasslands this summer month happens to be – grass! Britain has over 150 species in the grass family and, although they lack the colours of traditional flowering plants, many are beautiful in their own right – take **quaking grasses** and **tufted hair-grass** for example. They are wind-pollinated and don't tend to flower until this time of year. Most people take them for granted, but for enthusiasts they offer a lifetime of study.

On road verges everywhere, **hogweed** has taken over from cow parsley as the common umbellifer.

One of the glories of Britain's natural history is a chalk downland in early summer. There are a multitude of orchids, along with such delights as **kidney vetch**, **salad burnet**, **purging flax**, carline thistle, **marjoram**, **yellow rattle**,

Not many people take much notice of grasses, but midsummer is a time when many of them flower. There are more than 100 species in Britain.

squinancywort, **lady's bedstraw**, **cowslip**, **chalk milkwort** and many more. Chalk downland is a precious habitat, of which 20 per cent was lost between 1966 and 1980.

Globeflower appears in abundance on hay meadows.

The butterfly season is warming up. In areas with uncut long grass look for the large skipper, a species with low, whirring flight. It often feeds on blooms such as **burdock**. The dingy skipper is also flying now.

The unobtrusive small blue is also active at the moment, although you would be hard-pressed to call it blue. The male's upperside is faded blue at best, and the underside of both sexes is powdery blue-grey with black dots, making it similar to a mini-holly blue. Its flight is weak and low. This butterfly lays its eggs on kidney vetch, a few of which hatch out as adults to give a second generation in August.

Another butterfly in the 'blue' family that doesn't live up to its name is the brown argus. Both sexes look like the female common blue, with a brown upperside decorated with orange spots on the edge of the wing. This species flies low down and slowly, and also occurs on heathland.

Amidst all this modesty, one butterfly shines brilliant and proud. The Adonis

The gorgeous Adonis blue is only found on flower-rich grassland, where its food plant is horseshoe vetch. The larvae are protected by ants in return for the 'honey' secreted by the caterpillar's special glands. The ants will sometimes bury the larvae at night.

The handsome snow bunting is a rare breeding species confined to the tops of the Scottish Highlands. This is a male.

blue male is a stunning, almost shocking sky-blue, hard to miss even among June's opulent display of flowers. In common with the small blue, it is mainly a species found on chalk downland, and is localized in southern England. Ants in the soil often attend the caterpillars of this blue.

Look out, too, for the Duke of Burgundy on some chalk grasslands (see Woodland highlights on page pages 104–5).

On chalk downland, look out for the brilliantly red **five-spot burnet**, a day-flying moth often seen on thistle-heads and knapweeds.

Many deer (e.g. fallow, roe) have dropped their fawns this month, so take care in the countryside not to alarm the mothers. Keep your dogs on a lead.

MONTHLY HIGHLIGHTS: HEATHLAND, MOORLAND AND UPLAND

It is a busy time for reptiles. Sand lizards are laying eggs on southern heathlands, and slow worms laying theirs in damp, warm, rotting vegetation, including compost heaps in gardens.

Several plants best known for their berries flower at the moment, including **cowberry** and **cranberry**. The former is a common

The uplands of Britain hold their own special wildlife, with unusual butterflies, birds and flowering plants.

ground-hugging plant of northern moorland with modest white bell-shaped flowers, while the latter in mainly found in wet bogs, often with *Sphagnum* moss, and has small, nodding, lilac flowers.

Bilberry also blooms. This abundant dwarf shrub of moorland and open woodland on acidic soils has small, bell-like pink drooping flowers. Just as conspicuous are the bright green twigs.

In northern moorland, especially in Scotland, look out for the uncommon small pearl-bordered fritillary, which also occurs in woodland in the south. This intricately patterned butterfly lays its eggs on common dog violets or marsh violets. It shows a distinctive gliding flight that immediately separates it from most other butterflies of its size.

On southern bogs and heaths, an exciting bird of prey, the hobby, will often spend the afternoons skimming low over bogs and wet heaths in an effort to catch dragonflies, one of its staple foods. The birds are supremely aerobatic, sweeping, twisting and turning, locating each dragonfly by sight. When a hobby catches one you can see it transferring the body from its talons to its bill in mid-air.

On mountaintops, male ptarmigan finally lose their winter white colour and transform into cryptic plumage – a whole month later than the females.

The super-streamlined hobby specializes in catching tricky, speedy prey, including larks, pipits, swallows and swifts. At this time of the year it also spends much time catching dragonflies.

MONTHLY HIGHLIGHTS: RIVERS

Many popular riverside and aquatic plants come into flower this month. They include **yellow water-lilies**, **water crowfoots** and **water plantains** in the water, and **meadowsweet** on banks. Two deadly carrot-like plants also come out: the **hemlock** and its near namesake, **hemlock water-dropwort**.

A number of river fish may well still be spawning. The **gudgeon**, for example, needs the water temperature to reach 15°C or so before it will breed. It is found in the shallows over gravel in swiftly flowing water.

One of Britain's oddest migrations begins in late June. Leaving the females and young on British rivers, male goosanders embark on a journey to a special area to moult. Where do they go? Arctic Norway!

MONTHLY HIGHLIGHTS: LAKES, PONDS AND FRESHWATER MARSHES

Toadlets often emerge in June and it is an excellent time to see grass snakes in rivers and lakes.

Towards the end of the month, all newts finish egg-laying and the adults leave the pond. They become terrestrial until next spring.

June is the peak flying time for one of our rarest butterflies, the swallowtail. Although common on the Continent, in Britain it is restricted to the Norfolk Broads and only lays its eggs on a localized plant, the **milk parsley**. The swallowtail is very large, with a powerful, fairly slow-flapping flight.

Most red-throated divers lay their eggs on a large pile of weeds close to an island or the edge of the small moorland lochs on which they breed.

The **common carp** often spawns in June, and sometimes as late as July. It requires the water to reach 17°C and remain so for fourteen consecutive days.

It is a very good month for dragonflies and, especially, damselflies, which peak in abundance in the early summer. Each has different habitats, but look everywhere for **azure**, **emerald**, common blue and **white-legged damselflies**.

In summer a number of interesting plants, such as sea holly and yellow horned-poppy, can be found on shingle by the sea.

MONTHLY HIGHLIGHTS: COAST AND ESTUARY

June is the peak breeding season for **common seals**, much earlier than that of **grey seals**, which pup in autumn. They are also much more difficult to observe. Common seals don't form obvious colonies as grey seals do, and almost as soon as the pup is born, usually on a tidal sandbank, it is compelled to start swimming.

June sees a notable increase in the variety of flowers by the seashore. Those blooming include **sea campion, sea-spurreys, yellow horned poppy, sea stock, sea rocket, sea pea**, various clovers, **seaside centaury** and **sea plantain**.

One of Britain's great sights, at least as far as flowers are concerned, is the machair (a kind of Hebridean grassland) of the Western Isles and some beaches on mainland western Scotland. This is a low lying habitat based on sand mixed with the fragments of seashells,

often inundated by water and grazed at certain times of the year. The calcareous, thin soil and sympathetic farming technique makes machair phenomenally rich in plant-life, with incredible rich, colourful meadows for a short season in June. The flora includes many orchids.

For the masochist, June is a good month to brave attacks by hyper-aggressive great skuas on islands and maritime coasts of Scotland. Young skuas hatch throughout the month and their parents protect them by dive-bombing intruders, striking at the head and sometimes drawing blood. Humans are frequent targets and the attacks are genuinely intimidating. By the way, you do not need to intentionally invade the territories and disturb the birds; they will probably find you!

WEEKLY HIGHLIGHTS: WEEK ONE

🌿 First flowering of orchids: **narrow-lipped helleborine** (uncommon in beech woods

on chalk and limestone in southern England), **dune helleborine** (rare on dunes and spoil from North Wales to Scotland), **small white orchid** (mountain pastures to 700 m, cliffs; local, northern) and **southern marsh orchid** (marshes, meadows, dune slacks; southern England north to Yorkshire)
- Swallow first eggs
- Spotted flycatcher first eggs
- First weaned water vole young appear in rivers
- First great skua chicks hatch on Scottish coastal moors and islands
- This is the best week of the year to see marsh harrier food passes
- Peak flight of beautiful demoiselle (fast-flowing streams with pebbles or sand, especially across heath and moorland; scattered and local)
- Peak flight of large skipper begins
- The first **northern brown argus** butterflies are on the wing
- The first Fallow Deer fawns are born

WEEK ONE A Seabird Colony

From a global perspective, one of Britain's greatest glories is its seabird colonies. For example, Britain and Ireland host two-thirds of the world's European storm petrels, and 70 per cent of the world's **northern gannets**, and you would be hard pressed to find such significant figures for many other aspects of fauna and flora. The position of the British Isles on the edge of Continental Europe in the north-east Atlantic, together with its landscape of islands, sea loughs and cliffs ensures that it punches above its weight in puffins and gulls.

So really, quite apart from being a treat, a visit to a seabird colony is also a patriotic duty. Now, at the beginning of summer, is one of the best times of the year to go, although any time between now and mid-July will guarantee that there is plenty to see.

There are many types of bird colonies, but perhaps the most rewarding to visit are those on tall cliffs, sea-stacks and islands. It is here that you will find the greatest variety of different seabirds, and the accompanying scenery is a big bonus. If you can get up close you will find that your senses are assaulted: by the sight of teeming multitudes, the sound of birds crying, the sometimes overpowering stench of bird poo, and the dizzy height of the cliffs. If you stand and stare for a little while, another aspect of the colony becomes apparent – a succession of small incidents in the lives of the cliff-dwellers. You can witness a fight between neighbours, a raid from a marauding gull or skua or an intimate moment between members of a pair, all within a few minutes. A bird colony is the sum of thousands of small real-life cameos.

The cast of characters varies, but there are several mainstays found in most cliff colonies. The noisiest of these, and often the most abundant, is the **kittiwake**. It looks like a gull, and it is a gull, although one with unusually good manners – no killing of other birds, visiting rubbish tips, or stealing fish and chips – apart from being hideously noisy. Its trumpeting calls have a wailing quality, and have two settings – loud and very loud, echoing around the cliffs. Pairs of birds build quite a substantial nest with minimal anchoring on sheer cliff-faces. Once the young hatch they do not, in contrast to other gull chicks, wander far!

Alongside the kittiwakes on the sheerest edges are guillemots – which basically look like small penguins, except that they can fly. You won't find a nest anywhere because guillemots don't build nests; they simply lay their single egg onto a narrow ledge and incubate it standing up, often shoulder to shoulder with their neighbours. It must be uncomfortable, and the egg is in constant danger of being knocked off the cliff; it is pear-shaped to roll in a tight circle, but accidents happen. Every guillemot egg has its own unique, squiggly pattern.

Nearby to the guillemots will be their close relative, the **razorbill**, which is darker-backed, with a blade-like, laterally flattened bill, as opposed to the spiky, dagger-like bill of the guillemot. Razorbills select broader ledges, usually with something of a roof or canopy, and lay a single, rounder egg. A feature of the seabird colony is the coming and going of both these birds of the auk family. Throughout the day you can see groups of 50–100 of them swimming in the water below the cliffs, while at the same time groups will be flying low over the water, either on an errand out to sea, or returning. You might witness them landing at the cliff face, too, which they do with a complete lack of aerodynamic competence. Their wings are too narrow for finesse, and a crash-landing is commonplace.

Another character to mention is the northern fulmar. Living next to one of these must be like having neighbours with a large house and several Audis. They tend to use generous ledges near the cliff-top for their single egg, and they career around the airspace with effortless expertise on their long, narrow and stiffly held wings, like a mini-albatross. They wear a slightly disagreeable expression and, should anyone get too close, they can spit at them with stomach-oil. Charming!

Many sea cliffs will have other inhabitants, including gannets, cormorants, shags, herring gulls and even puffins, and in Scotland there might be **black guillemots** too. However, every sea cliff is a spectacle in its own right, with its own mix of species. All will be worth a visit during the busy seabird summer.

WEEKLY HIGHLIGHTS: WEEK TWO

The gannet is Britain's largest seabird, with a two metre wingspan. The adults need draughty sea cliffs and islands for their colonies, which are densely packed. Gannets are the only British birds to incubate their eggs with the soles of their feet.

- First flowering of orchids: **dark-red helleborine** (limestone pavements and cliffs; North Wales and Yorkshire northwards) and **bee orchid** (quite common in chalky habitats, clay, sand; widespread north to Cumbria and Durham)
- Blackbird last eggs
- Hobby first eggs
- Peak in clutches of reed warblers
- Turtle doves lay their first clutch of eggs
- Young moles begin to disperse, making this a good time to see one above ground
- The first adult common shrews begin to die, having bred for just a single season
- First flight of **small skipper** begins
- First adult cuckoos leave Britain to head south
- First flight of emerald damselfly, **scarce emerald damselfly**
- Last flight of orange-tip and green hair-streak
- Main flight of small skipper begins
- Main flight of **heath fritillary** begins (to end of July)
- Main flight of **dark green fritillary** begins (to end of August)
- Peak flight of **white admiral** begins (to second week of August)
- Peak flight of speckled wood begins (to end of August)
- Peak flight of **meadow brown** begins (to end of July)
- Chaffinch stops singing

WEEK TWO Orchids

A great many British wildflowers are loved and admired, but none arguably have quite the charisma and star quality of orchids. With their tall straight stems, fleshy spear-like leaves, garish colours and bizarre blooms, which vary from a very good resemblance to a bee to a jewellery stand with miniature dolls hanging from it, orchids are singular to look at and much admired, so much so that significant numbers of people will travel considerable distances to pay homage to them in season. And if you're unconvinced, now is the time to see what the fuss is about. Mid-June is the rush hour of the orchid highway. Of the fifty or so species which are known to flower naturally in the UK, four-fifths can be found in June.

Few parts of Britain lack orchids, but to see them at their best you need to visit a place where many are on display together, which is often a chalky hillside or down. Dunes can also be good and, perhaps surprisingly, so can quarries, golf courses and abandoned industrial sites with lime. If you then find that your fuse is lit, your attention will shift to rare gems in shaded woods or bogs. But

Like works of art from a great master, the flowers of burnt orchids may take years to produce – in this case up to fifteen years from seed to bloom.

WEEKLY HIGHLIGHTS: WEEK THREE

- First flowering of orchids: **fen orchid** (fens in Norfolk, dune slacks in south Wales and Devon; very rare), **musk orchid** (short turf on chalk downs, southern England) and **pyramidal orchid** (chalk downs, dunes, limestone pavements, quarries and industrial sites; north to Northumberland)
- Wild cherries appear in woods; they are among the first of the berry crop
- First flight of **Essex skipper** begins
- The last Duke of Burgundy butterflies are on the wing
- Main flight of **marbled white** begins (until end of August)
- The rare **mountain ringlet** begins to fly in the Lake District and central Scotland

most people get hooked first in open places with row upon row of opulent spikes.

The appeal of orchids lies not just in their unusual appearance, but in their unusual life histories. For example, it's astonishing to think that a relatively small plant such as the burnt orchid may take fifteen years to flower for the first time after it has set seed. Many orchids take six or more years to mature, and after all this time, some specimens only ever flower the once, for a single season (such as the early purple orchid). Clumps of orchids may disappear for one flowering period, only to reappear the next year. **Butterfly orchid** seeds may remain in the soil for many years, only flowering when conditions become suitable above ground.

Indeed, even flowering once for these plants can seem like a miracle. Orchid seeds are very small (a tenth to a quarter of a millimetre long) and carry no food reserves, so even if they fall into perfect soil with the correct conditions of acidity, light and moisture, they still rely on the attentions of a fungus to germinate properly. On first contact, the fungus attacks the orchid seed in parasitic fashion, but the seed fights back and breaks down

- The **large heath** begins to fly (until first week of August)
- Peak breeding of common seals
- The first migrant **green sandpipers** turn up in ditches, gravel pits and freshwater marshes; these are usually birds that failed to breed up in Northern Europe
- The first common sandpipers leave their breeding grounds (along rivers and beside lakes; mainly in the north)
- The first dunlins, mainly females, leave their upland bogs and moors
- Robins stop singing (between now and the end of July is the only time when they are quiet)
- Wren stops singing
- Smooth, palmate and great crested newts finish egg-laying

The bee orchid flower resembles an insect, and the mimicry is so good that bees will sometimes attempt to copulate with the bloom. If this happens the plant is pollinated. Many bee orchids, however, can self-pollinate if this doesn't happen.

the fungal cells to release vital nutrients. Over the next months the fungus and seed battle together, one gaining the upper hand and then the other. This bizarre ding-dong battle is essential for the survival of the orchid, and some plants retain these fungi in their roots up until adulthood.

If the germination is intriguing, the way that orchids pollinate is another well-known aspect of their lives. The unusual flowers, which are unique in make-up (the ovary is below the sepals and petals and the reproductive organs are carried on a specialized structure called the column), can often seem to be mimicking insects; such species include the spider orchids, bee orchids and **fly orchids**. They might even exude insect-attracting pheromones, as in the case of the fly orchid and early spider orchid. Insects are so taken with the mimics that they attempt to copulate with them and, in doing so, act as vectors in pollination. The plant's pollinia stick to their head and thorax and are thus carried to the next plant. Despite what appears to be an enormous 'effort' to mimic and attract insect pollinators, the bee orchid seldom relies on this form of pollination, instead simply pollinating itself by allowing the pollinia to fall onto its own stigma (female reproductive organ).

In most cases, though, insects do pollinate the showy flowers. The glorious, copious blooms of the butterfly orchids are fragrant at night and attract moths. Twayblades are visited by small insects, and as soon as they touch the right spot flaky lumps of pollen explode and cover the stigma. Different orchids have different mechanisms, but the truth is that the insect pollination of orchids is quite a poorly known subject, even in Britain.

As mentioned above, the bizarre appearance and lifestyle of orchids have charmed botanists for centuries, and their human history has had some interesting episodes. The famous lady's slipper orchid has always been rare and was almost wiped out by collectors, until just a single tiny colony held the fort for more than fifty years under heavy guard in Yorkshire. It has since been reintroduced to a number of former sites by Natural England and the Wildlife Trusts of Yorkshire, Lancashire and Cumbria, including Gait Barrows National Nature Reserve in Lancashire, where it is thriving. That is definitely not the case for the incredibly rare **ghost orchid**, which has been seen barely twenty times in the history of botany in Britain. It disappeared after 1986, when a single plant was found in Buckinghamshire, and in 2005 was officially declared extinct. Then, in 2009, it was rediscovered in Herefordshire. Rare flower guru Peter Marren believes that it is the hardest British flower to see. 'It can live underground without flowering properly for years on end, and it only flowers when conditions are just right. It flowers in the thick leaf mould in the darkest parts of the woodland, where there is no other vegetation.'

It is no wonder, then, that orchids capture the imagination. Nothing about them is entirely ordinary. If you take a trip to see some this week, beware their idiosyncratic allure.

The nightjar feeds on nocturnal insects, such as moths and beetles, catching them in flight, often using the moonlight to find them.

WEEK THREE Summer Night Birds

Mid-June is perhaps the sweetest time of the year to be out at night, with its long evenings and short times of darkness. For this local expedition the quarry is a trio of summer night birds. If you hear one, it's a success; two is superb; and three would be sweet indeed.

The night air is full of insects, which many of us know to our cost. Good conditions for these (still, warm) are also ideal for one of Britain's most mysterious birds, the nightjar. An owl-like bird, it has large eyes and a huge gape but, rather than catch small mammals, the nightjar specializes in larger insects, such as beetles and moths that patrol low airspace at night and twilight. In some ways it is the nocturnal equivalent of a swallow, sweeping low over the ground, jinking, turning, sometimes hovering as it chases its aerial prey. Over the heaths, moors, woodland glades and young plantations where it lives, it moves with superb aerial expertise.

What makes a nightjar trip special, however, is not so much seeing these birds (which is certainly good), but hearing them. The male makes one of the oddest sounds of all British birds. Known as 'churring', it is a long, drawn-out, somewhat hollow-sounding trill, which swaps between two frequencies, a little like a two-stroke motorcycle. Another way to imagine it is to think of hitting a hollowed-out piece of wood very fast, or even to compare it to a soft pneumatic drill. You will gather that it is difficult to describe, but in the wild it is instantly recognizable, even if you've never heard it before. An unearthly, eerie noise, it seems extraordinary that it is made vocally by a bird, but it is nonetheless.

In many of the places where nightjars occur, **woodcocks** do too, and yet the birds have completely different diets. While nightjars are catching aerial insects, woodcocks, which are a type of wader related to a snipe, will be probing their long, straight bills into damp ground for earthworms. They are equally nocturnal feeders, though, hiding out on the ground during the day, using their remarkable cryptic plumage for camouflage. The reason that woodcocks and nightjars are often seen at the same time is that, on a summer night, male woodcocks must take to the air. On the shady woodland floor it's hard to meet a member of the opposite sex, so woodcocks have an aerial display, called 'roding', which advertises their presence to local females.

The woodcock display is, essentially, a regular flight in a rough circle just above treetop height. This means that a single bird may appear several times during an evening, following the same path. The flight style looks unusual, with the bird periodically giving extra quick beats, or flicks of the wings, while it also utters a very loud 'hwick' call, often preceded by some quiet murmuring croaks. Although not as odd as the nightjar call, this sound is certainly distinctive. If a female hears and sees the display and likes it, she will give a quiet 'come-on-down' response and the birds will mate on the forest floor.

There is another unusual night bird that sings in June (and July), but in quite a different habitat, that of grassland and arable fields. This species, the quail, is no less mysterious than a nightjar or woodcock but, in contrast to these, it is virtually impossible to see. It gives a soft 'wet-me-lips' song with a ventriloquial quality. The song is apparently best heard between midnight and 2 a.m. Nowadays few people ever hear them.

WEEKLY HIGHLIGHTS: WEEK FOUR

- First flowering of orchids: **red helleborine** (very rare, woods on chalk in southern England), **green-flowered helleborine** (shade in woods, also sand dunes; scattered as far north as Northumberland), **frog orchid** (chalk grassland, limestone pavement, dunes, machair; widespread), **lizard orchid** (chalk grassland, dunes, golf courses; southern England, rare) and **late spider orchid** (chalk grassland in Kent, very rare)
- Nightjar first eggs
- Nightingales are typically seen for the last time, despite the fact that they don't migrate until August; they just become very elusive
- First **Lulworth skipper** flies, only on chalk downland in Dorset
- The rare **black hairstreak** flies for the first time in mature stands of blackthorn in the East Midlands
- The **white-letter hairstreak** also begins to fly (scrub and hedgerow with **elm** suckers; widespread in England)
- The first **silver-studded blues** are flying on southern heathlands
- The rare **high brown fritillary** flies for the first time (south-facing heather-covered woodland edge, mainly in Lake District)
- The rare **purple emperor** flies for the first time in southern mature deciduous woods
- The **ringlet** butterfly is on the wing for the first time this year
- Peak breeding of common seals
- Young weasels disperse from territory of their birth

WEEK FOUR Moth Trapping

Moth trapping is one of those activities that, from a distance, seems frankly bizarre. Why would anybody wish to trap insects that gnaw away at clothes and fly annoyingly against the house lights, unwanted and uninvited? To the urbanite, the idea of moth trapping probably confirms all their worst fears about those strange people that enjoy wildlife.

Yet there are few activities in natural history that seem so unpromising at first, yet when the toe is dipped in the water, reveal such wonders that the debutant is invariably blown away. I could not count how many times people make comments such as 'I had no idea there were so many species' or, more tellingly still, 'I didn't realize that moths could be stunningly beautiful'. Join in with a local moth trapping session on a June night, and if you are a first-timer, expect to be at least pleasantly surprised, if not stunned.

What people don't realize about moths is that,

The profusion of moths in Britain is one of its hidden glories. Even suburban gardens may host nearly 100 species on a warm June night, including such beauties as the lime hawk-moth.

to all intents and purposes, butterflies are simply showy, day-flying moths — there is no consistent, significant difference between the two groupings. Thus, some moths are considerably more colourful than some butterflies. And because there are many more moths than butterflies (2,500 versus 60), any sample will contain lots of goodies. Even more surprising is the sheer variety. On a good night in June or July, as many as 100 species could find their way into a single trap in a wood. Even in an urban garden, you can catch forty to fifty species in a single night in the peak summer season.

There is probably no better time to bask in the variety of moths than late June, although any time between the beginning of June and the third week of July will be excellent. The best nights are warm, still and overcast, without much moon. For some reason, thundery weather often brings a bonanza.

How do you appreciate the moths around you? There are two ways to do it. I recommend that you join an organized group, who will bring specialist equipment and will tell you the names of the species, which are often elaborate or remarkable (**setaceous Hebrew character**, anyone?). You can either join them on an evening or, better still, be present when the trap is opened on the morning of the following day. In the morning you will see the moths well and they will be drowsy, often allowing handling.

Of course, it is possible to do a DIY job also. All you need is a warm night, a bright bulb and an old sheet. Spread the sheet on the ground. The moths will be attracted to the light, will become disorientated and some will land on the sheet, allowing easy capture.

Whether or not you find moth trapping fascinating, it is worth a try. The biggest benefit is the realization that there is so much biodiversity out there — in this case, filling literally every corner of our land on the short summer nights.

JULY

The nightjar is found mainly on heathland and open woodland, and can be heard from mid-June 'churring' away at dusk

INTRODUCTION

July just pips August to the title of the warmest month of the year. In England as a whole, the average maximum temperature is 20.9°C to August's 20.7°C. In Scotland the average maximum is 16.9°C in July, while in Wales it is 19.1°C. On the whole, July is slightly wetter than April, May or June, although this is partly caused by the greater likelihood of thunderstorms.

Few people look forward keenly to the autumn and winter as they do the spring, and as the summer turns, there aren't the equivalent eagerly awaited markers such as snowdrops and daffodils to point the way. That isn't to say they don't exist – cuckoos depart, amphibians take to the land, the commonest dragonflies are big or red, some trees and herbs (docks, for example) tint red, berries become widespread and there are characteristic late summer blooms, such as foxgloves, **rosebay willowherb** and **hedge woundwort** to point the way. We don't ignore these signs, we just ignore the direction they are taking us.

Instead, we revel in the summer richness. June and July compete for the title of best month for wildflower blooms, butterfly and moth diversity and dragonfly species. The

Waterside places can be a little sleepy in July.

lushness and vivid green of the summer might be past – and the woods often can appear to be slumbering – but, like the end of a sale, there are still plenty of bargains to be had, despite the fading décor. Take purple emperor butterflies in woodland, pyramidal orchids on grassland and a rash of edible berries on northern moorland as three examples. There are many more.

Britain is, of course, a big island with varying climatic zones. July is the height of summer in many upland areas, and a great time to admire some rare mountain flowers.

HEDGEHOG DIARY: Now is the peak of hedgehog births in northern Britain, a little later than in the rest of the country. Down south the babies quickly become recognizable. Their eyes open when two weeks old, they develop fur and darker spines grow among the white ones. Before the month's end the young – looking like toy versions of the adults – will accompany their mother on feeding excursions.

BADGER DIARY: At last the young can feed for themselves, but late summer is actually a testing time for badgers. The range of food available declines, although wet weather at least ensures that some earthworms will be near the surface. Feeding trips are often social affairs, and a certain amount of bickering will be inevitable.

GREY SQUIRREL DIARY: July is the time when some squirrels give birth to their summer litters. Not all females breed twice in a year, and they only do so now if food supplies are adequate – a hot summer drought will discourage them. Indeed, this is sometimes a difficult time for squirrels, whose favourite food, nuts and fruits, will not become abundant again until the early autumn. The young from the spring litters will have dispersed away from their mother's territory.

BLUE TIT DIARY: Adult blue tits start to replace their plumage from late May onwards, but July is the main season of moult, when you might well find blue-tinged feathers on the ground. The moult is hard work for all birds, requiring considerable energy (it could be thought of as a kind of annual adolescence), and it is perhaps not surprising that small birds sometimes seem to lose a little vitality in the late summer. As they are no longer looked after by their parents, fledgling blue tits effectively 'leave home' in July. They disperse away, usually just within 1–2 km, sussing out potential territories, and join flocks of similar aged birds setting out in life.

COMMON FROG DIARY: July is a quiet month for frogs, although some tadpoles, still not fully metamorphosed, leave their ponds some time during the month. The adults are quite secretive and live on a diet of insects, spiders, earthworms, snails and small slugs found in the long grass, marshy ground or even woodland edge. They are often extremely active, detecting prey by sight and using their long tongues to reach and grab food.

MONTHLY HIGHLIGHTS: GARDEN

One of the most interesting garden wildlife events of the year typically happens in the last week of July – the mating flights of flying ants. For most of the year, these ordinary **black garden ants** live in their colonies in the ground. However, in order to found new colonies, they literally have to spread their wings.

Scientists studying this phenomenon have discovered that, although the precise day of the nuptial flight can be any time in late July or early August, it tends to occur between the hours of 4 p.m. and 6 p.m. This shields the ants from some predation (if they emerged in the morning they would be feasted on all day), while also allowing the queen to find somewhere to land before darkness falls.

Another consistent factor is that the flights happen during periods of warm, settled weather, and especially after a shower or rain. Too much wind or cold will postpone the great day.

Another fascinating piece of behaviour that you often witness in July comes from a quite different creature – the song thrush. For a large part of the year the diet of this familiar garden bird mirrors that of the blackbird: it searches on the lawn for worms and the in-leaf litter for insects and it binges on berries in the autumn. When the weather

If ever you needed convincing of the beauty of moths, finding the peach blossom in your garden would do the trick.

It doesn't always go to plan. Only today, writing this, I have witnessed a song thrush using decking as an 'anvil'. Unfortunately, the thrush didn't hold tight enough, and as soon as it launched the snail on the wood, the mollusc bounced right off the decking and into nearby long grass.

Be careful where you park your car in summer – or at least, try not to park it under a **common lime** tree, which are frequently planted in urban and suburban streets. The leaves attract heavy infestations of aphids; they make sticky honeydew which literally drips down.

MONTHLY HIGHLIGHTS: WOODLAND

Clumps of foxglove stain woodland edges purple at this time of the year, but the impressive, tall, flower-heavy spikes are a sure sign that spring is truly over. The leaves are famous for being the source of digitalis, long used in the treatment of heart complaints, but the plant itself is toxic.

Look along woodland edges for another mid-summer delight, the **wild strawberry**. With its broad, heavily-serrated leaves and yellow-centred pure white flowers, this small creeping herb is attractive enough. But that's not why we love strawberries, of course. Many commentators say that the fruits of true wild strawberries are tastier than those that we buy in the shops (which are a hybrid of two related American species). The only trouble is that wild strawberries are relatively tiny, easy to miss

is especially dry, however, as can easily happen in the latter half of summer, the song thrush has a secret weapon: it is able to smash the shells of snails. No other British bird does this, and it could be seen as an emergency procedure when other food is scarce. Finding large snails is easy enough, even human beings can do this, but the skill lies in the opening. The bird holds the outer edge of the shell in its beak and, with a motion that has both a vertical and sideways component, it thrusts the shell onto a hard surface. Surfaces are specially chosen; they could be a rock from a rockery, some paving stones, or perhaps even a bottle; favoured spots are often betrayed by a pile of shattered shells.

even when at your feet. They make a delicious snack, but harvesting enough to make a decent pudding can be hard work. You might be fortunate to find a location full of them (recently felled woodland clearings are good, apparently), but instead why not just savour the occasional nibble? Children, in particular, will be excited to find and taste these favourites in their wild state – reason enough for a family woodland walk.

Lords-and-ladies produces its berries for the first time. They are highly conspicuous on the woodland floor, a spike of clustered bright red beads.

One of the UK's most beautiful trees, the **small-leaved lime** flowers in July, later than its rare relative the **large-leaved lime**. The hybrid between the two, common lime, is frequently planted and also occurs naturally.

The flowers are drooping clusters of yellow blossom that smell fragrant, and attract insects in great abundance – the buzzing of bees around a lime can be incredible. The flowers of this tree can be collected and brewed to make lime blossom tea, and the leaves are a decent salad vegetable.

Sweet chestnut also blooms in July, producing long (12–20 cm), narrow spikes of yellow-green flowers.

You might not immediately notice it, still less appreciate it, but at the moment deciduous woodlands can simply resound to the gentle cooing of the wood pigeon, so much so that it can create an atmosphere all of its own. These birds often breed late to coincide with an abundance of grain at harvest time. The birds eat grain and convert it into a kind of highly nutritious 'milk' to feed to their young.

A few woodland butterflies reach their peak abundance in July. Look out for the large, showy and very orange **silver-washed fritillary** in deciduous woodland. It often flies high and powerfully, but will drop down to feed on nectar-rich blooms such as bramble, thistles or **hemp agrimony**. In common with other fritillaries, it lays its eggs on violets. Often found in the same places at the same time, the showy white admiral is another splendid butterfly with powerful, gliding flight; the upperside is black with bold white markings, while the underside is a pattern of clean white and burnished orange. It lays its eggs on honeysuckle.

Topping them all, though, is the magnificent purple emperor. It has everything going for it – good looks, size, power on the wing, and an enigmatic nature. Add in rarity and you have a mix that has lured butterfly enthusiasts, siren-like, to its lairs for centuries. It isn't easy to find, though. It only flies between late June and mid-August in a few scattered large woods, particularly in Hampshire, Surrey and Sussex.

Bird song has all but evaporated, but two species of warblers, blackcaps and chiffchaffs, continue through to the end of the breeding season. The truth is that most singing birds have now fallen silent for another year.

MONTHLY HIGHLIGHTS: FARMLAND

July is a major month for harvesting crops, including winter barley and winter oats. Then, at the end of the month, the first oil-seed rape may be cut; the black seeds are used in the production of vegetable oil. Rape is often used as a break crop, planted every other year to replenish the soil with nutrients.

Once the cereal crops are harvested, the leftover stems can be used to make straw, which is baled. Straw can be used as bedding, as fuel or as the roughage component of fodder.

Other crops still need maintenance. Potatoes, for example, will need irrigating and spraying. Less usual produce such as cherries and strawberries will be available now.

Meanwhile, beef cattle should be fattening up well on rough pasture at this time of year. Pigs, on the other hand, sometimes suffer from overheating or even sunburn, and need plenty of shade and water.

Now is the time that common poppies are seeding. If you enjoy foraging, collect some seed-heads on the point of ripening and opening. Leave them a few days until they rattle when you shake them, and then turn the head upside down and cut it open to reveal the seeds. They have an excellent nutty flavour, good on bread.

Another intriguing farmland weed is **pineapple weed**. It is an ancient import that doesn't look much, but crush the round green flower-heads and you will enjoy the sweet smell of pineapple on your fingers.

The days in July are long and, on the whole, warm, and if there is one appropriate bird sound for the season, it is the soporific purring of the turtle dove. Most often heard as a gentle disembodied sound from a bird hidden in a hedgerow, the advertising call is really quite similar to the purring of a cat close-up.

MONTHLY HIGHLIGHTS: SCRUB AND THICKET

Traveller's joy comes into flower in scrub and hedgerows on calcareous soils. Much more conspicuous are the large, white, trumpet-like blooms of **hedge bindweed**, looking like mini-loudhailers.

Brambles are flowering abundantly everywhere. Their flowers are rich in nectar and much used by a variety of insects, including butterflies.

Wildlife of all kinds thrives in untidy corners, especially in summer. What most people would walk past without noticing can keep a botanist absorbed for hours.

Wild raspberries begin to appear in the second half of the month, until early August. In the northern half of the country, fruits appear on the **bird cherry**, a small shrub. They are hardly distinguishable from those of the wild cherry, a large tree.

Look out also for the white, flat-topped hydrangea-like blooms of the **guelder rose**, with small fertile flowers inside an outer rim of large white infertile ones, making it distinctive.

In July the abundant high-summer hedgerow butterfly, the **gatekeeper**, emerges, each individual with a flash of orange on the forewings and with two white-centred black spots. It is smaller and brighter than the similar meadow brown, which has a single white-centred black spot and is in its prime in June.

Nearby, in lush grasslands as well as hedgerows, look out for the much duller ringlet, which is smaller than the gatekeeper and is named for its neat yellow-rimmed black spots on the underwings. As befits a British summer butterfly, it is capable of flying in dull, cool weather as well as on sunny days.

A classic hedgerow and scrub butterfly is the white-letter hairstreak – but only because all that remains of its food-plant, elm, is suckers rather than the mature trees. The butterfly is difficult to see with its fast, erratic flight and it has a tendency to stay around treetop height.

If ever a moth proved that butterflies don't have all the bright colours, it is the scarlet tiger. It even flies during the day.

MONTHLY HIGHLIGHTS: GRASSLAND AND ROADSIDES

The July grasslands are still floral master-pieces, with much the same sort of blooms as in June.

If you take a rest by lying on any grassland in Britain for the next few months, you will probably hear a chorus of **grasshoppers** and **bush-crickets**. There are thirty-three species in Britain, each with a distinctive voice.

The burnets are characteristic of slightly different grasslands. **Great burnet** grows on neutral to alkaline, slightly damp soils, while salad burnet is characteristic of chalky soil (and the leaves are a tasty salad supplement).

Meanwhile, the **six-spot burnet** moth can be found in grassland of any light soils; five-spot burnet moths prefer chalk grassland.

Several distinctive roadside plants come into flower in July. You can hardly miss the delicate pink trumpets, often with white longitudinal stripes, of the **field bindweed**, frequently draped over roadsides, banks and shrubs. The tall stems of agrimony, with their outward-facing, yellow, star-shaped blooms, appear by roads and paths. **Wall penny-wort** (or **navelwort**) grows on western walls and cliffs, a ramrod-straight spike of green flowers with peculiar rounded leaves, each with a central dimple looking like a human navel.

It is best to avoid **giant hogweed**, an introduced plant that flourishes on roadsides. Like a giant cow parsley, but taller than a human being, it is extremely poisonous.

July is a good month for many butterflies. One of the most abundant is the meadow brown, which usually peaks in numbers this month. It is most abundant in grassland, but wanders to many other habitats as well, including gardens. It is one of the few butterflies that manages to fly when it is cloudy, or even raining.

In long grass look for two very common moth-like butterflies with golden forewings, the small skipper and the Essex skipper, with their low, whirring flight. Both lay eggs on grasses: small skipper on **Yorkshire fog** and Essex skipper on **cocksfoot**. These species are easiest to see on blooms such as **black knapweed**.

Up north, July is the best month to see the northern brown argus, a mainly Scandinavian butterfly that inhabits chalk or limestone hillsides in Scotland and the Lake District. Its food-plant is **common rock-rose**.

On the downs, the late-blooming **chalkhill blue** is now flying, replacing the Adonis blue that has a spring flight in June. The male has silvery-blue forewings, making it easily distinguishable from the more intensely coloured common blue that flies in the latter half of the month. This butterfly's food-plant is horseshoe vetch.

July is also a good month to see the marbled white, which, despite its name and neat black-and-white appearance, is most closely related to the browns such as meadow brown or gatekeeper. It is colonial, usually found on unimproved grassland and untended verges, especially on chalk. The underside is as neat and intricate as a newspaper crossword.

MONTHLY HIGHLIGHTS: HEATHLAND, MOORLAND AND UPLAND

Some July blooms to look out for on heath, moor or uplands include **wintergreens**, **dwarf cornel**, **cloudberry** and **Alpine lady's mantle**.

On lowland heaths, the parasitic plant **dodder** flowers, draped over its host plants, heathers.

In wetter areas of northern and western bogs, wild cranberries, red and shiny, become available. The commercially grown cranberry is an American relative. At the same time cowberries are found on upland and moorlands, mainly in Scotland. Their fruits are similar to cranberries, but the plant is more robust. Just to confuse you, there is also a plant called **crowberry**, with black berries.

Perhaps the classic butterfly of southern heathlands, the silver-studded blue, begins to fly at the end of June, but is at its peak in July. This butterfly has a close relationship with ants, which abound in heathland at this time of the year. The smaller insects attend the caterpillars and presumably deter some predators, in return for licking honeydew from their bodies.

There could hardly be a greater contrast to another July butterfly, the mountain ringlet. It is confined to the Lake District and parts of the Scottish Highlands, where it inhabits grassland above 350 m and up to about 700 m; as such, it is our only butterfly confined to the uplands. Even so, it is difficult to see except on sunny days. It almost invariably flies close to the ground. Next month you are much more likely to see the similar **Scotch argus**.

Much commoner on moorland and bogs, but usually found below 500 m, is the **large heath**, which is quite widespread in Scotland, parts of northern England and North Wales. It is much paler than the mountain ringlet and is also less fussy about weather conditions, regularly flying when it is dull and murky – probably sensible for where it lives!

These habitats are superb for dragonflies, including rarities. The **small red damselfly** and **keeled skimmer** are insects of lowland southern heaths, while the Scottish bogs and other habitats host rarities such as **northern**, **brilliant** and **downy emerald**, **azure hawker**, **northern damselfly** and **Highland darter**.

The moorland-loving ring ouzel has now finished breeding and begins to move around in search of berries to sustain it for its migration. Individuals will visit high altitudes for bilberries and then gather in flocks in late July to feed on rowan berries.

While most birds have now finished breeding, the eggs of the hobby, a bird of heathland and farmland, only now begin to hatch (in mid-month). This species feeds its young mainly on birds, including swallows, meadow pipits, larks and even swifts. It delays breeding so that it can feed its nestlings on juvenile birds, which are easier to catch because they are less experienced.

Ptarmigans undergo their second moult of the year (of three). They turn from cryptic mottled brown to a much greyer colour.

MONTHLY HIGHLIGHTS: RIVERS

Rivers can appear to be sleepy places in July, above and below the surface. By now most

Purple loosestrife is an attractive waterside plant that tends to form dense closed-shop patches of its own species

river fish have finished spawning, although this does depend on the weather. The **chub** will often spawn as late as mid-July, as its young require warm weather to thrive. If this doesn't happen, river spates in winter can kill them all off.

The vegetation beside rivers will be thick and rank, and several new waterside plants will be opening this month. **Purple loosestrife** is one of the most attractive, with its tall, copiously flowered spikes of deepest purple; it also grows in patches, magnifying the effect. Indeed, these patches are no coincidence, as the plant grows profusely to crowd out any competitors.

MONTHLY HIGHLIGHTS: LAKES, PONDS AND FRESHWATER MARSHES

During the month, young common toads emerge from their natal ponds and wetlands en masse – usually later than common frogs. During the month, hundreds of black 'toadlets' less than 10 mm long can be seen crawling in the long grass near to wetlands. They are heading for such habitats as open woodland, hedgerows, grassland and gardens where they will eventually hibernate.

Many aquatic plants come out in July. Look out for **white water-lily** and **amphibious bistort** in the water itself, **yellow iris** on the margins and **great willowherb** on the banks of lakes and ponds.

It feels like summer, but the autumn migration has already started. July is the peak month in Britain for green sandpipers, waders that breed in Scandinavia and are now returning south for the winter. Adults arrive first in marshes, riverbanks and lagoons, often from mid-June, with juveniles arriving from the end of this month.

Local families of Canada geese gather together with non-breeding birds to form large moulting flocks.

Coots are also moulting, and their numbers often build up on larger lakes and ponds in the late summer. They are flightless for a time.

On wet days, or those with heavy cloud cover, take a trip to the nearest large pond, marsh or reservoir. In these conditions birds that feed on flying insects, such as swifts and house martins, are forced to visit water. In the normal, still conditions of summer, these birds feed high up, above rooftop height, where they can catch aphids, ants and even airborne spiders (propelled by strands of web, like parachutes) by sweeping across the airspace. They snatch their food items one by one, using sight. In inclement conditions, however, the hunters are foiled by the fact that the air whisks their prey away, making it unavailable or simply much more difficult to catch. However, one reliable place to find food in these conditions is the water surface. Here the appearance of prey is more predictable and the insects are at higher density. The birds are attracted and, in the right conditions, they will often skim low over your head as you watch them. It is a compelling sight.

Incidentally, when a large area of low pressure sweeps over the country in mid-summer, some swifts are known to avoid the lack of food by simply flying away from the meteorological disturbance. On occasion they can be seen hundreds of kilometres from their colony, even leaving the nestlings untended. The youngsters are specially adapted to cope with short periods of starvation, but they are still vulnerable to the vagaries of food supply at any time in summer.

Ospreys may provide high entertainment on Scottish lochs and a few sites in England. The young begin to fly in the second half of July and the adults must work hard to feed them. On Rutland Water, central England, special cruises to watch the birds in action take place.

MONTHLY HIGHLIGHTS: COAST AND ESTUARY

July is the peak month for the mating of common seals, being just after the peak of births. The young seals are weaned after three to four weeks and it is evidently then convenient for the female to mate. Mating occurs in the water; the fertilized egg doesn't implant until the autumn, delaying births until next summer.

July is a good month for seeing **minke whales** in Britain, one of the few whales that enters shallow water and can be seen from headlands, as well as from boat and ferry trips. They are currently entering the waters around the Inner Hebrides, Shetland and the southern North Sea, in each place remaining for a month or two. They are easily identified by the obvious blow, their large size and sickle-shaped dorsal fin.

Quite a number of coastal fish move inshore in summer, so if you go fishing you have a much wider variety to catch. Fish may move into harbours, or estuaries, or the sub-littoral zone. Examples of fish that make these movements include **grey mullet**, **red and grey gurnards**, **sprat** and **pilchard**.

In July a curious thing happens in the life of the **shelduck**. Most adults set off on a journey to a special place for moulting – the majority go to the Heligoland Bight, off the north coast of Germany, while others go to Bridgwater Bay in Somerset. Currently they still have dependent young, in crèches, but these they abandon and leave in the care of a few selected adults, known as aunties. It is their job to see the chicks through to the flying stage.

The last **great auk** seen in Britain was found (and later killed) on Stac an Armin, in the St Kilda group, in July 1840. It is the only British breeding bird known to have become globally extinct in modern times.

Tamarisk comes into flower, throwing out sprays of soft pink flowers any time until October. It is a small tree with feathery foliage, abundant by watersides in the Mediterranean and widely planted by the seaside in Britain.

The distinctive sea holly comes into flower.

Sea bindweed, perhaps the deepest pink and most attractive of the bindweeds, also blooms.

Thrift is a mainstay of cliffs and seaside throughout the summer. Its pink blooms can be seen from April right through to October.

WEEKLY HIGHLIGHTS: WEEK ONE

- First flowering of orchids: **marsh helleborine** (marshes and fens on chalk, also dunes; throughout England and Wales) **broad-leaved helleborine** (mainly woodland, especially along paths; widespread north to Central Scotland) and **creeping lady's-tresses** (pine woods in Scotland, northern England and Norfolk)
- Latest greenfinch eggs
- Latest skylark eggs
- Latest pied wagtail eggs
- Most breeding cuckoos have now left Britain (but their young may not be out of the nest yet!)
- Song thrush stops singing
- Smooth and palmate newt eggs hatch and the young begin their metamorphosis
- Red squirrels begin to moult their tails

and will soon look very meagre and scraggy, indeed
- Main flight of small skipper begins
- Main flight of large skipper begins
- Second (summer) peak of green-veined white begins
- Second peak flight of holly blue begins (until first week of September)
- Main peak of small tortoiseshell begins (to first week of September)
- Britain's only migratory Canada geese gather to moult in the Beauly Firth in Scotland
- The annual World Worm Charming Championships take place in Cheshire (around this time)

WEEK ONE Dragonfly Watching

High summer is the peak of the year for dragon-flies. These insects are the divas of their world: good-looking, well-turned out, fast-living, and with more than a hint of a predatory nature. It is only right that they should come out on the hottest days, and shimmer.

Most people would recognize a dragonfly, but many would be surprised that there are more than fifty species on the British list. Their varied nature is reflected in their names: damsels, emer-alds, hawkers, chasers, skimmers and darters. The idea of this local expedition is to go dragonfly watching and get an idea of this variety of forms.

You can start off dragonfly watching on your own. You need a book and, usually, a close-focusing pair of binoculars, because these insects have excellent eyesight and are generally wary, not allowing a close approach. These insects are very active and, even if you don't disturb them, they are often fidgety. It may take a long time for an interesting species finally to settle.

A garden pond is actually a great place to look first, because it is good dragonfly habitat, and some ponds can attract as many as ten species in the course of a summer, including **large red**, common blue and **azure damselflies**, **broad-bodied chasers**, **common darters** and various hawkers. As with all natural history, getting a handle on the common species is the best way to start. Incidentally, dragonflies are distinguished from damselflies by being larger, more robust and faster flying; at rest, they hold their wings out and flat (damselflies tend to hold their wings up when at rest, often closed together over the back).

Sooner or later you will want to extend your search beyond the garden pond. If you are going further afield, note that good weather is essen-tial for dragonfly watching. Ideally, you want a sunny, hot day (above 20°C is best) without too much wind. The peak of activity will be around the middle of the day.

Most aquatic freshwater habitats are good for dragonflies, but obviously the more types of habitat you visit, the more species you will see. Local ponds and gravel pits, unshaded woodland ponds, canals, lowland rivers, marshes and fens, bogs and upland watercourses – all have their own suite of species. Dragonflies are actually quite difficult to identify, because males, females and developing individuals (tenerals) all look different, and there are many similar species.

To this end, you could consider joining a dedi-cated dragonfly field trip. Many are organized by local natural history groups and the British Dragonfly Society (http://www.british-dragon-flies.org.uk). The latter holds its annual Dragonfly Day in the first week of July. The advantage of going with enthusiasts is that they will be used to netting and handling individual dragonflies. If you do join a trip, you will actually be part of a growing trend. Once the preserve only of a few eccentrics, dragonfly watching is increasingly popular (a lot of eccentrics), especially among birders, who find the dragonfly-rich months of mid-summer less captivating for birding. You can even go on dragonfly watching holidays abroad.

Of course, the so-called 'dragonfly' is only the mature form. Dragonfly and damselfly larvae are mainly aquatic and, in many ways, a completely different field of study from the adults. You will have to do some pond-dipping to find them, but once again, on dedicated field trips, there is often somebody on hand to do this.

In 2009, the UK's first Dragonfly Centre was opened at Wicken Fen in Cambridgeshire, a site with twenty-two species on its list. If you are anywhere near the area in the summer, it would be worth a visit. It is run by the British Dragonfly Society and the National Trust.

Dragonflies, like this four-spotted chaser, hold their wings out horizontally at rest, whereas damselflies hold their wings up and often closed over the back

A swarm of honey bees at a natural tree site. The queen will be somewhere in the middle.

WEEKLY HIGHLIGHTS: WEEK TWO

- First flowering of orchids: **bog orchid** (bogs of *Sphagnum* moss, widespread but localized)
- Latest house sparrow eggs
- Many adult shelducks leave our estuaries and depart to spend summer and early autumn in Germany
- The first **curlew sandpipers**, adult males, arrive on British lagoons and estuaries after breeding in the Arctic
- Skylark stops singing
- Blackbird stops singing
- First young common lizards hatch out
- Main flight of Essex skipper begins

- Main flight of Lulworth skipper begins (very rare, chalk on south coast, mainly Dorset)
- Main flight of chalkhill blue begins (to first week of September, mainly southern on chalk and limestone)
- Second peak wave of large white butterflies begins (until the end of August)
- The summer peak of small white also begins, but carries on longer, until the second week of September
- Main flight of silver-washed fritillary begins
- Main flight of red admiral begins (to fourth week of September)
- **Purple hairstreak** begins to fly (until mid-August)

WEEK TWO Bee Watching

This is a day for appreciating something that most of us take for granted – bees. Most of us adore honey and a warm summer day resounds to the humming of bees, especially with plenty of blooms about. They may sting – and can be dangerous – but on the whole humans have a positive attitude to bees; they are the only biting or stinging insects that we don't curse and kill.

These days bees are hitting the headlines for being in long-term decline, certainly since the 1960s and at an accelerating rate since 1998. The situation is indeed alarming: Great Britain has apparently lost 20 species of bees and a quarter of the remaining 267 are at risk. Look out for the annual Great British Bee Count. This allows people to count bees and help to monitor their populations. It would be worth contributing to the data, which is easy even for beginners to do.

Of course, you can also enjoy the antics of bees as entertainment. The visits of bees to flowers, the regular entering and leaving colourful blooms, is as relaxing as smooth running water or ocean waves, especially with the accompanying buzz. It is also relatively easy to pick out some types of bees, such as bumble bees and honey bees. Honey bees are in fact a fully domesticated insect, while the various sorts of bumblebees are all wild animals, as are solitary bees, which don't live in hives or colonies, but as individual breeding units.

Honey bees are extraordinary animals, with their complex colony structure of the queen, drones (males) and workers (non-breeding females). The workers are particularly famous for their 'waggle dances' performed on return to the hive. The way they are aligned as they dance indicates the position of good nectar resources to other workers – in which direction and how far. When the flowers are precisely in line with the sun, the worker dances directly up the vertical cone, and if the nectar-rich flowers lie at any angle left or right the bee progresses at the corresponding angle to the vertical on the comb. Meanwhile, the distance of the nectar source is indicated by the duration of the waggle-run. Amazingly, if a bee is detained in the hive for some time before being able to communicate its instructions, when it finally gives its news it will adjust its dance to compensate for any movement in the sun in the meantime.

Bees also flap their wings to keep the hive cool. Worker bees have many functions (these vary through the life of the bee), including cleaning, defence and foraging. Some workers are charged with the task of undertaking – removing dead bees from the hive. These insects are incredible.

One of the ways to appreciate these astonishing insects is to visit a beekeeper or an open apiary event. There are about 20,000 beekeepers in the country and, in common with most enthusiasts, they are always pleased to meet and encourage new faces. An afternoon at a bee event will be illuminating and, if nothing else, you can always buy some honey.

The British Beekeepers' Association has many local branches. Contact www.bbka.org.uk.

- Summer flight of small copper begins (until second week of September)
- **Grayling** (the butterfly) is on the wing for the first time (to mid-September)
- Peak flight of gatekeeper butterfly begins (to end of August)
- Peak flight of banded demoiselle (slow-flowing streams, rivers, canals; southern half of the country)
- Great crested newt eggs hatch and the young begin their metamorphosis

WEEKLY HIGHLIGHTS: WEEK THREE

- Latest goldfinch eggs
- Latest kingfisher eggs
- First sand lizard eggs hatch
- First births of hazel dormice in nests up in the trees
- The roe deer rut begins, well before that of other deer (except muntjac, which breed all year)
- Peak flight of scarce emerald damselfly (coastal ditches clogged with vegetation; southern England, rare)

- Summer peak of the brown argus butterfly begins (to the beginning of September)
- Summer peak of common blue begins (until end of September)
- Lesser whitethroats begin to move south, usually making short movements at first. Eventually they will move east and winter in East Africa
- Common whitethroats start at much the same time, although their eventual destination is West Africa. Two species of whitethroat in the same British scrubland could be 3,000 miles apart by November
- The southward passage of willow warblers begins
- Dunnock stops singing
- The World Snail Racing Championships are held in Congham, Norfolk. The world record for covering the thirteen-inch course is two minutes exactly, set by a snail called Archie in 1995 (he promptly went to stud – an interesting thought for a hermaphrodite animal)
- The first swifts leave Britain for Africa

WEEK THREE Seeing Stag Beetles

There aren't too many insects that attract attention from the British public. And there is only one beetle that does so, and it only does so by being huge and lumbering and having horns, and perhaps also for being seen in people's gardens. The **stag beetle**, Britain's largest, is also becoming rarer; indeed, it is actually endangered in Britain.

The stag beetle is named after the outsize horns of the males, which have a resemblance to the antlers of a stag. The males use them to grapple with each other when competing for the attentions of females, as well as during courtship. The females have much smaller mandibles, but they aren't for show and are more effective at giving you a nip. Males can grow as long as 70 cm, while females can be as short as 25 cm.

Stag beetles can fly, although it would be fair to say that they aren't the most aerobatic of creatures. Indeed, the maximum they can manage is about a kilometre, which makes dispersal difficult. It also means that stag beetles always carry the look of learner-flyers, swerving alarmingly and not quite being in control. It tends to be on warm summer nights, at dusk, that they embark on their airborne adventure, and that is the best time to see them. Parks and gardens with old trees in southern England, particularly the London area, have the healthiest populations.

Stag beetles take flight for two reasons: to seek a mate or to seek a place to lay their eggs. The latter has become an increasingly difficult task, because the beetles need to find a damp, rotten tree stump – something that is unloved in the tidy culture of many urban and suburban areas. Here the females lay up to seventy eggs, and these hatch to produce large, whitish, maggot-like larvae that can grow to 11 cm in length. They chew the wood for at least three years (and up to seven) before pupating, then emerge as an adult in the autumn, rapidly disappearing into the leaf-litter and soil. Only the following spring do they take flight.

The stag beetle is localized in southern England, but a relative, the **lesser stag beetle**, is commoner and more widely distributed. The males lack the formidable mandibles of the larger species, but they are still impressive insects.

If you see a stag beetle, make sure you log your sighting: http://ptes.org/get-involved/surveys/garden/great-stag-hunt.

WEEKLY HIGHLIGHTS: WEEK FOUR

- First yew berries ripen
- First rowan berries ripen
- Latest swallow eggs
- Latest yellowhammer eggs
- Latest nightjar eggs
- First litters of the year of harvest mice are born, in a well-woven ball-like structure in the herb layer
- Young stoats, especially males, begin to disperse from their natal territory
- 'Flying ant mating day' is usually this week
- First **silver-spotted skipper** flies
- Peak autumn flight of brimstone begins (to second week of August)
- Peak flight of emerald damselfly, until third week of August (typically acid bogs, luxuriant ditches with brackish water; widespread)
- Some small tortoiseshell butterflies go into hibernation, even as early as this, selecting dark, dry places, including corners of sheds and houses
- The last ringlet butterflies are seen in numbers, although the odd one will hang on until the end of September
- The first Scotch argus butterflies appear on acid grasslands, mainly in the Highlands
- Reed warblers begin their autumn migration
- Some great crested grebes begin to leave their breeding lakes and fly to their winter quarters, which may be on the sea.
- The first bar-tailed godwits return to British estuaries after breeding in the far north (**Black-tailed godwits** also return, from Iceland)
- Juvenile dunlins begin to arrive on British estuaries and lagoons

There are many species of molluscs to be found on Britain's shores. These are periwinkles, but others include cockles, tellins, mussels and razor shells.

WEEK FOUR Rock-pooling

This might be a local or a long-distance expedition for you, depending on how close you live to the sea. But most holiday seasons take you to the beach, and near most beaches are some of Britain's best wildlife sites for sheer, weird variety: those that are in the intertidal zone.

Rock pools are actually only a small part of the intertidal zone, the area left on a beach between high and low tide, covered twice a day. There is also sand, mud and those areas of rock that have no pools. It is a profoundly different world to the one we are used to, a stepping stone to the marine. The creatures seem far more removed from us than birds or mammals, or even butterflies and freshwater fish, and somehow they seem more menacing. Children recoil in terror at the thought of crabs. **Sea anemones** could be creations from the TV series *Dr Who*. That is part of the appeal of rock-pooling: bizarre life-forms that you can touch with your hands.

That, incidentally, is one of the tips for exploring this habitat – use your hands, not a net, as that might damage the creatures you are looking at; few will bite or sting you. Another is to make sure that you go to the beach at low tide, preferably during spring tides, when more rocks or mud are exposed. Arrive about two hours before low tide. Approach the pools carefully, avoiding casting your shadow on the water – your fear of the aliens is nothing compared to theirs of you.

Other than that, simply stare, and feel. Every rock pool is like a gallery of exhibits, each one slightly different; deeper, further from the sea, differently sculpted. Some might change in character on the next tide.

Rock-pooling is easy to do, but it is also subject to dangers. Recently uncovered rocks can be slippery and treacherous, and seaweed can be like ice on a road. Rock pools are often deeper than they look. Remember to bring sun-cream in this exposed habitat – the water may reflect the sun back at you. And sorry to repeat the obvious: the pools are tidal, which means that, sooner or later, the tide will come in and cover them. For goodness sake, don't get cut off – rock-pooling is very absorbing.

If the intertidal zone is treacherous for us, it is a very challenging place to live for the creatures that reside there. Imagine it: half the time it is covered by sea, the rest it isn't. The action of wind and waves on the rocks and sand makes it very easy to be dislodged. There is a wide variation in temperature. It sounds horrendous, and the residents have to live with it. Some, as you know, cling to rocks – barnacles and limpets, for example. Others, such as shrimps and crabs take shelter in rocky fissures or under rocks or in the seaweed, and these can be the best places to find them. Still others keep themselves buried in the sand when the tide is out, and a little gentle digging in a rock pool may reveal them.

If you bring a cheap plastic net and a couple of Tupperware boxes or ice-cream containers, use these to put your free-living animals inside. Don't leave them there for very long, however. A magnifying glass might be useful to get a close look at the many shellfish, seaweeds and small fish.

Although every rock-pooling trip is different, there are certain species that everybody wants to see (especially children). Any kind of fish will be a big bonus – these will often be **shannies**, **blennies** or **gobies**. You will need to be able a handle a **shore crab** (hold on either side of the carapace). Make sure you find at least one sea anemone, a **hermit crab** and a **starfish**. Highly sought after creatures include the **snakelocks anemone** and **blue-rayed limpet**.

One thing you should consider is that rock pools are at their very best when they aren't pools. In other words, if you can revisit at high tide and snorkel over the area, you will see the creatures at their best, and in a completely different light. In many places this is easily possible, and adds to your enjoyment of the seaside.

Some good rock-pooling sites:

- Helford Passage, Cornwall
- Shoalstone Beach, Devon
- Kimmeridge Bay, Dorset
- Thanet, Kent
- Seven Sisters Country Park, East Sussex
- West Runton Beach, Norfolk
- Redcar, North Yorkshire
- Whitby, North Yorkshire
- South Landing, Flamborough, North Yorkshire
- Porth y Pwll, North Wales
- Cold Knap Point, Barry, near Cardiff
- Hilbre Island, Merseyside
- St Bees' Beach, Cumbria
- Seaham Beach, County Durham
- Cresswell Shore, Northumberland
- Rockliffe, Kirkudbrightshire
- Roome Bay, Crail, Fife
- Calgary Beach, Isle of Mull
- Isle of Skye

August

Several birds take their leave of Britain very soon after breeding – few pied flycatchers remain after August

INTRODUCTION

August is a month when many humans migrate; the summer holidays see widespread movements in all directions, as we all know to our cost. Interestingly, people often end up travelling to the same places as wildlife, and at the same time. Just as many of us head for the coast, so do migratory birds, for example. August isn't as spectacular for birding as September, but the movements are still highly significant. Species such as the swift, pied flycatcher and nightingale leave our shores.

Another type of migration also heads for the coast, although few ever see it happening. The warming of the seas, however, sees a large number of marine organisms – everything from **basking sharks** to **jellyfish** – come closer to shore in the summer than they are for the rest of the year. Anglers rejoice in the extra diversity, and you might well see it reflected in summer rock-pooling trips. Further out, the generally calm seas mean that this is the peak season for seeing dolphins and other sea mammals.

As summer draws to an end, so depressions coming out from the Atlantic begin to affect our weather more, making August wetter and windier than June or July – as

A moody August morning by a lake in Snowdonia.

every holidaymaker wryly observes. On the other hand, if high pressure holds sway for any length of time it can also be extremely hot, with Britain's high temperature record set in August 2003 at Faversham, Kent (38.5°C, 101.3°F). The average for August is 20.7°C in England, 16.6°C in Scotland and 18.8°C in Wales.

Inland there is still plenty to admire. An excellent diversity of flowers persists into August, especially if the weather has been good. And the heathlands and moorlands are at their most colourful as the heather blooms.

HEDGEHOG DIARY: Young born back in June will now be weaned and soon become completely independent. They will feed voraciously, and need plenty of food such as beetles, caterpillars and earthworms, their usual favourites. In the garden they also eat slugs and snails, of course, so should be encouraged as much as possible.

BADGER DIARY: Late summer can be a difficult month for badgers, especially in dry conditions. Their favourite food, earthworms, are hard to find when the ground is baked, which means that they need to do a lot of digging. Badgers are omnivores, though, and they might well dig out wasps' nests, take beetles and **leatherjackets**, and also look for summer fruits such as blackberries and strawberries.

GREY SQUIRREL DIARY: For most squirrels August and September are months of preparation. They begin to moult into their winter coat, tail and ears first, and they devour the crops of the year – acorns, hazel and beech – in order to put on weight. Meanwhile, the summer litters, born last month, become independent. They face a challenging time ahead fattening up enough to cope with the winter to come.

BLUE TIT DIARY: Late summer sees big changes in the life of blue tits. Firstly, their diet begins to shift, from an essentially insectivorous one, with an emphasis on caterpillars, to a largely vegetarian diet, in which tree seeds, such as those of beech, predominate. Another change is still more noticeable to us: from being territorial birds found in pairs, blue tits become more sociable. In July the juveniles join together, often with other bird species, to form flocks that wander neighbourhoods; by mid-August, the adults have joined them. Dozens of birds of several species, including blue tits spend a few weeks roaming about.

COMMON FROG DIARY: Most adult and young frogs are now found away from the pond, in damp places such as ditches, long grass, under logs and stones and in gardens. However, if the weather has been particularly dry, they will need to return to the water.

MONTHLY HIGHLIGHTS: GARDEN

Common wasps could hardly be considered a garden highlight at any time of year,

The arrival of the setaceous Hebrew character in the garden is a classic sign of late summer and autumn. Setaceous means 'bristle-like' and the moth has a mark like the Hebrew character *nun*. This super-abundant moth is found throughout Britain, Europe, northern Asia and North America.

but why is it that they annoy you so much during your summer barbecue? The reason is most intriguing, because for a large part of the year wasps really aren't much trouble at all. In the spring and early summer, the workers are living up to their name, busily feeding on pollen to keep themselves in good health and catching enormous numbers of smaller insects, including aphids and caterpillars, to feed to their grubs (it is estimated that workers from a single nest catch 500,000 insects in a single year). Their discipline is impressive, as they nurture new generations of workers, first, and then new queens.

Once the new queens hatch from the colony after mid-summer, however, the workers' main task is accomplished. Now, you might say, they have time on their hands before dying in the autumn. At the same time, the queen's influence on the colony wanes. Previously she controlled her colony by means of exuding chemicals, but now the effect wears off. The lack of control and the lack of useful work is a perfect storm for wasp trouble, both in the colony and abroad. Violent anarchy leads to internal fights, and wasps emancipated from the nurture of grubs go in search of food, including sweet things. Not surprisingly, they are strongly attracted to all sorts of pleasant picnic and barbecue foodstuffs, and make a shameless menace of themselves.

You can swat wasps with some abandon in late summer. But remember what a useful garden pest-controller they are earlier in the year.

There are plenty of more popular insects flying at this time of year, not least butterflies. One well worth looking out for is the holly blue, which is often seen flying around hedges, higher up than other blues. This species has two food-plants, holly and ivy. It lays on holly in May, and caterpillars from these eggs hatch in July, metamorphose and will lay their own eggs on ivy in early August.

Most bats have now weaned their young and their attention will turn to mating. Bats come together in the autumn.

MONTHLY HIGHLIGHTS: WOODLAND

August isn't the best month for woodland flowers, but one you might well notice is the exotically named **enchanter's nightshade**, which had magical powers attributed to it. The plant is a little disappointing, with small, white flowers densely packed on spikes in the understorey, but it is distinctive.

Purple hairstreak is the classic late summer woodland butterfly. It is usually seen flying around the canopy of oak trees, particularly towards the late afternoon. Individuals only occasionally descend, when the attractive purple colour can be glimpsed.

There are two very different insects to look out for at the moment. Hornets are giant wasps with a tasteful chestnut-brown colour on the thorax and abdomen. They live in colonies in holes in trees, and have a worse sting than a typical wasp; happily, however, they are as gentle and benevolent as an old English sheepdog and won't attack unless severely provoked. Of course, that doesn't mean you don't get a shiver down your spine when one flies past your nose.

Completely different but just as sociable is the **wood ant**. These insects build mounds on the woodland floor, and feed partly on insects for which they forage, but mostly on honeydew from aphids. They are highly active at the moment, but the queen hides in the depths of the mound during the winter. Wood ants bite, so stepping on a nest is not recommended.

MONTHLY HIGHLIGHTS: FARMLAND

Harvested crops look beautiful and succulent, but harvest for the farmer means hard work and long days – indeed, sometimes long nights as well.

August is a key month in the arable farming calendar, when farmers have to harvest many of their crops. It's a time when you can often see combine harvesters working the fields of winter- and spring-grown wheat, and spring barley, even at night. The weather is important at this time.

As soon as the cereals are harvested, the ground is prepared for the next crop. The fields are cut for straw and the stubble is ploughed. Muck left over from the indoor housing of livestock may now be spread over the fields.

At the very end of the month, early-sown oil-seed rape may be drilled. Peas and onions are harvested. On some farms an increasingly popular crop, maize, can be collected.

House sparrows often congregate in grain-rich farmland in August. Indeed, it is the only time of year that sparrows regularly leave their territories; the rest of the time they are stay-at-homes. However, the lure of bounteous food tempts them to join together in large foraging flocks. After a brief festival of feeding, they return to their territories, often with potential young new colony members in tow.

At this time of the year, collared doves will also perform an exodus from suburbia and binge on spilled grain in cereal fields and farms. Large flocks may form here.

MONTHLY HIGHLIGHTS: SCRUB AND THICKET

Scrubby blooms are everywhere, and there is much to enjoy. A selection of popular blooms to look for include teasel, various **evening primroses** and the smart and well-dressed hedge woundwort.

Rosebay willowherb is something of a selfish plant. Seeding itself in places that have been disturbed, often after a fire, it quickly grows up in large patches, keeping everything else out. It is, nonetheless, a tall and handsome bright pink herb that adds colour to railway embankments and other waste places.

Climbing over the taller vegetation using shoots known, in science fiction-like jargon, as 'tendrils', two common members of the pea family are difficult to miss. The jewel-like **tufted vetch** has one-sided spikes (between 2 and 10 cm long) of between ten and thirty vivid purplish flowers, while the **bush vetch** is like an economy of the same, with fewer flowers of a less consistent bold colour.

There are thus plenty of flowers still around, but the fruit and berry season will soon be in full swing. The **wayfaring tree** is unusual for the fact that its dense clusters of small berries begin as green, then quickly turn red and then black, but you can often find red and black together on the same cluster. Once the berries are black, birds can eat them.

August is the perfect month for seeing a classic 'scrubby' butterfly, the **brown hair-streak**, although it is never straightforward.

In common with other hairstreaks, it is an unobtrusive insect, spending much time flying around the treetops, especially of ash.

At this time of the year, scrub – and coastal scrub in particular – can be a haven for migrant birds. Particularly towards the end of the month, birds such as the common redstart, pied flycatcher, willow warbler and whinchat become widespread all over the country as they migrate south on a broad front.

MONTHLY HIGHLIGHTS: GRASSLAND AND ROADSIDES

For many of us, the summer holidays are a time for taking long road trips. If you are unfortunate to get caught up in a traffic jam, one unusual way to quell the frustration is to look at the profusion of late summer flowers that grow on roadside verges and the central reservation. One of my personal favourites is **chicory**, a tall plant with glorious large, sky-blue flowers, which you can hardly miss where they grow, mainly on calcareous soils. Their roots are often put into coffee mixes and their leaves are a tolerable component of salad, but on high summer mornings they are good as a balm for road-rage.

Some other distinctive flowers to look out for are **bladder campion**, a sort of bloated version of the ubiquitous **white campion**; the tall, regal spikes of **great mullein**; the yellow pea-flower **yellow vetchling**; the tall spikes of **melilot**; and the tropical-sea blue of **field scabious**.

Ragwort is a trash-common yellow

Moorland comes into its own in late summer, turning pink with the blooms of heather, here contrasting with the green of bracken.

daisy-type flower found almost anywhere, but at this time it plays host to one of Britain's most distinctive caterpillars, the yellow-and-black larva of the **cinnabar** moth. At times plants can be overrun with the caterpillars, so they are hard to miss.

August is the only month when you can see the rare silver-spotted skipper flying. Similar to the large skipper, it is confined to south-facing chalk grassland and lays its eggs on **sheep's fescue** (grass). It tends to bask on bare ground.

More catholic in its habitats is the common blue, which occurs anywhere close to its near-ubiquitous food-plant, **bird's-foot trefoil**. Nonetheless it is colonial and is missing from some suitable areas. It is best looked for in the morning or early evening, when it takes a break from its frenetic fluttering to rest and bask.

MONTHLY HIGHLIGHTS: HEATHLAND, MOORLAND AND UPLANDS

Late summer transforms the austere, treeless landscapes of upland Britain into shimmering purple, as the heather flowers, making the scenery softer and more welcoming. The commonest heather, **ling**, used to be used as bedding, and the stems can be tied together to make an effective brush.

The other common species of heather are **bell heather**, with larger and brighter flowers than ling (looking like mini-designer lightbulbs) and **cross-leaved heath**, which occurs in damper areas.

Just as abundant on some heaths and moors is the bilberry. The fruits of this low-growing shrub, available in great quantity, are blue-black and very tasty. They are virtually unknown in cultivation.

Growing on many moorland edges, including in upland areas, the rowan adds its own colours to the landscape. The bright orange-red fruits in dense clusters contrast with the rich green of the leaves, which are arranged on the twig in opposing rows (pinnate).

August is the month when young adders hatch. Anywhere between a handful and twenty young may comprise a litter. The young snakes are not helped by their mother, but may remain near her for the first few days.

The classic August butterfly on heathland is the grayling, although it begins to fly from mid-July. It also occurs on chalk grassland and, particularly, on coastal dunes, a major requirement being sunny places with low vegetation. This is an inconspicuous butterfly that spends much time hidden by its perfect camouflage when basking on the ground.

Meanwhile, the equivalent in upland areas of Scotland and northern England is the Scotch argus. It only begins to fly at the very end of July and is rarely seen in September. This species prefers acid grassland and bogs up to a height of 500 m above sea level. It is difficult to find except on sunny days.

MONTHLY HIGHLIGHTS: RIVERS

The riverside flora is beginning to decline, but the various species of water crowfoot are still flowering. **Water mint** is still flowering, and so is **gypsywort**. The latter is so-called because, in far off times, the Roma were supposed to stain their skin with the juice of this plant.

Most river fish have finished spawning, but not the minnow, which will lay eggs at intervals right through from May to August.

MONTHLY HIGHLIGHTS: LAKES, PONDS AND FRESHWATER MARSHES

You might not immediately notice it, but something strange happens to our ducks in mid- to late summer. Have a look and you will see that there is either an absence of males, or those that are recognizable have turned distinctly unkempt and blotchy. What happens is that these males have assumed a special sober, female-like plumage – ducks in drag, you might say – known as 'eclipse' plumage. It occurs because, after breeding, all ducks moult their flight feathers almost simultaneously and become virtually flightless. This is a risky state of affairs, but it would be riskier if the males maintained their bright colours. Instead, then, they dress down until their bright plumage grows again.

Life in the reed beds and among waterside plants has generally quietened down, but that isn't to say that nothing is happening, including one fascinating confluence of different lives intertwining. At this time of year, **plum-reed aphids**, which live most of the year on plum or blackthorn move into reed beds to feed. This insect is small

An upland lake in August. It will be full of young fish at this time of the year.

and unassuming, but its body is packed with protein and, to a sedge warbler, it is a super-food. The birds move en masse to reed beds at this time of year (some move to northern France) and feast almost entirely on the aphids, which seem to have an effect akin to spinach for Popeye. The birds can fly direct to West Africa on a single flight. Their colleagues the reed warblers have a broader diet in autumn, with fewer plum-reed aphids, and they migrate in a series of shorter hops.

The aquatic flora is still copious although the number of species is falling. The **monkeyflower**, with its huge yellow snap-dragon-like flowers that apparently look like a monkey's grinning face, is blooming well.

MONTHLY HIGHLIGHTS: COAST AND ESTUARY

August is a good month to see basking sharks off the west-facing coasts of Britain. The second largest fish in the world, about 10 m long, the basking shark uses 'combs' in its gill-slits to filter plankton and other small organisms out of the water. It is readily iden-tified by its large triangular dorsal fin sticking out from the water as the animal feeds near the surface. Good places to see them include Cornwall, the Isle of Man, Skye, Mull and also Malin Head in Northern Ireland.

Great crested grebes may appear on sheltered coasts, often in small, well-dispersed groups. Having left their breeding lakes inland, they will moult here.

In the Scottish Highlands, young red-throated divers fledge and move to inshore waters, gradually migrating south, often in family parties.

Great skuas begin to leave their breeding grounds on Scottish coastal moorland and gradually drift south, soon passing most coasts of Britain.

Look out for black-tailed and bar-tailed godwits on estuaries and beaches in their black-red summer plumage. The adults have returned from the breeding grounds and the juveniles will follow next month.

The late summer blooms are still plentiful and include **sea knotgrass, red** and **saltmarsh goosefoot, sea beet, sea purslane, glasswort, sea-blites, sea spurge, tree mallow, sea carrot, oyster-plant** and **autumn squill**.

WEEKLY HIGHLIGHTS: WEEK ONE

- Best week for harvesting bilberries
- First ripe elderberries
- First flowering of orchids: **violet helleborine** (heavy shaded deciduous woodland on chalk; Midlands and southern England), **Irish lady's-tresses** (by lochs in north-west Scotland; rare)

The common lizard can often be found basking on paths and walls.

- 'Flying ant mating day' may take place
- Main departure of swifts away from Britain, on their way to Africa
- Robin begins singing and continues until next summer
- Wood pigeon stops singing
- Corn bunting stops singing
- Young fox cubs born this year begin to disperse
- Main flight of silver-spotted skipper begins (to end of month)
- Peak flight of gatekeeper
- Now is the peak time for adult curlew sandpipers to pass through Britain, with the juveniles following in a month's time
- The peak southward movement of adult willow warblers begins (juveniles are slightly later)

The smooth snake is our rarest native terrestrial reptile, found only on heaths in the extreme south of the country.

WEEK ONE Reptile Watching

Britain has only six native species of reptile, plus the occasional visiting sea-turtle. Several other species have been introduced, but as a temperate island cut off from the European mainland after the last Ice Age, we are cruelly impoverished in regard to this part of our fauna. The same applies to amphibians. At least, though, that means that it doesn't take long for an enthusiast to tick them all off.

But what is the best way to appreciate reptiles in Britain? The answer is to visit a southern heathland in summer, where you might be fortunate enough to see all six species in a day (or even more if you visit some introduced species). If this option is not available, a variety of open habitats, including moorland, commons, cliffs, sand dunes, downland, railway embankments and woodland rides will hold at least some reptiles. Reptiles require two main things: basking spots to take in the heat of the sun, and dense ground vegetation where they can hide away if threatened by predators.

The easiest species to see is probably the slow worm, a legless, brown lizard that is often found in compost heaps in the garden, pretty much throughout the country. Grass snakes also commonly visit gardens, but what they really like is wet areas such as ponds, marshes, rivers and lakes. If you see a snake swimming, it is almost always a grass snake, at least in England. As for other lizards, the common lizard is (unsurprisingly) widespread, while the sand lizard is rare and localized in southern England. Common lizards have a useful habit of basking on boardwalks in many places where they occur. Adders are widespread, while Britain's rarest terrestrial reptile is the smooth snake, confined to heaths in southern England.

Reptiles do, of course, have cold blood, and need to warm their bodies using the rays of the sun. This necessity often leads people to think that the hotter it is, the better it will be for looking for reptiles. This isn't the case, because cold-blooded animals don't wish to overheat, either, and usually retreat into the shade if the sun is too hot. It is actually much better to look for them in the morning or evening, or on a dry, cloudy day, especially during the warm month of August.

Locating reptiles is by no means easy, although it does seem second nature to some people. The suggested technique is to walk slowly forward looking about three metres ahead of you, scouring open sunny spots where reptiles might bask – low grass, logs and piles of brush are popular, and man-made objects such as paths and path-sides are, too. Try to avoid casting your own shadow where you are looking.

Another, rather more convenient way to find reptiles is to provide some habitat yourself. There is one piece of equipment that does make life a great deal easier for herpetologists, and that is the large, rectangular sheet of corrugated iron known in the trade as a 'tin'. It doesn't have to be corrugated iron, in fact, since roofing felt, or even old carpet, will also do. The tin can be placed in the reptile habitat and used to monitor numbers. Snakes and lizards find them irresistible because they keep the ground below them warm and dry, and it also allows the animals themselves to be concealed. They are particularly popular with slow worms, which prefer not to bask out in the open, and grass snakes. Adders use them more sparingly.

As mentioned above, there are a few extra species in Britain that have been introduced, and if you are interested in reptiles, they are worth a visit. The commonest is the **wall lizard**, well established on the south coast of England (with some inland colonies), while the **green lizard** appears only to be established in the Bournemouth area. There is a colony of **Aesculapian snakes** near the Welsh Mountain Zoo in Colwyn Bay and another near London Zoo. Town parks throughout the country also have populations of introduced **red-eared terrapins** in their ponds, originally from the Americas.

WEEKLY HIGHLIGHTS: WEEK TWO

- First ripe fruit of beech, and first tints of its autumn colour
- First ripe hips of dog rose
- Slow worms begin to give birth. The young are born 'live' (not as eggs) in groups of up to twenty-five. Look for them in compost heaps or under pieces of corrugated iron
- Peak flight of silver-spotted skipper begins
- Second brood of dingy skipper flies for a short time
- Peak flight of brown hairstreak begins
- The peak departures of common whitethroat occur (until the end of the month)
- The so-called 'glorious twelfth' of August marks the beginning of the shooting season for red grouse (and ptarmigan).
- The young of the hobby only now fledge; they are among the last British birds to do so

WEEK TWO Seeing Dolphins and Whales

Britain's sea mammals are a marvel that most people seem either to ignore, or disbelieve the existence of entirely. A few years ago I visited Bournemouth Beach, where a whale had spent the last couple of days frolicking offshore. When I arrived, I expected a crowd to be gathered, but how many spectators had the animal attracted? None. The only explanation can have been that people simply didn't believe they could see such an animal there. It wasn't disinterest – once I pointed the animal out (a **northern bottlenose whale**), plenty of people were excited. It seems that, to most of the public, the riches out there just seem somehow out of reach.

There is no better month to cure 'sea mammal disbelief' than August. Being a time of holidays, people expect magical memories, while at the same time calm seas are ideal for finding sea mammals. In the UK we have several places where it is easy to see **bottlenose dolphins**, the world's best-known species, and then why stop there? **Harbour porpoises** are common and easy to see in some places such as the west of Scotland, and even minke whales are regular there, too. You don't even have to get your feet wet.

There are two ways of seeing sea mammals in Britain, and the method you choose depends on your sea-legs. By far the most reliable way is to take a dolphin cruise into suitable waters where bottlenose dolphins are commonly seen. You might spy nothing but a few dorsal fins momentarily showing above the surface of the water, but on the other hand you might see playful animals bow-riding (swimming fast at the front of a boat) or breaching (leaping clear of the water). Whatever happens, on these dedicated cruises, you usually see at least something.

An enhanced nautical method is to take the ever-burgeoning number of more specialist dedicated trips. These may target bottle-nose dolphins, but there are other species to look for, too, including **common dolphins** and **white-beaked dolphins**, the latter an Atlantic speciality. It depends where you are. Some of these trips are real adventures, lasting some hours, and you will need to be happy with bumpy water, or be able to trade seasickness for views of an unusual cetacean.

Ferries are an ideal compromise for whale and dolphin lovers who prefer larger boats. A whole range of commercial ferries plies the waters of western Scotland, and these regularly turn up sightings, especially of porpoises. The ferry that travels to the Western Isles is a good one for minke whales. For the more adventurous, ferries travelling across the Bay of Biscay to Spain can, in the right conditions, offer some of the best cetacean watching in the world.

But what about those who cannot tolerate boats – what hope is there for them? The answer is – plenty! It is easy to see cetaceans from land, although you need a little more effort than you do from a boat, and you will usually need a calm sea and good lighting conditions. On the whole, a cliff-top on a peninsula will give you the best chances of success. You generally need plenty of time, a pair of binoculars (or better, a telescope) and a comfortable seat. Check the water for seabirds. If you see a whole mass of gulls or terns concentrated at one point in the sea, that may well indicate a large shoal

Bottlenose dolphins are not the most numerous cetaceans in Britain, but because they often come inshore and there are several very reliable places to view them, they are one of the easiest to see.

of fish; check carefully for any fins in amongst the masses. Certain watchpoints are superb for land-based records of cetaceans – check the list below.

A word of warning is appropriate here: cetaceans are notoriously difficult to identify and are frustrating to see, from land or boats. If you're expecting wonderful views of animals jumping out of the water or coming close, nine times out of ten this won't happen.

Having said that, the most famous watchpoint of all is Chanonry Point on the north side of the Moray Firth, not far from Inverness, where bottlenose dolphins are almost guaranteed. The animals here are seen all year round and often very close. The best time is from about an hour after low tide; as the tide comes up the dolphins chase the fish in. They will often play and breach at the same time. Many observers have had truly magical encounters here.

Good land-based places to see cetaceans:

- Moray Firth (especially Chanonry Point): bottlenose dolphins
- Gwennap Head, Cornwall
- Newquay, Ceredigion, Wales
- Strumble Head, Pembrokeshire
- Girdleness, Aberdeenshire
- Flamborough Head, East Yorkshire
- Huntcliff, Saltburn, North Yorkshire
- Sumburgh Head, Shetland
- Neist Point, Skye
- Ardnamurchan Point, Highland

Check the following for details of boat operators:
- www.seawatchfoundation.org.uk
- www.orcaweb.co.uk

WEEKLY HIGHLIGHTS: WEEK THREE

- Peak time for honeysuckle berries
- First autumn tint of elder leaves
- First hazelnuts begin to ripen
- First horse chestnut conkers begin to ripen
- First flowers of ivy bloom
- First oak leaves begin to change colour
- The flowers of rowan begin to change colour
- First main autumn tint of silver birch leaves and sycamores
- First flowering of orchid: **autumn lady's-tresses** (mainly chalk grassland, also cliff-tops and dunes; England and Wales)
- Latest wood pigeon eggs
- Young pine martens begin to disperse
- Last Essex skippers
- The summer peak of green-veined whites ends
- The summer peak of Adonis blue begins (to third week of September)
- The last common redstarts leave their breeding areas

- The first wave of migrant spotted flycatchers passes through scrub and light woodland (until early September)
- The peak southward departure of garden warblers occurs
- Peak departure of reed warblers from south coast
- Starling starts singing again
- Yellowhammer stops singing

WEEKLY HIGHLIGHTS: WEEK FOUR

- Grass snakes hatching
- The first swallows leave the country on their way to South Africa
- Last small skippers seen
- The fruits of hawthorn (haws) begin to ripen

- Peak departure of lesser white-throats away from Britain (until early September)
- Peak departure of whinchats from Britain (until early September)
- The middle peak of three migration peaks shown by the grasshopper warbler: late July, late August and late September
- First main southward movement of chiff-chaffs (females leave first)
- There is a peak in the numbers of **little egrets** seen around the country, many of which are juvenile birds dispersing
- Young polecats disperse from their birth territories
- Red deer have now grown their antlers and will begin to rub off the velvet

WEEK THREE Buddleias and Butterflies

This week's highlight can be undertaken quite readily in the garden, so long as you have buddleia growing. Otherwise, a friend's garden, a garden centre or even a patch of untended ground will suffice. All you need is a few bushes of buddleia, a warm, sunny, still day, a cup of coffee and a little time.

Britain's butterfly fauna is restricted to about sixty species, which is as many as you can see on a single meadow in a morning in many parts of Europe. To compound the impoverishment, the clouds of butterflies that were regular in our countryside before pesticides and high intensity farming intervened have all but gone. However, at the end of the nineteenth century, a previously obscure shrub called **Buddleia davidii** was introduced from its home in China into Britain. It thrived, partly because of the ability of its small wind-blown seeds to travel far and wide, and partly because it quickly became popular because of its colour and butterfly-attracting potential. It is hard to imagine how our butterflies could cope without it these days, especially in the urban environment, such a magnetic attraction does it have for these colourful insects. These days, remarkably, some of the best butterfly watching anywhere happens to be in the garden.

This week's challenge, then, is to watch butterflies come and go during a chosen idle moment on a warm August day. Why not set yourself the challenge of seeing ten different species, which should readily be possible? And as you do so, you can reflect on the life histories of some of your visitors. Their lives are vibrant and eventful, their comings and goings surprising.

For example, consider the origin of your red admirals, which are almost certain to be enjoying the blooms on this August day. The red admiral is partly a British butterfly and partly not. Most individuals you see now will be the offspring of the year's immigrants, which arrived here in the spring from the continent, having crossed the Channel. These immigrants laid eggs in May or June, and the subsequent caterpillars will have fed on British nettles and hatched out in late summer. They are very much second-generation British butterflies, but the link with this country is then broken. Vast numbers of red admirals try to hibernate over here, but very few succeed, so the population will more or less be wiped out and needs to be boosted by more immigration next year.

A similar story occurs with the painted lady. Waves of immigrants start coming in during the spring, with vastly different numbers year on year. But not a single egg or chrysalis will survive the winter here, and its presence each summer again depends on immigration. The painted lady you might be watching today is doomed as an individual and as a breeder, sad to say.

A very different case concerns the Comma. The butterflies you are seeing today are the year's second generation, having hatched from eggs laid in the spring. However, these individuals will be responsible for next year's first generation; after feeding in late summer they will hibernate as adults and reproduce next May or June. The same applies to peacocks, so these insects will have quite a few months still to live.

Other home-grown butterflies that you might see this week are Large, Small and green-veined whites, and brimstones (although some large whites, in particular, could be Continental immigrants). Each of these species has a spring brood, which lays eggs (on cabbage plants in the case of the Whites, on **buckthorn** in the case of the brimstone), which then metamorphose during the summer and emerge as the adults you are seeing in the autumn. However, while the brimstone hibernates as an adult (and is often the first butterfly to be seen each year), all the adult Whites die and leave their eggs to overwinter.

Another common autumnal butterfly, the speckled wood, has a similar lifestyle, with a spring brood and autumn brood. However, it does something that no other British butterfly does — it overwinters as a chrysalis, not as an egg or adult.

Thus, the comings and goings of butterflies on a single buddleia bush reflect many different stories. If you live on the south coast of England, however, there could be one more twist. Red admirals, in particular, are sometimes seen flying south in autumn, as birds do, leaving our coasts for the Continent. Their fate isn't fully known, but some could get far enough south to survive and breed next year. One of the red admirals you see could be in this category – about to go south to a future unknown.

Common butterflies flying in the third week of August:

- Brimstone
- Large white
- Small white
- Green-veined white
- Holly blue
- Brown argus
- Common blue
- Small copper
- Red admiral
- Painted lady
- Small tortoiseshell
- Peacock
- Comma
- Speckled wood
- Gatekeeper
- Meadow brown
- Small heath

A badger hole is quite easy to recognize by the shape of its entrance, rather like a capital 'D' on its side.

WEEK FOUR Badger Watching

Few wildlife encounters are quite as exciting as those with badgers. This is partly because these animals are instantly recognizable, with their black-and-white striped faces and grey back; it is partly because badgers are iconic, with a long and often fraught history with people. But perhaps the most remarkable fact is that such a large, supposedly conspicuous predatory animal somehow manages to survive in our human-dominated country. Indeed they don't just survive, they thrive. Southern England holds the densest population of badgers found anywhere in the world.

Various badger authorities recommend conflicting times when badger watching is at its best. Some quote February, when courtship is at its height and the animals are very noisy; others quote May and June, when you can see the cubs. But since the spring is so chock-full of other wildlife to admire, why not set out to see a badger in the balmy days of early autumn? The cubs are still around, albeit well-grown, and the ground has largely dried out, meaning that badgers may have to work harder to get at their favourite earthworms and will have to vary their diet a little more. They may be distracted and slightly easier to see.

Badger watching has never been easier than it is today, for three reasons. One is that the badger population is very high, despite the absurd cull that has taken place in a few counties. Secondly, more and more places have seen the commercial potential of badgers and hire out time in hides, bed and breakfast cottages and even restaurants with viewing areas, many offering almost 100 per cent guarantees of seeing the animals in the wild. And thirdly, there is a network of active badger groups all over the country where you can receive information about how to see badgers. Many members of these groups will have the animals regularly visiting their gardens. So really, if you want to see a badger, it shouldn't take much effort. Another advantage of watching at this time of year is that the commercial enterprises are less likely to be full than they are in the summer.

The reason that badgers can be so reliable, a selling point for entrepreneurial cottage owners, is that their centre of activity never changes. The badger sett is a network of tunnels and chambers that may be occupied by different generations of animals over centuries, meaning that, unless some catastrophe happens to the sett (invariably a human one), some animals will return to the same place every day, leaving after dark and returning in the early morning, without fail. True, on some nights they remain underground, particularly during sharp frosts, but most nights will see at least some activity. On the whole, other carnivores have many different dens within their home range and move around, so they are far more difficult to see.

Another advantage of looking for badgers is that each sett is occupied by a group of individuals, rather than a single individual or pair, so if one or two have an off-night, others might be on the move. The average number in a badger sett is six adults, which includes a breeding pair and a number of youngsters, typically older young that have stayed within the social group. However, one or more youngsters will sometimes leave to join groups elsewhere – they might even disperse as a sibling group – and this often happens at this time of the year. You never know what you might see from night to night.

Much as it is fun and convenient to watch badgers from a hide or from the inside of a house, an open-air encounter is a whole new level of experience. Out in the wild the slightest cough, rapid movement or change in wind direction can ruin your chances of seeing anything. On these occasions there is a raw meeting between badger and human, which can be unpredictable. The chances of observing anything are suddenly in the balance, and it enhances the excitement.

If you are going wild, then you need to arrive at the sett well before dark and find a position upwind from the entrances, and preferably above them in case the wind changes (some people climb trees). You need to wear dark, comfortable, non-rustling clothing that will keep you warm as the night sets in; some people take a mask to cover their pale face. It is best to keep a tree or rock behind you so your silhouette isn't visible. At first, you should remain at least 10 m away from the sett, which probably means that you will need a pair of binoculars to see the animals properly. Once settled in, keep quiet and still, regardless of the attentions of biting insects, and be patient. If you do manage to see something, taking all these things into account, it is a genuine achievement. Whatever you see and wherever you see them, though, badgers are memorable.

SEPTEMBER

Throughout September it is worth watching the coast for Arctic skuas passing through – you might see these birds chasing smaller seabirds, hoping to intimidate them into regurgitating food

INTRODUCTION

September is officially the first month of autumn, but it often doesn't feel that way. On average, September is warmer than May and it isn't far behind June, although there is generally less sunshine. In England it is on average almost as dry as August, but in Scotland there is a sharper distinction, with considerably more rain. The seas around the UK have been warmed up all summer long, and reach their highest temperatures now. The autumn equinox, when the day and the night are approximately of equal duration, occurs on 22 September.

Much as September basks, the decrease in day-length isn't to be denied. The number of species of flowers blooming falls dramatically and, while there are seeds and nuts everywhere, many plants have done their business for the year. At the same time the variety of insects at large also plummets, although the atmosphere can still be buzzing. Grasshoppers and hoverflies are as prominent now as any time in the calendar.

One of September's best-known changes is that of migratory birds, which collectively head south. The bulk of trans-equatorial migrants leaves this month, so it is a time of joy for birders. It's goodbye to many swallows, warblers, flycatchers, redstarts and so on. Next month is dominated by arrivals.

Birds are not the only animals migrating. Butterflies and moths are still coming into the country, and it is an excellent time for unusual moths such as the **hummingbird hawk-moth**; a few butterflies leave. Hover-flies also migrate in, along with aphids and other small insects wafted in by favourable winds. Meanwhile, in rivers, many fish begin their shift from the warmer, shallow waters where they breed in summer to the deeper water of their winter quarters.

September marks the breeding season for some animals, notably mammals. Most species of deer are rutting or are about to, rodents and rabbits are still producing litters and, perhaps surprisingly, it is the breeding season for bats. Boy bats meet girl bats in various ways. Some males hold territories, while others fly to traditional 'swarming' sites at the entrances to caves, tunnels or even buildings, where many before them have met to mate.

September continues a process begun after breeding towards a greater sociability. Birds, deer and even reptiles are far more communally minded than when breeding. It is the season of flocks and herds, as well as mellow fruitfulness.

HEDGEHOG DIARY:

It's a curiosity of hedgehog behaviour that these animals sometimes bear litters in September, or even October. It could be that an individual's attempts to breed failed earlier, or that they are emboldened by a successful attempt in early spring to try again. Either way, young-sters from these litters hardly ever survive, being rarely able to put down enough fat to cope with their winter hibernation – they must survive sometimes. Anyhow, the current hedgehog population is high and they can be easy to see, with their minds concentrated on eating as much as they can.

BADGER DIARY:

It's a busy time for badgers as they begin feeding prodigiously and collect large amounts of bedding for the sett, especially for the young to be born early next year (February). They also visit fields and take cereals such as wheat, oats and maize. Sometimes they will lie out in fields or bracken clumps during the day.

GREY SQUIRREL DIARY:

It's a month for eating, and then more eating. The abun-dance of tree fruits means that squirrels can put on weight to survive – and indeed breed – in the middle of winter.

BLUE TIT DIARY:

The transformation from insect-eater to seed and fruit-eater is complete, along with a lengthening of the blue tit's alimentary canal to help. Many birds eat blackberries at this time of year. Individuals now settle into two different strategies: they can be resident in one area, or they can live a nomadic lifestyle, moving locally from place to place.

COMMON FROG DIARY:

If any tadpoles have not metamorphosed by now in cold, northern lakes, they might overwinter as tadpoles and develop into froglets next spring. As the froglets grow, they shed their skins from time to time. They won't be sexually mature until their second or third winter.

MONTHLY HIGHLIGHTS: GARDEN

Red admirals are often at their most abundant this month. Look for them on fallen fruit, such as apples. The odd small white can still be seen, but butterflies are generally down in variety.

The autumn moth season is well and truly upon us. Look out for such common species as **black rustic**, **copper underwing**, grey shoulder-knot, chestnut, **lunar underwing**, **autumnal rustic** and the **thorns**: **canary-shouldered**, **August**, **dusky**, **September** and **early**.

In general, September is an interesting month for insects, and two groups are particularly obvious now. You can hardly miss craneflies, also known as daddy-long-legs. They are true flies with just the one pair of wings, and they do everything badly: they can hardly fly properly, they seem to have no sense of direction and they have a habit of carelessly losing their legs. The larvae of these flies are the notorious leatherjackets, which cause damage to roots and stems.

The other group you might notice are the hoverflies. Superficially similar to wasps or bees, they are also true flies and are famous for their ability to hold almost motionless in the air. They cannot bite or sting. Of the 300 or so species in Britain, many visit gardens

Confusingly, there is a brimstone moth (as here) as well as a brimstone butterfly. The moth is abundant.

and there is a growing interest in them among naturalists. Hoverflies often feed on plants with platform-like inflorescences with many flowers, such as umbellifers.

MONTHLY HIGHLIGHTS: WOODLAND

By mid-month the nuts of hazel will be ripe, and it will be well worth searching for them on the edge of woodland. They taste excellent (cobnuts are the cultivated form), especially when ground up, and pack more protein, fat and carbohydrate weight for weight than hen's eggs.

It's the season for nuts and berries, but a few flowers are hanging on, too. One of the most attractive is **herb Robert**, a member of the geranium family with its five white-striped purple petals peeking out from the shade. Its leaves turn a brilliant red in autumn, and the leaves have an unpleasant, acrid smell. In some parts it is known as 'stinking Bob'. **Wood sage** is also still going strong, but its flowers are greenish-yellow and, with the crinkly leaves, the plant looks faded even when it is at its best. Sadly, even the leaves aren't pleasantly aromatic.

Ivy begins to flower, and will soon be attracting large numbers of insects.

Sycamore begins to drop its distinctive seeds. They are paired and winged, perfectly adapted to spin like a helicopter blade so that they are more effectively dispersed.

Its close relative field maple also has paired, winged seeds, although they are opposite rather than at an angle. Late September sees the best of native maple colour, a brilliant yellow.

Oak trees are also dropping their acorns this month and next.

MONTHLY HIGHLIGHTS: FARMLAND

Sometimes harvesting continues well into September, especially when the weather has been poor. Otherwise the ground will be ploughed and fertilized and, later on in the month, new crops such as winter wheat, winter oil-seed rape and winter barley will be drilled. Almost immediately afterwards

The kestrel is the bird of prey you most often see hovering over roadside verges and fields. It feeds primarily on small mammals.

the winter rape crop will be treated with herbicide.

At the same time, some harvesting of crops such as potatoes, sugar beet and beans continues. In orchards, apples and pears are in season.

The lambs that looked so delightful in early spring are now prepared for market, as meat. If they aren't ready yet they will be known as store lambs, liable to be sold at any time during the winter and early spring.

Meanwhile, many dairy and beef cattle are calving.

This is the month that we wave farewell to many of our swallows. A sure sign that they

An autumn sunset over a weedy corner, one of many priceless unkempt patches in the countryside. The flowers are sow-thistles.

are on the move is their habit of gathering on overhead wires, chattering excitedly, flying out and back, and looking in silhouette like so many crotchets on the musical cleft. In these early days swallows are not great travellers, but just make irregular short movements south-eastwards.

MONTHLY HIGHLIGHTS: SCRUB AND THICKET

Summer is the time when hedgerows and fields are at their most colourful and bounteous, but it could be argued that autumn is the time when waste places and scrubby patches shine. Not only are shrubs adorned with berries, but many herbs display a last hurrah around Britain's neglected corners.

One of the true delights of early autumn is to come across a large thistle patch – yes, really. If you can forgive thistles for what they do to you when you sit injudiciously during a summer picnic, you can appreciate them now as they set seed. Ordinary fields in an autumn breeze have the look of a sort of botanical heavy industry as the white, fluffy flower-heads puff out plumes of floating seed. There are always a few still in flower, with their purple nodding heads adding colour to the scene. Banks of seeding thistles large and small attract flocks ('charms') of goldfinches, which may number in the hundreds locally. Before they discovered garden feeders, goldfinches used to take a third of their annual diet from thistle-heads, extracting the seeds by inserting their thin beaks into the bracts and prising them apart. All the time birds hold on dexterously to the herbs, often clinging upside down and fluttering their wings to keep balance, showing off their brilliant yellow wing-bars.

If you see a charm of goldfinches, look out for the young birds of the year. Some will still have fawn-brown heads, lacking the familiar bold pattern of the adults.

As summer fades away, several other blooms are still going strong and come into their own. One of these is the **common mallow**, with its large, indented purple flowers that look like those of its relative, **hollyhock**. Mallow grows as tall as a metre and decorates roadsides and waste ground throughout the summer. The young shoots, leaves and nuts are all edible.

When it comes to the berries of autumn, however, none are more obvious, abundant and tasty than the fruit of the humble bramble, also known as blackberries. Early September marks the peak time for collecting them, since it is still early season before they get affected by mould or flies. The blackberry is probably the wild produce that more people forage than any other, but that does not make it any less delicious. Blackberry picking is a delightful family activity, healthy in every way with, as the doyen of foraging, Richard Mabey reminds us, 'just enough discomfort to quicken the senses'. A few scratches from the bramble's fierce thorns, and perhaps the odd sting of a wasp, are the price we pay for our natural feast. Brambles go into any number of excellent recipes, including blackberry and apple pie, bramble mousse and bramble jelly.

All the foraging sages tell us that the berries at the end of the shoot are the largest and sweetest.

Another shrub almost as ubiquitous as bramble is the elder. The berries are ripe at this time of the year and provide very important provisions for many birds, especially starlings and song thrushes.

Dogwood is one of the earliest deciduous shrubs to tint, and the rich claret of its leaves is a sign of things to come.

MONTHLY HIGHLIGHTS: GRASSLAND AND ROADSIDES

It's conker season, when children everywhere open the thorny fruits of horse chestnuts to get the large brown fruits with a large pale scar, then put them on a string and attempt to break the opponent's rival 'weapon'. Conkers also have medicinal properties.

Although it is September, roadsides are still packed with flowers, not all of them popular. The **broad-leaved dock** is still going strong, although the wide leaves are acquiring their crimson autumn tint. **Common vetch**, **meadow cranesbill**, **common toadflax** and **common milkwort** are all looking good. **Black medick** and both common **clovers**, **white** and **red**, adorn many a path and right of way.

Japanese knotweed, a much-disliked plant introduced from Japan in 1825, begins to flower.

In autumn mountains and moorland can quickly become somewhat devoid of life as many of the breeding birds, for example, migrate down to the lowlands.

MONTHLY HIGHLIGHTS: HEATHLAND, MOORLAND AND UPLAND

The summer has faded, but some butterflies are still on the wing, including the gaudy small copper, with its bright orange forewings with large black dots. Although tiny, it is a turbo-charged, restless species, usually fluttering close to the ground.

Another small butterfly is also around on heathland, living up to its name. The small heath has been around since May, except for an inter-brood gap in July, but the second-generation adults are still going strong now. The butterfly is like a very small meadow brown or gatekeeper, and it flies low down. The fast, erratic flight is quite similar to that of the small copper.

The number of flowers on show is beginning to diminish, but **sheep's sorrel** is still very much in flower. **Louseworts** are out and **bog asphodels** are still blooming on acid bogs.

MONTHLY HIGHLIGHTS: RIVERS

The **Indian balsam** in still in flower, adding some patches of pink colour to riversides. It is also known as 'policeman's helmet', owing to the peculiar, irregular shape of the flowers. It was introduced in 1839 from the Himalayas, and finds our climate very much to its liking.

Common and **marsh figworts** are flowering.

Black knapweed has now set seed but, along with the various thistles, provides food for goldfinches.

You would hardly expect to be going hunting for crocuses and gentians in September, but in fact one species of each can be found on grasslands at the moment. The **meadow saffron**, a mauve crocus, is in peak flowering season on unimproved grassland in parts of England, while **autumn gentian** is more widespread on chalk.

Some river fish migrate downstream in autumn, to deeper water where they can pass the winter. Diminutive three-spined sticklebacks may even swim to coastal and estuarine waters.

MONTHLY HIGHLIGHTS: LAKES, PONDS AND FRESHWATER MARSHES

Among the blooms still going are **marsh woundwort** and **brooklime**, the latter a type of speedwell.

September is an excellent time for large **dragonflies**, typically the **migrant**, **common** and **brown hawker** and the **emperor**. Rare dragonflies are being recorded all the time these days, so look out for **lesser emperor**, **yellow-winged darter** and even **banded darter**.

This is the peak time for great crested grebes moulting. They often gather on larger lakes in numbers. At the same time, though, other individuals may still have young, or even eggs.

September marks the beginning of the movements of some of our fish into deeper water for the winter. The **common perch** is an example of a species that retreats to the depths and becomes sluggish in the winter.

MONTHLY HIGHLIGHTS: COAST AND ESTUARY

Sea lavenders are still in bloom. There are a number of different species in different habitats, but each can turn their patch of saltmarsh mauve.

Birdwatchers will spend more time than usual this month watching the coasts for seabirds. One of their targets is skuas. These predatory and piratic seabirds are solidly built and gull-like, and their feet are fitted with both webs and sharp claws. Part of their

One of the tastiest of all autumn forage, the fruits of the sweet chestnut are well protected by their sharp spines. It is well worth the effort of harvesting, though. Originally, the sweet chestnut was introduced here by the Romans from southern Europe.

feeding strategy is to fly rapidly and low towards other seabirds and tail-gate them until their victims disgorge any food they have recently eaten. Watching skuas chasing other seabirds is gripping stuff. The various species of skuas have different targets: **Arctic skuas** harry kittiwakes and terns, while great skuas may attack large gulls and birds up to the size of gannets.

September is a good time to see both basking sharks and **blue sharks** in British waters. If you are interested in sharks go to www.sharktrust.org.

One of the most conspicuous seaside plants at this time of the year is sea buckthorn. That's not because of the narrow, willow-like leaves of this spiny shrub, often used to stabilize dunes, but because of its remarkably generous, dense clusters of bright orange berries, which seem to load the shrub to its absolute limit. They are much appreciated by inbound migrant birds.

WEEKLY HIGHLIGHTS: WEEK ONE

- First autumn tint on ash
- The leaves of wild field maple begin to turn
- First leaves of hawthorn begin to turn
- First autumn tint of hazel
- First oak acorns begin to ripen
- This is generally the best week of the year for blackberry-picking (the last week of August to the second week of September are also perfect)
- Most peacock butterflies go into hibernation
- Last gatekeeper butterflies are seen
- Peak of juvenile curlew sandpipers on lagoons and coastal marshes
- The first pink-footed geese arrive in Britain for the winter, touching down in Scotland

WEEK ONE Foraging

Foraging is collecting free food from the countryside, which you can eat on the spot or add to your meal at home. Most of us have done it in the form of blackberry picking, but blackberries are just the tip of a delicious iceberg out there waiting to be gathered. If you stop at blackberries, you are hardly doing justice to the bounty of the hedgerows and woods.

According to the foraging *cognoscenti*, early September is the best time to go out and gather. John Wright in *The River Cottage Handbook: Hedgerow* says: 'Many summer fruits are around and the autumn ones are just beginning, roots are plump and green vegetables such as watercress and **fat hen** [are] still in leaf'. That very sentence alone should be enough to send anybody to their nearest open space.

Why should we forage? It certainly doesn't save any significant money, and it costs plenty of time, far more than 'normal' cooking. We forage, as with many of our interactions with the countryside, because there are deeper pleasures involved. Doubtless the process massages our ancestral gathering instinct. The time and effort could hark back to when life was slower and we were more dependent upon the work of our hands.

Well, for whatever reason foraging is a delightfully satisfying experience – but how do we do it? The best way, unless you are prepared to put in some hard preparation in learning how to identify plants and to follow foraging cookbooks, is to join in a professional field trip. These are becoming extremely popular. If you are a complete beginner, this is the way to go.

However, if you can identify some plants (not mushrooms, there is no reason why you cannot start off slowly. Quite a few genuinely good foraging plants are probably in your own garden, if you have one: for example, dandelion, stinging nettle, **hairy bittercress**, chickweed, yarrow. Other plants are very easy to identify so you are unlikely to make a mistake, such as elder, mallow and wild garlic. And of course, at the moment several well-known nuts and berries are around, including sweet chestnut, hazel and bilberry. As it happens there are more than 160 wild plants in the UK that are edible, and up to ninety can be available at any one time.

There are a few rules about foraging. If you are in a public place, including a public footpath and road, it is fine. However, you are not allowed to forage on private land and some places have byelaws that prevent any kind of collecting. You should avoid nature reserves. On a purely practical level, ensure that you don't forage from roadsides that are subject to very heavy traffic, avoid areas that have recently been sprayed with herbicides or pesticides, and be careful to wash your produce carefully.

Here is a list of plants available at this time of year, to give you an idea of how plentiful they are (from *Food for Free* by Richard Mabey):

- Beech nuts
- Bilberry
- **Black mustard**
- Bramble
- Dandelion roots
- Elderberries
- Hawthorn berries
- Hazelnut
- Heather flowers (for tea)
- Hop fruits
- **Jack-by-the-hedge**
- **Juniper**
- Poppy seeds
- Raspberry
- Rose hips
- Sea beet
- **Wild service tree**
- Wild strawberry

- Early berries of blackthorn (sloe)
- First leaf fall of ash
- First leaves of beech begin to fall
- The first holly berries begin to ripen
- A second wave of migrant spotted flycatchers passes through scrub and light woodland, two weeks after the first wave
- The main southward passage of Manx shearwaters occurs (Manx shearwaters breed in Britain but winter off South America – the only bird species to do so)
- The red deer rut begins in some places

WEEK TWO Bat Walks

The autumn is a surprisingly good time to go on a bat walk. You might think that, by being among the few British mammals to hibernate, bats would be winding down at this time of year, making just intermittent, bleary-eyed appearances in the night sky. However, this is a long way from the truth. The autumn is the bats' breeding season, when they are at their most bullish and frisky. They also use this season to wander more widely than normal, sometimes travelling from their summer roosting sites to their winter roosts, and even to special breeding centres where the sexes can meet. They must also feed well, in order to get themselves in good condition for hibernation.

So, autumn is a good time for 'batting', but really, any time in the summer will also be good for a bat walk. Many wildlife trusts and bat groups run public events, so the time when you do this expedition will depend on what's available locally. The point is that it is worth tagging along.

Britain has a surprising number of bat species, with more than a dozen relatively widespread breeding species, around eighteen in all (this figure may change because more and more is being discovered about British bats all the time). They constitute a significant proportion of our mammal fauna. Yet, while wildlife watchers rave about otters and dolphins, squirrels and badgers, they rarely get quite so stoked up about bats. But these flying mammals are full of interest, and if you dip your toe into the subject you might get hooked. There should be a word of warning attached here: bat watching, counting and study does have an effect on some people, making them strangely addicted.

For now, though, I simply recommend that you attend a bat walk on a warm evening. You'll need an expert on hand, not just to point out bats but also to bring a bat detector along. This piece of kit, as important to a bat specialist as a net is to a butterfly lover, is a small box that magically transforms the calls of the bats – above the range of frequencies that our ears can hear – into audible signals. It does this more or less in real time, so that, as a bat flies past emitting its ultrasonic sonar to locate food and avoid obstacles (it emits sounds and can detect their echoes), you can hear it, albeit in translated form. The useful thing about this is that different species of bats emit different calls, often at different frequencies and making different patterns. In certain circumstances you can therefore identify the species of bat that flickers past you. For example, a common pipistrelle, when feeding, can be heard to make vaguely flatulent buzzes which are, on the bat detector's setting, loudest at 45 kHz, while **soprano pipistrelles** make a similar echolocation signal with peak energy at 55 kHz. Meanwhile, **noctule** bats make sounds like loud raindrops falling on a plastic roof, while a **Daubenton's bat** sounds through a detector like the crackling of a fire. The actual details here might sound complicated, but the exciting part is discovering that, in many places, there are several species of bat coexisting. Many people, despite living in close proximity to bats, simply don't register their existence.

A bat walk, therefore, can be a revelation. In ideal conditions, for example if the air is warm and still and you are standing beside a lake next to open fields, you can both hear and see several species at the same time, and multiple individuals of each. This could enable you to get a handle on identifying some for yourself, even by casual observation: the Daubenton's bat, for example, is the only species that will fly very close (a few centimetres) to the water and catch insects from the surface. Equally, noctules are the bats most often seen in the clear airspace at or above treetop height, typically moving fast and with the occasional acrobatic dive or tumble to sweep up an insect. **Brown long-eared bats**, meanwhile, can be seen flying very low over a bush or next to a tree with slow flight, often with much hovering. The more you experience bats, the more you will begin to appreciate their characteristics.

If you do find yourself fascinated by bats, there are specialist bat groups all around the country. These run lectures, counts of bats, bat-box checks, hibernation checks and even bat mist-netting sessions, as well as the walk you might have attended. There's a world of flying mammals out there.

The network of bat groups is co-ordinated by the Bat Conservation Trust: www.bats.org.uk.

WEEKLY HIGHLIGHTS: WEEK THREE

- Elder leaves are at peak autumn colour, and the first leaves begin to fall
- The first leaves of hawthorn begin to fall
- The first leaves of horse chestnut begin to fall
- The first leaves of rowan begin to fall
- First main leaf fall of silver birch and sycamore
- This week sees the biggest departure of swallows from British shores as the birds leave for South Africa
- Conversely, the first barnacle geese arrive in Britain from the Arctic (Svalbard), to spend the winter (mainly in Scotland)
- The main departure of breeding black-caps occurs
- Fallow deer begin to moult into their dull winter coat

WEEK THREE Sparing a Thought for Spiders

Of all the suggestions in this book, taking a close look at spiders is probably the one that most people will ignore. Spiders have more than an image problem, it goes much deeper; many people are genuinely afraid of them. It happens that, if spiders had psychiatrists' couches, a fear of humans would be high on their list of manias — and with much better reason. Yet these small and often fragile invertebrates terrify us. Indeed, about now, in spider season, the newspapers are already carrying articles with words such as plagues, enormous and invasion.

It is true in autumn spiders are very difficult to ignore. Not only do they begin to enter our pleasantly warm houses in the autumn, but their webs are more obvious now that at any other time of year. That's because many species of spider bred over the summer and their young are beginning to become larger and more conspicuous, especially if it has been a good summer for their small invertebrate prey.

The idea of this week's challenge is not to cuddle up to spiders — just to appreciate them a little, if just for a moment. You don't even need to appreciate the arachnids themselves. On autumn mornings, if you take a walk anywhere in the countryside, you are bound to see hundreds, if not thousands of webs encrusted with dew, and they can look magnificent, covering every weed like dust-sheets in an abandoned house. Spiders' webs are one of nature's great constructions, and spiders' silk one of its greatest building materials.

The sheer number of webs that are highlighted by morning dew gives you an idea of just how abundant spiders are — in fact, it can be an interesting exercise to count the number of webs in a small defined area. This, though, is only the tip of the arachnid iceberg. One study found that a single hectare of rough grassland may play host to 5.5 million individual spiders. Most of these, admittedly, are the very small money spiders and their relatives, but that is a pretty large number.

About 650 species of spiders have been recorded in Britain, and these have adopted a wide range of lifestyles. For example, the web-builders like the **garden spider** are the patient ones that set their trap and wait for something to fly or crawl into it. The others wander around looking for prey by sight, and might not use silk at all – the large number of **jumping spiders** fit into this category. So do the **wolf spiders**, which chase down prey like a wolf, although they don't live in packs. Most wolf spiders have a lair to which they retreat after a hunting session, often lined with silk. These spiders are extremely successful and are often found in tough habitats, including uplands, where other spiders find it hard to live.

About half the world's spider species spin webs as traps. The best-known one in Britain is the garden spider, which has a brown body with a whitish cross-shape on its abdomen. The webs of this spider are often impressively wide and have the familiar 'cartwheel' struts; there may be several of them on your garden fence or across insect flyways in flower beds and shrubs. There may be 20–30 m of silk in a single garden spider web, which makes it all the more remarkable that it is renewed every day. In the evening the spider

rolls the silk back in and liquefies it with its digestive juices, eventually renewing the silk proteins and re-spinning the web before the morning. It takes, on average, about an hour to make the web from scratch. It is an astonishing effort, and some of the lazier web-spinners let their traps almost fall into disrepair before renewing them.

Of course, everybody's least favourite spiders are those that run across the bedroom floor at a disconcerting speed, or impertinently find their way into the bath just before it's about to be filled with water and used. It's good to know the source of your fear by name, and in this case the guilty party is usually *Tegenaria domestica*, although there are several closely related species that are equally drawn to human domestic bliss. A large male *Tegenaria* is capable of running at 50 cm per second, and the overall leggy-ness and span makes them intimidating. They can bite, too, but their real interest is actually sex. Their perambulations about the house are aimed at discovering a mate; they aren't even hunting food. If truth be told, they are actually making themselves very vulnerable.

The trouble is, nobody can quite accept spiders being fragile and vulnerable. So this week, all you have to do is to give a thought to spiders. Admire a web for a few seconds, and put a spider out to the garden rather than squashing it. Be kind to them, grudgingly if you have to, and at least understand what extraordinary creatures they actually are.

WEEKLY HIGHLIGHTS: WEEK FOUR

Spiders' webs are so commonplace as to be unappreciated. Many spiders re-make theirs every single day.

- Last week to pick blackberries (if you pick them after Michaelmas (29 September), the story goes that the Devil will have spat on them – so beware!)
- The leaves of our wild field maple are at their most colourful
- Last slow worms go into hibernation, often in an abandoned small mammal burrow
- Last natterjack toads go into hibernation, digging their own burrows in the sand
- Peak flight of small tortoiseshells ends
- The first **whooper swans** arrive in Scotland for the winter after a single-leg flight from Iceland

- The first brent geese turn up on British estuaries to spend the winter there, having bred in Arctic Russia
- The first white-fronted geese arrive in Britain from Greenland to spend the winter in the Inner Hebrides (their colleagues from Russia arrive much later, in November)
- The first wild greylag geese arrive in Scotland from Iceland
- The first large numbers of lapwings begin to turn up on British fields and estuaries – most of these are visitors from the Continent and will spend the winter in the UK

WEEK FOUR Small Mammal Trapping

Britain's small mammals are, to say the least, underappreciated. **House mice** and common rats have appalling reputations, with some justification, but the rest of our small mammal fauna, with a pot-pourri of voles, mice and shrews, have much appeal. If you've never done it before, may I suggest you try attending a small mammal trapping session? They are frequently run by the local Wildlife Trust or mammal group – try contacting the Mammal Society for information.

You might ask: why now, in late September? The reason is that, ever since the spring, our mice and voles have been building up their numbers. Most species have multiple litters throughout the warmer months of the year, leading to very high populations. Before the colder months set in and decimate these populations, the chances of catching some interesting mammals are never better than in early autumn.

The practice of mammal trapping consists of setting some purpose-built humane traps overnight in good habitat. There may be anything up to about thirty traps scattered over a selected location. The interesting part is opening them up in the morning, and that is when you need to attend. Incidentally, the person operating the traps will have been trained to catch and handle small mammals. Technically, you are not allowed to catch a shrew without a licence, although nobody ever tells the shrews that they should refrain from entering unauthorized traps.

The field vole, along with the wood mouse and the bank vole, is thought to be Britain's most abundant mammal. It is seldom seen, however, as it hides in long grass in an attempt to avoid predators.

Humane mammal traps have two parts, an entrance 'lobby' (which is tripped when the animal has entered) and a holding box, which is invariably stuffed with straw and provides a variety of foods both to entice the mammal in and to keep it fed overnight. When you are inspecting a trap in the morning, there is a frisson of excitement as soon as you see that the entrance has tripped and the door is shut – you have a guest.

Strictly speaking, the contents of the trap, which are disgorged into a polythene bag or a bucket, could constitute any one of two species of voles, four of mice and three of shrews. You are most likely to see wood mice, along with bank voles, field voles and perhaps common shrews.

You will learn the difference between a mouse and a vole (mice have big eyes, long tails and big ears; voles have small eyes and small ears), and you might see how peculiar shrews actually are. These animals are voracious predators and must eat something every hour in order to live (a common shrew is estimated to eat 570 small creatures a day). With their small eyes and ears and long snouts, they are the Daleks of the mammal world.

You might not find many species, but as long as you see something, this doesn't matter. Unless you are particularly averse to rodents, a spot of small mammal trapping should greatly increase your regard for these abundant neighbours.

In common with many small mammals, bank vole exhibit their highest population in autumn, after what is usually a prolific breeding season.

OCTOBER

From October redwings migrate into the country to spend the winter here – on clear autumn nights it is often possible to hear their calls as they fly overhead

INTRODUCTION

Although it is the second month of autumn, October often sees the first real signs of the season – the first widespread frosts and big Atlantic storms. The latter are caused by cool polar air moving southwards and meeting tropical systems, producing a turbulence that may be exacerbated by the fact that the waters surrounding Britain are at their warmest. Sometimes they are warmer than the land, causing condensation and precipitation. All of this translates into rain and wind. Temperatures countrywide drop sharply and rainfall leaps upwards – in England from an average of 69.7 inches in September to 91.7 inches (Scotland goes from 139.7 inches to 162.6 inches; Wales 123.8 inches to 152.9 inches). The average daytime temperature in England drops from 17.9°C to 13.9°C, with similar reductions elsewhere.

Even if the weather doesn't seem turbulent, the wildlife is certainly in a state of high flux. Most things are doing something active and even the trees seldom seem to be static, one day swaying in the wind, the next dropping leaves into the still air. Birds are still migrating in force, but now it is the incomers who outnumber those departing.

Our country's borders are always open to birds, and millions of European birds pour here to enjoy our mild, wet winter, avoiding the snow and frost further east and north.

Just as conspicuous as the celebrated falling leaves are the seasonal fruits, nuts and berries now starring in a hedgerow or understorey near you. They are produced for the incoming birds, now abundant and nomadic, spreading seeds to order. They come in bright colours, and are abundant enough to make a hedgerow as well-stocked as a supermarket display.

Many smaller animals depend upon nuts and berries to get them through the coming months, and they appreciate the overproduction. Some, such as dormice eat and get fat and hunker down. Some eat and get fit, reaching peak physicality as weather conditions bite. Some store the food away, such as jays by day and wood mice by night. Nuts and seeds have the advantage of lasting, making them perfect larder material.

October is a month of change. And notice this: every time you look into the sky, you see something, be it a leaf, a seed, an insect hastening to a late bloom or a bird travelling somewhere. Not every month is like this.

HEDGEHOG DIARY: This month sees a flurry of activity, a little like last-minute packing. There are still enough mild nights for foraging, but the ready supply of invertebrates dwindles rapidly. The animals begin to build their winter shelter, or hibernaculum.

Grey squirrels thrive in the autumn, feasting on the different nuts and fruits that can be found everywhere. Their special favourite, however, is acorns from oak trees, which they often stash away in underground caches.

BADGER DIARY: In preparation for lean times in winter, badgers eat hungrily at every opportunity and put on weight quickly. Their diet is as broad as their bellies, and they take a great deal of fruit such as windfall apples, pears, acorns and beech mast.

GREY SQUIRREL DIARY: The autumn peak in tree mast means that well-fed squirrels are at their fittest and healthiest in the winter, when most of them mate. For now, though, all they need to do is to seek out acorns, hazelnuts, beech mast, maple, ash keys, hornbeam or coniferous cones – whatever is available. At no time of year do squirrels spend so much time on the ground, where they will bury caches of excess food. Apparently, grey squirrels usually forget where they have stored their bounty, whereas red squirrels have better recall. This can be immaterial because most squirrels can smell out caches anyway. By now, all the young squirrels born this year are independent of adults and siblings.

BLUE TIT DIARY: Now is a time of survival and preparation. Many individuals depend on good stocks of beech mast at this time of year, which will help them right through the winter. They need to be in peak condition for the next few months.

COMMON FROG DIARY: Frogs go into hibernation (really a state of torpor rather than true hibernation) from the second half of October onwards. Some enter the mud at the bottom of a pond, while others remain in damp, sheltered places.

MONTHLY HIGHLIGHTS: GARDEN

The number of 'weeds' in the garden begins to diminish – to the relief of the gardener! However, look out for some indestructible weeds still going, such as **annual mercury**, petty spurge, groundsel and **red dead-nettle**. Daisies are giving their last display of the year!

Several autumn moths exhibit the colour of fallen leaves, including this frosted orange.

On quiet starry nights, if you venture out into the garden, you might be treated to the sound of migratory birds flying low overhead. In particular, listen for the sharp, high-pitched 'tsee' of the redwing and the 'shack-shack' of the fieldfare, our 'winter thrushes' (see page 186). Hearing these overhead can bring the thrill of wild bird migration literally to your doorstep.

Another, perhaps unexpected arrival in gardens is the goldcrest. Thousands of these minute birds (our smallest) arrive as winter visitors from the Continent to augment our resident population, and many newcomers are seen in gardens.

The butterfly variety has dropped severely, but mild October nights can be fruitful for moth trappers. Several autumn moths are truly stunning, among the very best of them being the gorgeous **merveille du jour**. Other good ones include red-green carpet, **figure-of-eight**, **beautiful gothic**, brindled ochre, black rustic, **Blair's** and **grey shoulder-knots**, **green-brindled crescent**, **red-line quaker**, **yellow-line quaker**, **brown-spot pinion**, **beaded chestnut** and lunar underwing.

Several common and widespread moths have the most perfect camouflage among brightly-coloured autumn leaves. These especially include the gorgeous sallows: **barred sallow**, **pink-barred sallow**, **sallow**, **dusky-lemon sallow** and **pale-lemon sallow**.

MONTHLY HIGHLIGHTS: WOODLAND

The woodland floor is buzzing right now, and not just because each day there is a refurbished carpet of fallen leaves. Many nuts have fallen, too, and many more await on the trees. For many woodland animals it is a bounteous time, and for the wildlife enthusiast a little time spent watching the woodland floor may be well spent.

Watch, for example, how tits and nuthatches have swapped the canopy, where they foraged for insects, for the ground. They, plus chaffinches and bramblings, will spend much time foraging among the colourful leaves, especially of beech. Grey squirrels and jays will be on the lookout for acorns, while during the night small mammals such as wood mice, **yellow-necked mice** and bank voles will scour the leaf-litter for winter food supplies.

The jay is the most obvious forager among them. This colourful bird spends many hours a day in October simply collecting acorns, which it then stores away in its territory, one by one. A single jay may collect up to 3,000 acorns between late September and early November and store each in a different hiding place. These acorns and other seeds are used as emergency winter supplies, and the bird seems to remember where most of its caches are hidden.

Jays with territories in gardens and other places may have to commute many times every day to collect the acorns they need. That is why jays are often so conspicuous at this time of the year.

There are plenty of fruits around. Honeysuckle has formed its blister-like cluster of sticky red berries.

It is a fulsome time for tree seeds. A treat for all is the crop of sweet chestnuts, so well protected by the fearsome spiky husks, yet so perfect when opened and roasted on an open fire – foraging heaven! Beech mast is also tasty, and when foraging under both these trees you can enjoy the glorious hues of their autumn leaves, especially in the sunshine.

Hornbeam produces its seeds now, too. They are in clusters of paired nuts connected to a distinctive three-point papery yellowing wing, which floats slowly down to the ground.

Barn owls will revel in the high numbers of mice and voles available in grassland in autumn, after the rodents' breeding season.

MONTHLY HIGHLIGHTS: FARMLAND

It's all change for pastoral farming, as dairy cattle are brought indoors for the winter. Beef cattle are often left outside and given supplementary feed when times are hard. Sheep, meanwhile, are dipped, wormed and taken to fresh pasture, often at low density to contend with the lower nutritional value of grass at this time of year. This is also the time sheep are put to ram, a euphemism for their breeding season, which continues into next month.

On arable farms the drilling of winter wheat and barley carries on apace. Sugar beet and potatoes are still being harvested.

MONTHLY HIGHLIGHTS: SCRUB AND THICKET

One of the lesser known berry-bearing shrubs that fruit in October is the buckthorn, a plant mainly of the chalk in southern and central England – and included here because it is forever confused with widespread and common blackthorn. The berries start off green, then turn purplish and black, slightly resembling small (6–10 mm across) grapes. They should, however, be studiously avoided, since they are a powerful laxative. A wonderful sixteenth-century warning cautions that they 'do purge downward mightily … with great force and violence and excess'.

A much more obvious October fruit is the crab apple, a small (2–3 cm in diameter) yellow version of the familiar apple. The crab apple is a native shrub commonest in scrubby habitats.

October marks the peak arrival of the birds known as our 'winter thrushes', the redwings and fieldfares. These species breed in Continental Europe, especially Scandinavia, and about a million of each spends the winter here. They arrive, along with many thousands of Continental blackbirds and song thrushes, on the east coast and quickly move inland, with the largest numbers appearing in the west by November. At first they concentrate on taking berries from bushes, so are most abundant in scrub and hedgerows, but later in the winter they will switch to searching for invertebrates in the soil.

Many of Britain's raw hillsides were originally clothed with woodland.

MONTHLY HIGHLIGHTS: GRASSLAND AND ROADSIDES

The flowering season refuses to yield to the shortening days, and in some places the colour is as good as at any time of year. On roadsides, waste ground and railway embankments, much of the colour is provided by imports such as the luxuriant **Canadian goldenrod**, tall with extravagant fingers of intense yellow. Another popular plant that will still be going strong into next month is the **Michaelmas daisy**. There are several species, but most have violet-blue florets with an orange centre. Both are North American plants, introduced 200 years ago or more. Curiously, while found in open habitats in Britain, they are woodland plants in their native land.

Several other native plants are still in flower. One of the most prominent is yarrow, but **black horehound**, **fennel** and common mallow are still going strong.

In parkland there can be some good rutting action going on, especially among fallow deer, for whom this is the peak month. Some fallow deer males set up their own rutting stands, while other males all display together. It makes for some intriguing viewing, further enlivened by the loud groans of the randy males.

Heathlands can still be colourful well into October.

On a few heathlands, October sees the arrival for the winter of a rare and exciting predator, the **great grey shrike**. An unusual combination of songbird and killer of small vertebrates and large insects, the great grey shrike has a large territory and can be difficult to pin down. It feeds on dragonflies, beetles, birds and small mammals.

Up in the mountains, on the chilliest, most open plateaux, ptarmigans complete their third and last moult of the year, changing from a greyish plumage with white belly into a virtually complete white-out except for black on the tail, the male alone also having a small black patch near the bill.

Red deer quite naturally steal the headlines, but October also marks the height of the rut of **feral goats**. Localized on various mountain ranges and cliffs, the hardy animals live quite independently of people. The billies can be seen attempting to ram each other, even on the steepest slopes.

MONTHLY HIGHLIGHTS: HEATHLAND, MOORLAND AND UPLAND

The flush of purple from summer has faded to brown, with very few heathers in flower, just a few blooms of bell heather. The light-bulb-shaped flowers of cross-leaved heath lost their colour in late summer, but still remain in place, brown and fading.

There is much colour to see, though, on heaths and moors. Birch leaves are now golden-yellow and bracken has turned earthy brown.

MONTHLY HIGHLIGHTS: RIVERS

This is the month that most mute swan cygnets are driven out of their home territories by their parents, often forcefully. The youngsters will soon find a local flock of other non-breeding birds and remain with these until they breed at three or four years old.

The autumn marks the downstream migration of the European eel, once common and widespread but now officially endangered. At night, usually around the time of a full moon, the mature adults of

While Brent geese breed in the Arctic tundra, they are just one of the many species of northern birds that use Britain as wintering quarters.

varying ages make their way from upriver – where they might have remained for twenty years – down towards the coast. They will eventually make their way to the Sargasso Sea near Bermuda and lay eggs there.

MONTHLY HIGHLIGHTS: LAKES, PONDS AND FRESHWATER MARSHES

Common reed is still flowering.

An odd sight that you might be fortunate enough to see at this time of the year is **bearded tits** 'high-flying'. This involves small groups of birds flying up above the reed beds as high as 20–30 m, calling excitedly. They often simply drop down again after a few seconds, but this high-flying can be the precursor for younger birds dispersing, eventually moving off away from their home reedbed for pastures new.

Most lakes play host to plenty of winter wildfowl. This is the month for peak numbers of **shoveler**, a small duck with a huge bill used for filtering small organisms from muddy water. Watch out for groups swimming in a circle, each dabbling in the other's wake.

WEEK ONE Salmon Leaping

Of course you've seen it on TV. You will have been taught the remarkable story of Britain's most famous migratory fish, and how it journeys far out to sea and back, returning following the chemical pull of scent, traversing various obstacles, including waterfalls, against the odds, to its home spawning ground to lay eggs for the next generation. But one thing is for sure – there is *nothing* like seeing it in real life.

Surging water has its own attraction, an elemental combination of power and freshness. And fish generally, which to many of us typically remain too hidden and too timid to understand, suddenly take on a new kind of life when they leap out from the water, with the unexpected loud splash. Put the two together and the scene is exhilarating.

It isn't particularly easy to observe, though. In most parts of Britain a salmon run only occurs for a couple of weeks in the autumn (although you can see leaping in March and April in Wales, for example), and only then in the correct conditions. The fish prefer to leap in the early morning and late afternoon, and often after heavy rain. The latter is because, although the surging water is flowing against them, the fish benefit from a 'hydraulic jump' – the opposite upsurge caused by the water cascading down at the foot of the falls and then rising up again a little downstream. There are also many other subtle factors that could come into play, influencing the journey in the preceding days. Therefore, a truly good run is not easy to predict in any particular place.

Having said that, even the sight of a single salmon could be enough to make a visit worthwhile.

MONTHLY HIGHLIGHTS: COAST AND ESTUARY

In some areas thrift is still blooming boldly, adding some pink to the scene. Other later flowering plants include **red goosefoot**, common scurvy-grass, sea purslane, **shrubby sea-blite**, **prickly saltwort** and sea spurge.

An unusual sight on the south coast could be butterflies such as the red admiral migrating south back over the sea, like a swallow. Such individuals will attempt to hibernate on the Continent.

There might still be seabirds on cliffs. Indeed, the shag has a very long breeding season and some youngsters don't leave the nest until October. A few gannets will still be present, with the occasional late chick finally departing this month.

By now there are large numbers of wild geese on British estuaries, including brent geese in the south and barnacle geese on the Solway and in western Scotland.

People are often surprised how big these fish are – many returning to their breeding grounds are over 60 cm in length and 5 kg in weight. Visitors are also surprised just how strong the currents are that the fish have to negotiate, and just how high they can jump (the record is 3.4 m up a vertical weir) It seems impossible, furthermore, that they can somehow summon the strength and poise to stay above the obstacle once they have ridden it. And yet studies show that most mature individuals do manage to make it to the spawning grounds, despite the intense effort of swimming upstream.

The act of leaping is, of course, just a small part of a remarkable life history that is worth recalling as you watch the fish in action. The hatchery is upstream of the leaping site, in the gravelly bottom of a river's upper reaches, and here the successful salmon lay their eggs typically in November and December (the actual season varies with location and weather). Exhausted by their journey and having not eaten since they entered fresh water, most now die. Their eggs, though, hatch in early spring and grow for about a year, sometimes more, by which time each young salmon is known as a parr. These immature stages head downriver and transform into the marine stage of the salmon (the smolt). After a short time of adjustment in an estuarine environment, they head out into the deep water and live the life of a marine fish, mixing with sharks, dolphins, jellyfish and turtles – it is hard to imagine a habitat more different from the rushing torrents of the British uplands. British salmon spread out into the North Sea, some going as far as the waters off south-west Greenland. They eat crustaceans and smaller fish and put on weight.

Wigeon also return to their winter quarters en masse in October and November.

WEEKLY HIGHLIGHTS: WEEK ONE

- The leaves of field maple begin to fall
- The leaves of hazel begin to fall
- Oak leaves have all changed colour and the first ones begin to fall
- Red squirrels begin their autumn moult, and will soon look immaculate
- The sika deer rut begins
- The fallow deer rut begins
- Last large whites of the year can be seen
- Last time comma butterfly is around in numbers
- Wintering blackcaps from Germany and Austria begin to arrive in British gardens and woodland
- The peak arrival of redwings from the Continent begins this week and will carry on for most of the month
- Dipper starts singing

However long the salmon remain in the sea, which may be anywhere between one and four years, the urge to spawn inevitably brings them back to the rivers and streams where they themselves hatched. How exactly they rediscover the spot is still not entirely certain, but they are thought to use both the earth's magnetic field and the arrangement of stars in the night sky as a guide; they could also use predictable ocean currents. Closer to home they seem to recognize the correct river by some sort of chemical signal. If so, they must be able to detect these markers in minute quantities.

The salmon's sense of direction, of course, needs to be just right, assuming that it would be unable to reproduce if it turned up at foreign spawning grounds. After all, if a fish got it wrong, imagine the waste of effort – all that swimming, all that leaping, just to arrive at the wrong place. The confidence – indeed certainty – of the salmon's drive is possibly the most impressive aspect of it all.

Some salmon-leaping sites:

- Philiphaugh Salmon Leaping Centre, Selkirkshire
- Falls of Shin, Lairg, Highlands and Islands
- Stainforth Force: River Ribble to the North of Settle in the Yorkshire Dales
- Falls of Braan: The Hermitage, Dunkeld Perthshire
- Cenarth Falls: Cenarth Pembrokeshire, South Wales
- Fish Ladder, Pitlochry
- Soldiers Leap, Pass at Killiecrankie
- Rocks of Solitude, Edzell
- River Tyne, Wylam Bridge
- Force Falls near Sizergh/Sedgwick on the River Kent
- River Tyne, Hexham Weir
- Castle Weir, Ludlow on the River Teme, Shropshire

WEEKLY HIGHLIGHTS: WEEK TWO

- Common lizards retire underground or into deep litter to hibernate
- Last grass snakes retire underground to hibernate, also in deep bracken litter
- Bank voles give birth to their last litters of the year
- Mountain hares begin their autumn moult, with white spots appearing on the fur
- Roe deer have completed their moult into the winter coat
- Last speckled wood butterflies make an appearance
- Small heath butterflies are on the wing for the last time
- The last lesser whitethroats of the year are usually seen in southern coastal scrub

WEEK TWO Red Deer Rut (Widespread)

They are big, they are noisy and they are super-charged with hormones. Who wouldn't want a ring-side seat to watch our largest land mammal, the red deer, at the height of the rut? The sight of well-matched stags clashing antlers, together with the remarkable belly-aching roar of territorial males, combines to remind you that these crowded islands still provide the stage for some world-class wildlife experience.

The red deer is quite widespread in Britain, with pockets of wild population in parts of England including Exmoor, the New Forest and Cumbria, as well as some well-maintained herds in deer parks (Richmond Park in London is a famous location). Arguably, though, the best viewing occurs in the animal's heartland, in the hills and glens of Scotland, where you have a magnificent backdrop to the antics of these impressive beasts. Wherever you do view it, however, the red deer rut has all the ingredients for great action: groups of large animals, intense competition, and the threat of violence. At its heart the rut is a competition between rival males for access to a harem of females. Studies have shown that about 80 per cent of all fawns are sired by just 20 per cent of males. One of the reasons for the level of aggression is that the stakes are high.

Preparation for the rut really begins in the early spring, when the stags shed last season's antlers. At this time of the year they have nothing to do with the females, usually associating loosely with other males, while the hinds live in extended family groups. The males spend the summer feeding up, putting on weight and growing new antlers; by August the velvet (the skin supplying

The red deer is well known as our largest native land mammal. It is also one of the loudest, its roaring during the rut being audible from over a mile away.

nutrients to the antler bone) is scraped off, and the antlers are sharp and ready for action. In the early days of September the stags move off on their own and go to a special rutting area, which is often in a traditional site used continuously over the years. Once there, they begin to round up females and form a harem, which may contain anything up to fifteen individuals.

Not surprisingly, a harem becomes a focal point for male competition. If a rival is brave enough to challenge an incumbent stag, it is a winner-takes-all situation, with all the harem females swapping sides. So the territory owner does everything in its power to intimidate an intruder – it will thrash the vegetation with its antlers, it will urinate and defecate, and above all it will roar, making a very loud, slightly complaining rumble that easily carries for over a mile across the glens. The roar, angry though it sounds, is the red traffic light, preventing most physical confrontations. There is a direct correlation between the size of a male and the amount it roars, and this gives any challenger enough information to back down if it isn't up to the challenge. Incidentally, one of the enjoyable features of the red deer rut is that you won't be the only observer. Groups of bachelor males gather close to a harem and take a keen interest in any fights, even though they will not make a challenge themselves. Together with the harem, it makes the rut almost a standing-room-only event.

If an intruder is a match for an incumbent, a skirmish will take place. The stags will first walk alongside each other, sizing each other up while still roaring; then, if nothing is settled, they will lock antlers. Like two wrestlers, they interlock, twist and turn. Ideally, one will gain the higher ground and push its rival downhill, away from the hinds. The fights are often brief, lasting less than a minute (five minutes is known), but they are brutal: some 20 per cent of stags that take part in a rutting fight will sustain injuries. However, they are rarely disabling, and only a very small proportion are ever fatal.

Nature is rarely fair, and it is invariably the case that the largest and heaviest stags will win the necessary battles and inseminate their females. Interestingly, there seems little direct correlation with the size and structure of the antlers, except that older males have larger antlers than young animals. Individual stags vary in the number of sharp points (or 'tops') that they possess, making them recognizable to the human observer (some males have sixteen tops while eight to ten is usual).

If you do manage to observe red deer rutting, you will be doubly fortunate if you manage to see a fight. But even if you don't, a good roar is a spine-tingling sound, and if you can admire the backdrop of the Scottish glens in their late autumn brown, you will certainly not be disappointed.

WEEKLY HIGHLIGHTS: WEEK THREE

- The last small copper butterflies are typically on the wing
- The last painted lady butterflies are usually seen
- The main arrival of Greenland white-fronted geese can be seen on Islay and in the west of Scotland
- Numbers of pink-footed geese reach a peak in Scotland. They reach a peak in Norfolk in January
- The first Bewick's swans arrive in Britain from Russia to spend the winter (more will arrive in the coming weeks)
- The last common whitethroats of the year are seen
- Large numbers of chaffinches begin to arrive from the Continent to spend the winter in Britain

The jelly ear fungus doesn't look particularly inviting, but is edible and nutritious. It grows mainly on alder and can be found fruiting almost all year around.

WEEK THREE A Fungus Foray

Everybody delights in the floristic delights of summer, when our fields, meadows, riversides and roadside verges are festooned with colourful flowers. Many fewer people realize that there is a second bloom in autumn, involving just as many species and an impressive range of hues. This second bloom is not of plants but of fungi – or at least, the fruiting bodies of fungi, known to just about everybody as mushrooms or toadstools.

While you really cannot miss summer's riot of blooms, the display of fungi is much more subtle. Few fungi are tall or large; many, indeed, are hidden in leaf-litter, on rotting wood and in long grass. This does not diminish the delight of discovering them, however; in some ways it embellishes it. It makes a trip to find fungi, universally known as a 'fungus foray', extra special.

The sheer variety of fungi in Britain is remarkable. There are over 3,000 species with reasonably identifiable fruiting bodies, and thousands more that live in the soil (mycorrhizal fungi). Some sites in Britain, such as the Savernake Forest in Wiltshire, have well over 1,000 species – how often does a site in Britain have 1,000 species of anything? New species are discovered regularly – and that's new species for science, not just Britain. Fungi come in many shapes – not just mushrooms and toadstools but also bracket fungi, puffballs, clubs, corals, earth stars and those that look like peeled fruit. They also exhibit just about every colour – red, yellow, purple, pink – and different textures. Some are abundant, many are rare. Many of them are beautiful, if not quite in the same way as the blooms of flowering plants. They are also important as primary decomposers.

Fungi are, however, a difficult group to get to know. Many species are extremely similar and there are a lot of them. A single species may change its appearance considerably as it grows. Their peak season is often quite short, too. To be honest, the only way to enjoy a fungus foray is to go with somebody qualified and knowledgeable.

One of the delights of a fungus foray is the question of what is, and what isn't, edible. People have been eating mushrooms since time immemorial, and equally, people have died from consuming the wrong sort of fungi all the way along. To be honest, this does imbue mushrooms and toadstools with a peculiar form of fascination. While some flowering plants, such as the deadly nightshade or hemlock, are as toxic as any fungi, they never seem to gain quite the same allure as the deadly fruiting bodies of toadstools. It is by no means unusual to go on a single trip and bring back a delicious meal, while growing alongside your dinner would be fungi that would kill you in a few hours. Indeed, it can be difficult to tell the deadly ones from the edible ones and, unfortunately, people do make fatal mistakes. Within the last decade a few people have died from toadstool poisoning, mainly as a result of eating the well-named **deathcap**, which is common in woodland and even on some garden lawns.

As for edible fungi, what is truly remarkable is the range of subtle tastes on offer. One experience that every keen British wildlife enthusiast must have is to sample a mixed basket of freshly gathered fungi. And it's not just the typical mushrooms that are good. One of my personal favourites is the **giant puffball**, a big white football-sized mass that is about as far removed from your typical **chanterelles** as it is possible to get.

There is also a half-way house between edibility and a tendency to poison, and this occurs with fungi that have hallucinogenic properties. The best known of these is also probably the most famous toadstool of all, the **fly agaric**. This is the large, red-topped fruiting body which looks as though it has small white sugar lumps stuck on top of it. This common toadstool, mainly associated with birch woods, is often pictured with fairies dancing around it, but the only way you will get to see the fairies is to cook and eat some of it (not recommended). And even then, the exact effect it has varies widely, from person to person and toadstool to toadstool. Some people get euphoria, others just throw up. It is undoubtedly better to just enjoy this toadstool visually *in situ*.

Speaking of leaving things where they are, much has been made in recent years of the scourge of professional collectors who scour the woodlands removing fruiting bodies for profit. The opinion of many mycologists seems to be: 'good for them'. If they are searching in a public area, it isn't much different from other forms of foraging. Also, most fungi are *fruiting* bodies, not flowers, so if the body is removed the actual heart of the plant, in the ground, isn't damaged. Over-collection over a longer period of time could be harmful, but on the whole, it is hardly the worst problem faced by guardians of our natural world.

On the contrary, mushroom collectors are only doing what our ancestors have been doing for thousands of years. Why not make a date this year to join them?

Bracket fungi is formed from the fruiting structures of many different fungi that cause heartwood decay in standing trees.

The fly agaric is everybody's idea of the perfect toadstool. It is widespread and especially common under birch trees. But if eaten, the flesh may induce hallucinations.

WEEK FOUR Hearing an Owl Hooting

The nights are drawing in quickly now. There's a melancholy about the end of summer, but night-time in autumn nonetheless has a definite magic about it, not least because it is the peak time to hear the tawny owl hooting. The idea of this expedition is to hear this atmospheric sound for yourself. The experience is at its best when the night is still and moonlit and you are waiting somewhere spooky, perhaps near an abandoned building or a graveyard … .

The tawny owl is the commonest owl in Britain, and the one you are most likely to hear in suburbia or woodland. It hoots most frequently in September and November, because that is when younger owls pair up. At the same time, all the adult owls in the neighbourhood also hoot, to ensure that no other individuals trespass on their territory. Once a young owl has survived its first few months of life, it has a decent life expectancy, up to twenty years. But at the moment, there is much tension in the frigid night-time air.

The tawny owl is Britain's commonest owl species, but it is difficult to see owing to its nocturnal habits. The autumn is the best time to hear its haunting hoot.

The tawny owl's song is the one that was rendered 'two-whit, two-oo' by William Shakespeare. It so happens that the 'two-whit' part is really the contact call between the sexes, but you have a good chance of hearing that on a November night, too. The hooting goes like this: there is an introductory, slightly resigned hoot, a short gap, and then a longer, quavering hoot, or series of hoots. To many, this last sound is full of menace, and you will certainly hear it on many a movie soundtrack to introduce a frisson of fear. On the other hand, it is one of nature's most evocative wild cries.

If you are intending to listen out for it, you need to select a still evening and go out quite late, perhaps 10 p.m. Almost any neighbourhood with old houses and large gardens is likely to host tawny owls, and you could always walk to a local deciduous wood, or stop in a woodland car park – the sound is, after all, far-carrying. Do take care, though. Even if owls don't do strange things at night, people do.

WEEKLY HIGHLIGHTS: WEEK FOUR

- The last whinchats of the year are seen, very late on their way to winter in central or southern Africa.
- The red deer rut finishes
- Great crested newts begin their hibernation

NOVEMBER

By November many winter visitors have already settled in – at this time short-eared owls arrive from the Continent and spend the season hunting for voles in grassland and open country

INTRODUCTION

The last month of autumn, November is statistically warmer than March, as well as the winter months. However, the light is sinking, with only December and January having fewer hours of sunshine on average, and it is also wet, with some significant rain on more than half of the days of the month. The areas of low pressure continue to roll in from the south-west, bringing storm systems. On the other hand, frosts are commonplace. In England the average daytime temperature is 9.9°C, a big drop from October (13.9°C). In Scotland it is 7.4°C, a couple of degrees above December to February.

November is a settling month as far as wildlife is concerned. The upheaval of autumn – leaves falling, birds travelling, animals hurrying to stock up for winter or cop out of it – begins to calm down (even if the weather doesn't). Most of the animals that are going to migrate have done. Most of the plant activity has been and gone, with most species having set seed and left leaves on the ground, at least by month's end. It is a settling month but also a diminishing month – light fades, variety fades, activity fades.

That isn't to say that November is a wild-life washout – not at all, there are plenty of fine things to see and they are often framed by a colourful background of deciduous foliage. But to stretch the metaphor, the overall picture is the looming reality of deep winter.

HEDGEHOG DIARY: You would be lucky to see a hedgehog in November, and if you do it could be an emergency. Late brood youngsters and animals in poor condition will be compelled to feed, even when conditions are less than ideal; they probably won't survive the winter. Well-fed, healthy animals will be well tucked up by the end of the month.

BADGER DIARY: The feverish food bingeing of autumn begins to subside, and animals tend to leave the sett later and later in the evening. There is less activity of all kinds and, for once, even mating behaviour calms down to almost nothing.

GREY SQUIRREL DIARY: The sap is beginning to rise, figuratively, in squirrel life, just as it has been withdrawn in the trees where they live; the bare lifeless branches and frost-covered trunks will soon host thrilling and hot-blooded chases. Male squirrels begin to become reproductively active, although they aren't ready to mate quite yet. Meanwhile, all squirrels have fully moulted into their thick winter coats.

BLUE TIT DIARY: For the most part, life is still relatively easy for blue tits in November.

There is plenty of food around, from tree nuts to rose hips and all kinds of seeds. Some individuals even visit reed beds for the flower-head seeds. For now, there will be modest numbers on the bird table, but that changes radically in very cold weather.

COMMON FROG DIARY: These are now all hibernating (for example, under rocks or in the water). It isn't a constant torpor, and individuals can move about and even catch food from time to time.

Much is changing in the world of moths. The autumn-flying Blair's shoulder-knot was recorded in Britain for the first time only in 1951, but has since spread to most of England and Wales.

MONTHLY HIGHLIGHTS: GARDEN

If you have ivy flowering in your garden, you can hardly have failed to notice that the pale, greenish-yellow flowers are a magnet for insects. At times dozens of wasps, hoverflies and butterflies may all be buzzing around at once. Nectar elsewhere is scarce.

The berries of yew may still be obvious in gardens and churchyards. They are waxy and bright pink-red and are extremely poisonous to us. However, birds are able to remove the toxic seed-cases and take the seeds, and some species simply swallow them whole without ill effects.

Among butterflies, the last small whites and green-veined whites hang on, while hibernating species such as peacock, small tortoiseshell and red admiral are still widespread. It isn't a great month for moths, but among the dwindling supply of resident species some rare migrants turn up to brighten the moth-shy gloom. Migrants regularly recorded in November include **vestal**, **gem**, **convolvulus hawk-moth**, **crimson speckled**, **dark sword-grass** and **scarce bordered straw**.

Most bats now enter their hibernation. They will spend most of their time torpid. Many go to attics and cellars, others to caves.

MONTHLY HIGHLIGHTS: WOODLAND

The tints of autumn are sensational in November, but one tree that barely contributes is the ash, with its narrow leaves simply turning a modest yellow before falling. The ash seeds, however, remain conspicuous throughout the middle of winter. The 'keys' are winged seeds that hang in dense, limp clusters, looking like dead leaves.

Large numbers of woodcocks arrive in Britain from the Continent, attracted by the damp and mild climate. They live by probing into damp patches of soil for earthworms, either inside woods or in meadows. The first big arrivals of immigrants usually coincide with the first full moon of the month.

In many parts of the country roosts of corvids, such as rooks, carrion crows and jackdaws, form, often mixing together in a single woodland. These gatherings can be very large and noisy, attracting birds from several kilometres away. Unpopular though corvids tend to be, these roosts are well worth visiting at a November dusk. The din is impressive and jackdaws, in particular, often perform aerobatics for a short while before settling down.

The secretive wild boar ruts in November and October. The normally solitary males begin to associate with female groups and rival males compete for access to them. Inevitably, the largest males attain the highest mating success.

MONTHLY HIGHLIGHTS: FARMLAND

Winter wheat, oats and barley crops should have been drilled by now, but if not, some final operations will continue into November. The growing crops will be closely monitored and treated with herbicides until they are established enough to complete with weeds.

Vegetables such as parsnips and cauliflower are in season.

The ground may well be ploughed in readiness for the sowing of spring cereals such as wheat.

On pastoral farms many herds or flocks need supplementary feeding because of the low quality of grass.

MONTHLY HIGHLIGHTS: SCRUB AND THICKET

They have been around since September, but to some extent, the fruits of the blackthorn, known as sloes, come into their own this month. They are deep blue, with a whitish lustre (similar to blueberries) and are 10–15 mm in diameter. Being relatively bulky, they are eaten only by larger birds such as blackbirds, song thrushes and mistle thrushes. Starlings will try to eat sloes, but they are generally rather big for them to swallow, and the birds use their sharp beaks to puncture them and take the pulp, with decidedly messy results.

Of course, birds are not the only consumers of sloes; people like them, too. Now is a particularly good time to pick them and eat them direct from the bush, since they are not as bitter to taste as when they first appear in September. But undoubtedly they are best when pulped and added to gin, with sugar. Sloe gin is tasty and warming, one of the delights of autumn produce.

Another popular native shrub plump with berries in November is the **guelder rose**. In this case the berries are bright red, small and in clusters. At the same time as they appear, the lobed leaves turn deep red, giving a fine autumn display.

Although hawthorn berries (haws) have been available since September, consumption by birds of the small red, shiny clustered globes tends to peak in November.

MONTHLY HIGHLIGHTS: GRASSLAND AND ROADSIDES

Only a few flowering plants now remain to adorn tired grasslands and waste places.

The delightful blue hanging flowers of harebell may hang on in grassland areas of all kinds into November

The screaming call of the rutting sika deer is one of the most remarkable of all British wildlife sounds. These are the females or does.

The late-flowering Michaelmas daisy is still going strong. **Mugwort** can be a dominant sight, although it is now all but over.

Many roadsides are adorned with wild roses. The bright red hips ripen early in the autumn, but they are hard at first and are only softening now, towards the end of November. They become a useful source of seeds for many birds and small mammals.

MONTHLY HIGHLIGHTS: HEATHLAND, MOORLAND AND UPLAND

November is a quiet month in this habitat after the buzz of summer. Unless, that is, you are in sika deer country. The rut of this introduced deer is at its height, and each day the stags emit an astonishing whistling squeal, a little like a very squeaky door. This amazing sound can be heard a mile away.

Look down at your feet, especially beside wet boggy patches on heathland, and you might spot one of nature's death-traps. The leaves of **common sundew** are still visible now, as they will be throughout the winter. They look like very small lavatory-brushes, stalked and fitted with long, red bristles. Catch the light right and you will see that these hairs are each adorned with a droplet

Otters are now found throughout Britain, both along freshwater rivers and along the sea coast. The latter are often mistakenly called 'sea otters', which is another species entirely. Otters are often active around lunchtime.

of fluid; originally it was thought that the leaves could retain dew throughout the day, hence the name 'sundew'. However, the purpose of the fluid is far more sinister. It is extremely sticky, and if an insect lands upon it (midges are apparently attracted to the fluid to lay their eggs), it often gets stuck. The leaves automatically furl inward to enclose the struggling insect, preventing its escape, and meanwhile juices are released that begin to break down the insect's body into nutrients that are useful for the plant. Being found in a habitat with few nutrients in the soil, it pays the sundew to be partly insectivorous.

On moorland the 'berries' of juniper are still available in quantity. Although birds do take these purplish cones from this evergreen shrub, which are highly nutritious, they never seem to rave over them as they do other fruits. The cones are edible to us and are excellent cooked with pork chops.

MONTHLY HIGHLIGHTS: RIVERS

November is the peak month for the **sea trout** to spawn in the upper reaches of rivers. They have a similar life history to salmon,

The estuaries of Britain are replete with birds, including gulls, ducks and waders so this ultra-predatory peregrine falcon has lots of choice.

but during their marine stage they are found in estuaries and coastal waters rather than far out to sea.

The late autumn is often a good time to see otters in rivers – not because of their annual cycle, but because there is less vegetation to hide them. Otters may breed in any month in the UK.

MONTHLY HIGHLIGHTS: LAKES, PONDS AND FRESHWATER MARSHES

There should be plenty of ducks around now on almost any water-bodies. If you watch them carefully, you might notice some interesting behaviour. Males of mallards, teals and **gadwalls** often gather in flocks and, if a female should swim past, they might all take part in some subtle posturing, such as shaking the bill and tail, stretching the head up, flapping the wings and sometimes lifting the bottom slightly out of the water. All of these are courtship displays, and they are often communal, with several males taking part.

MONTHLY HIGHLIGHTS: COAST AND ESTUARY

Some cormorants return to their breeding areas, having moulted out at sea.

November marks the first arrival of white-fronted geese from Russia to their English wintering grounds, for example in Kent and Gloucestershire.

There is a second big influx of dunlins (the first is in late summer) to British estuaries in late October and November, and their numbers build up to a winter peak. The birds are very site-faithful, wintering on the same estuary (or even part of estuary) each winter.

November is a good month for harvesting seafood from beaches and estuaries, as they are no longer so likely to contain contaminants. Cockles and mussels are abundant, tasty and 'alive, alive-o'.

WEEKLY HIGHLIGHTS: WEEK ONE

- The last adders enter into hibernation, often in groups crowding into abandoned mammal burrows
- Smooth and palmate newts begin to hibernate
- The last hazel dormice will go into hibernation, usually in a nest on the ground (often among roots), and not waking until at least April
- Most edible dormice also begin to hibernate, usually underground (e.g. in a hole) and with no nest material
- Young wildcats begin to disperse from the territory in which they were born
- Roe deer begin to shed their antlers (the other deer do this in the spring)
- The last decent numbers of red admirals of the year are seen before they hibernate
- The last few greylag geese arrive in Scotland to spend the winter

WEEK ONE Autumn Colour

This local expedition is hardly the most challenging one of the year. Autumn colour is all around us, and any visit to a deciduous woodland, especially in the sunshine, is going to be delightful. In Britain, with such a seasonal climate in the Northern Hemisphere, we have some of the best displays in the world.

The very familiarity of autumn colour may well, however, mask what an extraordinary event it is. Beyond the chemistry, which is well understood, the biological significance is still not entirely clear.

Most people know that the green colour of leaves is caused by chlorophyll, which is used to convert carbon dioxide in the air and water into simple carbohydrate compounds, using the rays of the sun – it is a plant's way of feeding itself. In spring and early summer chlorophyll production is at its height. As soon as the day length begins to decrease, even at the height of summer, changes occur in the leaves which, eventually, lead to the withdrawing of chlorophyll from the leaves, and their subsequent fall.

How and why, though, are the attractive colours – the browns, yellows, oranges, reds and purples – created? Well, the dullest brown colours are simply those of the cell walls that remain after various nutrients have been removed, and they show up when no other pigments are created. The yellows and orange colours, as well as the richer browns, are made by a set of biological pigments called carotenoids, which are present in many plants and animals, from bananas to caterpillars. These carotenoids are always present in the leaves, but are usually not visible because they are swamped by the green of chlorophyll. In autumn they come to the fore.

Chemicals called anthocyanins are responsible for the red, pink and purple of autumn.

Another set of pigments are of particular interest because they are not present at any other time of year. They are made by the breakdown of sugars in the leaf as the plant's phosphate supply is withdrawn to the twigs and the chlorophyll is reduced. They are known as anthocyanins, and they are responsible for most of the red, pink and purple colours. The amount of anthocyanins produced is related to the amount of light, which means that a sunny autumn produces the best colour.

The 'how' of leaf colour-change is readily explained, but the 'why', as so often in biology, is much harder to fathom. It is generally accepted that leaves are dropped because they do not provide enough nutriment in the low light during the short, cold days of late autumn and winter to make it worth keeping them going. They also provide more resistance to high winds than bare branches do, and this is another reason why they should be shed. Once you accept that leaf-drop makes sense, the withdrawal of chlorophyll and nutrients to leave some unwanted chemicals, such as carotenoids, *in situ* would explain the colour simply as a by-product of this natural event.

However, the fact that anthocyanins are 'deliberately' produced in the late summer during the reduction in chlorophyll suggests that there

Autumn colour (as here in the New Forest) is easily enjoyed, but the precise function of the change in leaf tint is not fully understood.

WEEKLY HIGHLIGHTS: WEEK TWO

🍃 The last wheatears of the year tend to be seen on the south coast of England

is more to leaf colour than just happenstance. An intriguing theory has been put forward that explains leaf colour-change as a form of defence against insect infestation. Bright colours could be a signal to insects that the individual tree's chemical defences are strong and vigorous, and the potential pests should therefore go elsewhere. The bright colours could also potentially attract birds to deal with such insects, and perhaps make them easier to find than they would be on green leaves.

However subtle the processes and reasons, the change in leaf colour is one of the most profound events in the wildlife year. Enjoy it while you can.

Some great places for autumn colour:

Several of these sites feature collections of trees and shrubs from abroad chosen especially for their bright colours.

- National Arboretum, Westonbirt, Gloucestershire (has the best collection of maples in the country). See www.forestry.gov.uk/westonbirt.
- Grizedale, Lake District. See www.forestry.gov.uk/grizedale.
- Sherwood Forest, Nottingham. See www.visitnottingham.com.
- The National Forest, Leicestershire. See www.visitnationalforest.co.uk.

No longer the unusual sight that it once was, the red kite is an exciting and spectacular bird.

The raven is a type of crow but is as big as a buzzard, allowing it to compete with other birds at red kite feeding stations .

WEEK TWO Red Kite Feeding

It really is hard to believe that the red kite was once on the brink of extinction in Britain. In 1932, the formerly widespread bird had suffered 100 years of persecution by shooting and poisoning, and was already gone from England and Scotland. It held on in a couple of Welsh valleys, with just two pairs and a few other singletons left. Things looked bleak.

In those valleys, though, lived conservation heroes who protected the kites voluntarily for the next few decades and numbers of red kites began to increase. Then in 1989, the RSPB, Natural England and the Welsh Kite Trust, among other bodies, threw their weight behind an ambitious reintroduction scheme, releasing birds from Sweden and Spain to southern England and northern Scotland. Ninety-three birds were set free in each of the Chilterns and the Black Isle schemes and the first wild breeding took place in 1992 in both places. Further schemes introduced red kites to the East Midlands, central Scotland, Yorkshire, Dumfries and Galloway and the Derwent Valley in north-east England. The results have been spectacular. According to the British Trust for Ornithology's *Bird Atlas 2007–11*, there are now 1,000 pairs in Wales, 800 in the Chilterns and 55 on the Black Isle, and red kites can be seen almost anywhere in the country.

By any measure, the reintroduction scheme has been a spectacular success. So successful is it that there are some places where it is hard *not* to see red kites. Travel along the M40 or M4 away from London and you might be distracted driving. The Chiltern population has done so well that it has spread over much of southern England. It is no longer surprising to see a kite in the Home Counties.

Having said that, there is nothing quite like seeing large numbers of these birds together, and there are two ways to do this. One is to find a roost site and visit at dusk. The other way is to visit one of Britain's kite feeding centres, which are found in Wales and Dumfries and Galloway (in the other regions the organizers prefer the birds to find their own food). The experience of seeing lots of them, all wheeling in the air at once, is simply fantastic.

The autumn is an excellent time to visit a kite feeding centre. There are large numbers of birds around, augmented by the juveniles from the breeding season. The colder weather encourages more birds to be lazy. And there is, of course, the fabulous back-drop of autumn colour on the hillside. Red kites look spectacular at all times, but if you have the gentle afternoon sunlight on them, as well as the seasonal hues, you are in for a true visual feast.

The kite feeding areas are, to be truthful, no more than glorified bird tables. The visitors are wild, but they don't always look it, and this is because of their lifestyle. Although red kites are exceptional fliers and are perfectly capable of catching live food, they are primarily scavengers, eating dead meat, scraps and almost anything they can find. Roadkill and dead livestock form part of the diet of 'wilder' kites. At the feeding sites they don't even need to look for these.

At the feeding stations red kites are the main attraction, but they are not the only one. Buzzards always join in the scrum, as do ravens, crows, rooks, jackdaws and magpies. Keener birders may well spot other raptors flying overhead. The feeding is a good opportunity to watch all kinds of aggressive interactions: kite on kite, kite on buzzard, crows on the larger birds – everything. And all the while the kites demonstrate their superb flying skills. You will hear calling – a breathy whistle – and you will see birds chasing, bickering and generally being a nuisance among their peers.

At all the stations the food is presented in the mid-afternoon, although it varies according to the time of year (make sure you find out in advance). Some kites will be waiting long before it arrives, and the birds fight it out between them for about forty-five minutes before everything has gone.

These days Gigrin Farm, the best-known site, may have as many as 400 birds present in a single day. When the feeding programme here started in 1992–3, there were six. Perhaps no other statistic illustrates the truly marvellous way in which wildlife can respond when we allow it to.

Kite Feeding Sites:

- Gigrin Farm, near Rhyader
- Bwlch Nant yr Arian, near Aberystwyth
- Black Mountain Feeding Station, Llanddeusant, Brecon Beacons
- Bellymack Hill Farm, near Castle Douglas, Dumfries and Galloway
- Tollie Red Kites, Dingwall, Highland
- Argaty Red Kites, Doune, Perthshire

WEEKLY HIGHLIGHTS: WEEK THREE

- The last departing house martin is seen on average this week. Their departure is something of a mystery because scientists still don't know exactly where they pass the winter. Many millions leave these shores, but there are few records of winter birds in southern Africa, just a few groups of hundreds or thousands here and there, definitely not enough to account for the European population.
- Male red squirrels begin to become virile and the breeding season will soon begin in earnest
- The last adult common shrews die. Normally, only the young born this season will overwinter
- Roe deer begin to grow new antlers
- Clouded yellow butterflies tend to make their last appearance of the year

WEEK THREE
Tracks and Signs

Everybody has seen the TV programmes: a presenter bends down to the ground, gives a look of concentration and says: 'A pine marten passed this way not long ago, probably this morning. The tracks are very fresh.' Or, on another occasion, somebody sniffs a pile of muck and says: 'Ah yes, otter'. Most people's reaction to such a stunt is simply to think: 'Very clever, but there's no way I could ever do that.'

Tracking animals and recognizing their signs has always been looked upon as an elite set of skills. And it is certainly true that very few people are really good at it. This, however, should not act as a deterrent, because everybody, whether they recognize

Some mammals can be tricky to see in the wild but leave behind various signs of their presence. This is the spraint of an otter.

the fact or not, can detect some animal signs. Not convinced? Then how about a molehill? The molehill is the sign of an invisible animal's presence. The holes in a rabbit warren are also distinctive. And can you smell fox?

There is no better time for looking for clues to mammal activity than the autumn. For one thing, the ground is often wet, so tracks appear in the mud. Most animals are active, sometimes feverishly so as they collect supplies for the winter (e.g. squirrels, mice), so there should be plenty of signs around. And also, many animals eat autumn fruits and nuts and process them in a distinctive way. The woodland floor, for example, can be littered with calling cards. If you are going to spend an hour or two checking for signs, you will need to buy a book with photographs or illustrations. Then you just need to walk around with a renewed mind-set.

If you are looking for tracks, then simply look beside a puddle, or along the edges of a river or stream. Tracks are pretty difficult to identify, although the familiar parallel two-toed hooves of deer are easy to recognize. Normally, you can only identify one of the more difficult creatures by finding a perfect print, and it will be helpful to measure it. Also, take a picture (include a ruler or something for size comparison) on a smartphone and post it on a wildlife forum, and somebody will identify it for you. You can also make casts of prints.

Animal dung, scats and droppings are not to everyone's taste as a study item, but they are among the most important signs left by animals, and for many mammals, scent is the primary sense. Many mammals, including foxes and otters, make scats and droppings intentionally obvious as territorial markers. And you can hardly miss the dung of grazing animals such as deer and sheep. There is poo everywhere, and if you can bring yourself to examine it by sight and smell, you can learn a great deal about the animals that have left it behind.

Another type of clue to an animal's presence is a feeding sign. This could take the form of something as small as a nibbled pine cone or hazelnut, or as large as tree foliage chopped by browsing. Indeed, one of the most obvious of all animal signs is the 'browse line'. This is the limit to which grazing animals such as deer can reach when feeding; above it there is growing foliage, below it the browse has been stripped bare. The browse line is usually about 1.5 m above ground.

As mentioned previously, now is an excellent time to find feeding signs on the woodland floor, by far the most obvious of which is a conifer cone that has been gnawed by a squirrel. It looks very like a corn on the cob that has been gnawed by a human, chewed neatly down to the core. Wood mice leave a tidy hole in the side of such delicacies as hazelnuts. These and bank voles also make collections of edible items that they store underground.

One other type of sign that you should look for is the den or other place of an animal's residence. Molehills and rabbit holes have already been mentioned. Badger setts (see pages 163–4) are easy to recognize, partly because these animals make multiple burrows in woodland areas, but there are usually obvious spoil heaps next to the holes, and the hole entrances are in the shape of a capital D, with the flat side downwards, and measuring at least 20 cm in diameter.

To some extent, almost every animal has a recognizable residence. A squirrel has a drey, placed high up in tree branches; it is usually distinguishable from a magpie nest by having more leaves. Field voles make runs and nests just beneath the sward of grass on fields. Hares make recognizable 'forms' in the ground, flattening down long grass. Hedgehogs make nests of straw. It is often simply a matter of learning these signs and spending a great deal of time outdoors.

Whether you ever become an expert tracker really doesn't matter. It is both fun and satisfying to recognize field signs, and even if you only know one or two, it will be proof of what the animals are doing away from prying human eyes.

One of the easiest mammal signs to find is a discarded conifer cone chewed to the core by a squirrel, much as we would toss away a nibbled corn in the cob

WEEKLY HIGHLIGHTS: WEEK FOUR

- The last departing swallow of the year is seen on average this week. In recent years, one or two individuals have over-wintered in southern England
- Foxes have now completed their autumn moult
- The sika deer rut finishes
- The Chinese water deer rut begins

These sanderlings are roosting at high tide. Winter waders cannot feed all the time, because their feeding grounds are covered up twice daily.

WEEK FOUR Waders at a High Tide Roost

Twice a day, throughout the winter, high tides cover the mud of Britain's estuaries. To most of us, this is just the cycle of life. To the masses of wading birds that cram into our coasts in the non-breeding part of the year, it is a headache.

It may not be obvious to many people that mud is a good thing. However, estuarine ooze is special. Brought down from upstream by the flow of a river, and deposited as silt when the flow ceases at the sea, it is regularly washed with nutrients from both sea water and fresh water and, as a result, is extremely fertile. Indeed, estuaries are among the most productive natural habitats in the world. A square metre of mud may hold more than 10,000 small creatures.

This mud is the waders' canteen, a rich and reliable feeding ground. There is both quantity and diversity available in great abundance, the sort that would even make a human being's mouth water. There are molluscs such as cockles, mussels, tellins and periwinkles; there are crustaceans such as small shrimps and crabs; and there are numerous worms, including those ragworms and **lugworms** beloved of anglers. Different parts of an estuary host different items in different densities, a seafood restaurant of many rooms.

The amount of food on offer is irresistible at any time of year, but in the autumn through to the spring the number of takers on the muddy expanses dramatically increases. That is because

British estuaries, perched on the edge of Continental Europe and rarely subject to heavy helpings of ice and snow, make perfect winter refuges for millions of birds that breed much further north, including the Arctic. A suite of species, including curlews, dunlins, **grey plovers**, knots, godwits and redshanks, all make a bee-line for British estuarine ooze, knowing that it will be a safe and bounteous place to spend the winter. Each of these species presents variations in size, bill length and shape, leg length and feeding technique that allow it to feed over the same parcels of mud as the rest without any species completely out-competing the other. The mud, therefore, can be a crowded place.

The idea of this trip is not to watch the different species of waders feeding over the mud in their different ways, interesting though that is. The idea is to watch what happens when the tide comes in – the feeding birds' headache.

Not surprisingly, as the tide rises, little by little there is less and less mud available over which the waders can feed. If you time a trip to a spring tide, the water will cover all the mud completely. This means that the waders will be forced by the rising water to abandon their feeding and find somewhere to stand. And that isn't as easy as you might think. There aren't too many places around an estuary where a bird can wait safely, especially a modern estuary, encircled by human activity. If there are well-protected islands, sand-bars and fields, they will be sought out by large numbers of birds. Demand typically outstrips supply, meaning that all the safe roost sites (and the birds do often sleep during high tide) are extremely crowded.

The very least you might expect from a visit to a high-tide wader roost is to see a lot of birds flying around. At the best sites, you can witness a real spectacle. As the tide rises many flocks of birds wheel around, often in large numbers, rivalling the aerobatics shown by, for example, starlings. Many waders have dark uppersides and light-coloured undersides, and as the birds turn, all in unison, there can be a shimmer of white. At a distance the wheeling birds look like plumes of smoke.

Certain species have a habit of gathering into large masses – knots, dunlins and bar-tailed godwits are examples. However, if you get your vantage point right you will be able to see many species of wader moving in flocks of varying sizes. Note that dunlins form large, dense flocks, while curlews spread out into much looser, more informal units.

The melee can be seen either side of high tide and, on spring tides, the birds may be wheeling around a good hour before and after this point. If you can catch a fine day and a sunset, you will be able to watch, and listen to, one of Britain's finest wildlife sights.

DECEMBER

Snow buntings come south to spend the winter on British mountains and coast

INTRODUCTION

December is a cold, wet and often stormy month. The average daytime temperature is just 7.2°C in England, the same as February, but warmer than January. In Scotland, the average temperature is 5.7°C, but both January and February are marginally colder, as they are in Wales. There are only 47.3 hours of sunshine on average in England, 35.4 hours in Wales and a paltry 24.7 hours in Scotland, adding statistic credence to the overall impression of darkness and damp. In Wales, December is by some distance the wettest month, while in Scotland it is the second wettest month (after January). In England both October and November are wetter. At least one good thing can be said of December; after the winter solstice on the twenty-first, the days at least begin to get longer.

As with the previous month, December doesn't have a good reputation for wildlife watching. This is partly because it is midwinter, with much wildlife in a quiescent state. Some animals are hibernating, some are torpid, some are in inert stages of life such as eggs and larvae. Plants might still be around, but without their signature blooms. The bare trees, set against grey skies and ever-impending dark, can make December seem lifeless.

A snowy scene like this could put most people off wildlife watching. But December has its very own charms and it is well worth getting out.

And yet, the inert state of the wildlife watcher is at least partly to blame. The cold and damp, plus the shortness of days, tends to keep us indoors by choice. The absurdly long preamble to Christmas can keep us indoors by necessity. As a result, December can seem stifling.

Yet need it be so? Recently I undertook a challenge: the idea was to see 500 species of plants or animals in the unloved month of December, including everything possible: fungi, seaweeds, mosses, galls, flies, fish – you name it – along with flowering plants and the usual animals. It took me twenty-one days to succeed, and I could have taken half the time; a friend undertaking the same challenge found 820 species, enlisting the help, as I did, of experts happy to lend a hand. I saw a butterfly (a peacock), a moth (the **December moth**, no less), an orchid (bee orchid, leaves only) and many invertebrates. I began with a silver birch tree in my garden and ended with a mother otter and her two cubs by a weir in a broiling river in the fading light of the last day of the year.

In truth, some important things happen this month, including the shortest day, usually on 21 December. Once this day passes the period of light in each twenty-four-hour period increases, little by little at first, but it is an important trigger. As a result you will almost certainly hear some birds beginning to sing, including blue and great tits and dunnocks. It is hard to believe, but this is the starting gun for the breeding season.

HEDGEHOG DIARY: All individuals will be hibernating, unless the autumn has been exceptionally mild. Hibernation is never total, however, and the odd animal may wake up and perhaps transfer to a new nest site.

BADGER DIARY: You might never have heard the term 'winter lethargy', although you will probably have experienced the concept yourself! It's the term used to describe the badger's state of activity in the winter, when it certainly doesn't hibernate, but it isn't its usual bustling self, either. A badger's body temperate may drop by as much as 8.9°C compared with late spring, but equally a run of mild nights may well usher it outside to go hunting for earthworms. One thing is for sure: badgers do spend most of the month underground in their sett, and you would be lucky indeed to see one.

GREY SQUIRREL DIARY: December is an important and exciting month for squirrels – and squirrel watchers. These mammals are often highly entertaining at bird feeders – leaping and somersaulting onto tables and seed-hoppers and showing off their acrobatic skills and intelligence – or annoying, depending on your point of view. Up in the treetops the males are now sexually charged and, by the end of the month and year, the females will be receptive. The stage is set for the squirrels' year to end as it began – with courtship chases and high jinks.

BLUE TIT DIARY: Major casualties take place in December among all small birds, as the weather gets colder and the days are pitifully short. At night, each individual has its own roosting site, usually in a tree hole or other crevice. Towards the year's end, the healthiest and fittest males will begin singing to defend a territory for next spring.

COMMON FROG DIARY: All individuals are hibernating.

MONTHLY HIGHLIGHTS: GARDEN

December should see an increase in the number and variety of birds visiting the garden, and this increase will gather strength early next year, or if there are particularly cold, frosty conditions. At such times the garden feeders can be busy all day long with visits from blue and great tits and, if you are fortunate, coal tits.

Every few years, **waxwings** turn up in unusually high numbers, both in gardens and, bizarrely, supermarket car parks. Usually confined to the Arctic and regions further north, these gorgeous birds rely almost entirely on berries, and one individual may eat 1,000 in a day.

Meanwhile, on supermarket roofs, and sometimes even Christmas trees, **pied wagtails** gather to roost. Fairy lights on Christmas

The angle shades is a common moth which breeds in Britain. However, it is also strongly migratory, with individuals coming into the country in the autumn, and even in mid-winter.

There are few flying insects around by day, save for winter gnats and the occasional late-hibernating butterfly such as a red admiral. There are, though, a few moths that you might catch in the garden using a light-trap. They include: December moth, red-green carpet, autumn green carpet, tissue, winter moth, **northern winter moth**, **mottled umber**, **sprawler**, brindled ochre, tawny pinion, pale pinion, grey shoulder-knot, red sword-grass, sword-grass, satellite, chestnut, dark chestnut, dotted chestnut, angle shades, oak nycteoline, silver Y, herald, Bloxworth snout and buttoned snout.

Most bats are hibernating, although the occasional individual might fly about on a mild winter's day. However, members of bat study groups often monitor hibernation sites and count the torpid animals at known sites, often attics and cellars.

MONTHLY HIGHLIGHTS: WOODLAND

The small, red berries of holly begin to ripen in the second half of September, but there is no doubt that they come into their own at this time of the year, together with sharp, spiny and shiny leaves. There is a tradition from ancient times of using holly branches indoors to ward off witchcraft and house goblins. Out in the wild, holly happens to come into its own in December as a food for birds, especially blackbirds and thrushes.

That other well-known Christmas evergreen, mistletoe, produces very unusual

trees may be a fraction warmer than ambient temperature, so they are drawn to these.

A few flowers hang on. **White dead-nettle** is still flowering (it never stops) and so is groundsel.

Ivy is beginning to produce berries, which will be critically important for birds in the late winter, as other food declines sharply. The odd wood pigeon will already be having a go, even if the berries aren't fully ripe.

Damp, muddy woodland in December.

MONTHLY HIGHLIGHTS: FARMLAND

All is relatively quiet in the arable sector, as the growth of winter crops slows in fields. Dry conditions allow for a little ploughing, getting the soil ready for tilling of spring crops. Swedes, carrots, red cabbage and Brussels sprouts are all in season.

Dairy cows will now be indoors, while beef cattle may stay outside. Indeed many are placed with bulls and pregnancies result; dairy cattle are usually artificially inseminated. Sheep are out in the fields and may well require supplementary food.

Out on the fields, look out for flocks of lapwings and golden plovers, as well as the winter thrushes redwings and fieldfares. At this time of the year many common farmland birds are in flocks, including skylarks, buntings and finches.

Those archetypal farmland birds, pheasants, will usually be found in small groups of a single sex in the winter. In the evening they call loudly to summon birds to their roosts, on tree branches.

MONTHLY HIGHLIGHTS: SCRUB AND THICKET

In the colourless December hedgerows, look out for the remarkable fruits of **spindle**. They are four capsules of shocking pink, as incongruous and indelicate as that jumper your granny knitted for Christmas, and there's nothing like them anywhere else in the countryside. Furthermore the capsules

white berries, which begin to ripen in November. The leaves are very easy to see at this time of the year, since they form rounded clumps on bare, deciduous branches.

Meanwhile, despite the season, quite a number of mammals' breeding seasons are in full swing. Male grey squirrels are full of testosterone, and the same applies to **red foxes**. Wild boar may still be rutting, and the introduced deer Reeves' muntjac can give birth, or indeed rut, at any time of year. With the woodlands bare, it is a good time to look for muntjac.

One of the most distinctive of all the 'berries' produced by British shrubs is actually a seed capsule – the shocking pink of the spindle.

split open to reveal violently orange seed-cases, as tacky as the season. A few birds, notably robins, eat the seeds, but they are best left alone by humans.

A common shrub used as a hiding-place for pheasants is the North American native **snowberry**. It would be easily overlooked were it not for its large berries, which are incongruously white, apt for the time of year. When opened, the berry pulp looks like crusty snow.

White bryony is another common shrub, this time with bright red berries that hang down like beads attached to string, or perhaps like small red Christmas lights. They look stunning in the hedgerows, but are extremely toxic (and the roots of the plant are even worse).

Yet another colour of berry can be seen in this tired month of limited hues: this time, black. The **wild privet** is a fairly common scrubby shrub with a better-known relative used in garden hedges. Its black berries, although poisonous to us, are eaten by birds throughout the winter.

The small black berries of dogwood grow in cherry-like clusters, but what stick out at this time of the year are the dark red stems of the new growth of this plant, adding a welcome touch of colour to chalk scrub.

MONTHLY HIGHLIGHTS: GRASSLAND AND ROADSIDES

Car journeys or walks along country lanes in December can betray the dormancy of the countryside, but it is an excellent time to learn how to identify deciduous trees and shrubs without their leaves. Take ash, for instance. This tree has very grey twig with distinctive blackish tips that look like small mittens, and the hanging seeds (keys) look like clumps of dead leaves. Other distinctive trees include oaks, willows and larches.

In a few parts of the country, such as Cornwall, primroses bloom for the first time.

MONTHLY HIGHLIGHTS: HEATHLAND, MOORLAND AND UPLAND

The uplands and moors can be seriously bleak at this time of the year, especially if they are covered in snow.

On southern heathlands, two small birds to look out for are the **Dartford warbler** and the stonechat. The former is a rarity and heathland is its only habitat in Britain. Dark,

Heathlands can be bleak places in the middle of winter. A covering of snow is bad news for resident Dartford warblers.

with a small body and very long tail, it tends to skulk in heather and gorse, but will show itself on sunny, still days. It is often found in company with the much more widespread stonechat, which is well known for perching upright on bushes and showing itself well. The male has an orange breast and bold black head, with white collar. The stonechat stands sentinel and the warbler uses it to be aware of predators.

MONTHLY HIGHLIGHTS: RIVERS

It can be a good month to see dippers on fast-flowing streams and weirs, mainly in the north and west of the country. Look for their white chest contrasting with dark brown body, curtseying and bobbing up and down on rocks and climbing into the water. They are remarkably hardy birds, sometimes moving in and around the winter ice, and they do something odd at this time of the year – they begin to sing. It's not a great song, like a sore-throated thrush, but it is encouraging to hear it on the short December days.

Winter heliotrope comes out, often by streams.

By now **Atlantic salmon** have reached their spawning grounds. The female makes

Of all the places to go wildlife watching in December, estuaries and tidal creeks are among the most reliable for seeing plenty of activity.

a depression known as a 'redd' in the gravel at the bottom of a river, which may be 15 cm deep. The gravel has to be of the right consistency, the water must flow at 30–45 cm per second, and the temperature must range between 2–6°C. The eggs hatch in the early spring.

Brown trout, meanwhile, often spawn in December, although it can be any time between October and February. In common with salmon, brown trout lays its eggs in gravel-bottomed rivers with swift flow. Some brown trout make a mini-migration upstream to their own natal spawning grounds.

Rivers don't always behave in winter, and heavy sustained rain can cause them to spate. This can have a catastrophic effect on the young of such fish as chub, if the summer has been poor.

MONTHLY HIGHLIGHTS: LAKES, PONDS AND FRESHWATER MARSHES

Bulrushes are still in seed and may attract such birds as blue tits away from neighbouring woods. In fact, compared to some habitats the riverside vegetation can still be quite lush. Reeds are very much still standing, together with other perennials such as **bur-reed**.

Occasionally, very late broods of great crested grebes, with their stripy heads and necks, will still be with their parents.

December sees a marked increase in the number of bitterns seen in our reed beds, especially in southern England. Some of these are forced westwards by hard weather conditions on the Continent.

On marshes and fens in East Anglia and the Home Counties, December marks the height of the Chinese water deer rut. Since the males lack antlers, they use their small tusks to stab at any rivals.

WEEK ONE Visiting a Grey Seal Colony

Do you fancy a trip to see a genuinely rare animal? If so, now is a good time to pay a visit to a grey seal colony. This animal, quite familiar around Britain's coastline throughout the year, is in fact one of the world's rarest seals: the British Isles plays host to about 190,000 grey seals, which is 36 per cent of the whole world population. So this trip is a privilege.

The breeding season of the grey seal runs from September to December, and peaks at different times in different places. In the south-west of England it is September to October, in most of Scotland from October to November, and there are sometimes births in spring in Wales. However, this expedition is timed to coincide with one of Britain's great wildlife sights, the pupping of grey seals on England's east coast. Nowhere is better to witness this than Donna Nook in Lincolnshire. Not only does it hold one of our largest colonies (up to 3,000 animals, and in a good year 1,000 pups born), but the animals themselves are astonishingly easy to observe. In most part of Britain grey seals give birth on remote beaches, but here you can almost walk up to them.

The grey seal drama plays out throughout the late autumn. In early November the bulls come ashore and set up territories in anticipation of the arrival of the cows later in the month. Having been inseminated the previous autumn, the cows give birth almost immediately to the pups, which are every child's idea of the perfect soft toy. They are covered by a creamy fluff and have big, rather sad-looking dark eyes. For the first week or two they feed hungrily on milk and almost double their weight, but after only eighteen days of life they are abandoned, and soon make their way out to sea, completely alone.

In December there will still be some pups about, but this coincides with an additional new phase of grey seal action. Seals follow a slightly odd breeding schedule (shared with badgers as it happens) of mating almost as soon as the females have given birth. The moment the nappies disappear, so to speak, the beach becomes the setting for meeting and greeting, not all of it friendly. Males compete together in corners of the colony for access to females, and most will hope to mate with several, if they possibly can. Competing bulls will make loud noises and rude gestures, but only very rarely fight. They are intimidating nonetheless and make excellent theatre.

Thus, Donna Nook can be a lively place at this time of the year – but it will rarely actually appear to be. When you arrive you will probably see little more than slumbering bodies, looking no more active than beached whales. You should get some wonderful views of pups and adults because, despite the fences, you can still see them very close-up. But any aggression you witness will be very much in fits and starts. One moment everybody is asleep, the next moment there is a conflagration, like volcanic hot springs.

But whatever you witness, remember what a rare sight this grey seal colony actually is.

Grey seals differ greatly from common seals in their breeding behaviour. The young are born in the autumn (not summer), the animals form discrete colonies, and the pups spend some time ashore before venturing into the sea.

MONTHLY HIGHLIGHTS: COAST AND ESTUARY

Compared to some habitats, the coast can be teeming with life in December. Estuaries, in particular, play host to enormous numbers of birds of various sorts, including gulls, waders and ducks. On an estuarine mudflat the food is plentiful at all times of the year, and in places may support 11,000 organisms in the top square metre of mud. These include cockles, tellins, ragworms, lugworms and spire shells.

Birdwatchers often go to sleep in December, with the anticipation of January, and a new birding list soon to come. However, it is an excellent month for gulls. In most areas five species are easy to find – black-headed, common, herring, **great black-backed** and lesser black-backed. In the south, **Mediterranean gulls** are increasingly common, while kittiwakes may be seen offshore. Two of the month's specialities, however, are visitors from northern waters, and both have suitably pale plumage. They are the very large and ferocious-looking **glaucous gull**, and the much smaller, more nimble **Iceland gull**.

WEEK TWO Beachcombing

There is a gentle joy about beachcombing in any month of the year, but in the winter it is a bracing joy as well. Why comb beaches now? The main reason is because of winter storms. These wrest more unusual creatures from further away than summer breezes and currents, and you might come across something extraordinary. But as everybody who visits the seaside in winter knows, especially around the madness of Christmas time, it is also the sheer thrill of being alone with the waves and sand that urges you to walk along the beach. It heightens the senses, and barges away the normal concerns of life, if only for a while.

The sea offers the slowest form of special delivery. Send a message in a bottle and you may wait years for a reply, or never. But there is some kind of post twice a day on every beach, as the high tide leaves something on the strandline. Winter storms could be seen, using the same metaphor, as something of a mass mail-shot. The beach will be covered with items washed up, all with stories and histories, lives and deaths, coming from destinations near and far. There will be routine items, revolting waste, and mysteries.

And on the strandline itself, living animals and undertakers can be observed.

The strandline hosts piles of debris left behind at the top of a receding tide, and it naturally moves in a lunar cycle up and down the beach, highest during spring tides and lowest during neaps. It usually looks like a pile of seaweed with various objects tangled within. What is contained within the strandline is an eclectic mix of the man-made and the natural, and both can be fascinating. One day you could come across a historical arte-fact, the next the remains of a marine organism. Tragically, whales and dolphins occasionally form part of the strandline, and if you do find a dead one it should be reported to www.ukstrandings. org (if you find a live one, ring the UK stranding hotline: 0800 652 0333). The fact that several species of cetacean are known in the UK only by dead stranded specimens shows just how poorly we really know the sea.

It is very rare to find a cetacean, happily, but there are plenty of interesting animals and animal remains that you might well find. A good example is the 'mermaid's purse', which

WEEKLY HIGHLIGHTS: WEEK ONE

🌿 Some field voles give birth to their last litters of the year
🌿 Most male foxes become virile

WEEKLY HIGHLIGHTS: WEEK TWO

🌿 Song thrush starts singing

is a shallow dark purse-shaped capsule with tendrils or 'horns' at each corner. It is the spent egg-case of a fish, usually a ray or skate or, if the tendrils are long and tangled, a dogfish (now called a catshark). The tendrils hold the case to the seabed. Look out too for the elongated, oval and bright white cuttlefish bone with a light, soapy texture. This is the internal structure of the mollusc that keeps it buoyant in the water. Another common find is the 'sea wash ball', which is a rounded mass of egg cases of the **common whelk** – the name arises from the fact that early sailors used these sponge-like splodges for washing. And, of course, there is a wide variety of shells to find, not just on the strandline but on the beach itself.

Most searches of the beach will reveal bird arte-facts, most often feathers. But a great many birds die during persistent stormy weather, and you can find anything from a complete corpse to skulls and other bones. Beached birds are monitored annually for research purposes by the RSPB.

Much of the strandline, however, is defined by seaweeds. Seaweeds become detached from their holdfasts by wind and waves and they often form temporary floating refuges in the sea for a variety of fish and other creatures. Many different species of seaweed may become washed up, including the deep-water **sea fan**, **hornwrack** and the **sea bean**, which comes from the Caribbean. Notwithstanding their innate interest, washed up seaweeds build up, become rotten and establish an ecosystem all of their own on the beach. This special habitat has been poorly studied, but is one of the richest in Britain in terms of biomass. It houses, for example, enormous numbers of **sandhoppers** and **kelp flies** and there are many other inver-tebrates, some very poorly known. Their plentiful supply attracts small mammals to the strandline, especially shrews, and also foxes and otters. In season, bats fly overhead. The strandline is a real frontier of discovery, ready to reveal more secrets – perhaps new species.

The strandline could be described as being made up from nature's litter, but the truth is that, in recent times, there tends to be as much human waste as natural waste on your average British beach. Human litter ranges from the frankly disgusting to the wondrously historical: artefacts from long ago turn up reasonably often. But nowadays, strandlines can become an eyesore, so much so that some of the pleasure of beaches can be lost.

There is plenty of opportunity to help remedy this, however, and that is to join an organized beach clean. These are run on a regular basis by the Marine Conservation Society (www.mcsuk.org) and are manned, as you might expect, by volunteers. If you love the beach, it is a good opportunity to show it. And, perhaps surprisingly, it is actually good fun.

WEEKLY HIGHLIGHTS: WEEK THREE

- On 23 December 2013 a **Nathusius' pipistrelle** was discovered in Holland with a British ring on it. This small bat had been originally caught near Bristol, 596 km to the west, in late summer 2010. This provided the first ever proof of a British bat crossing into Continental Europe
- Stoats have completed their moult. In many northern areas, this means that they are white, except for the black tail tip

WEEKLY HIGHLIGHTS: WEEK FOUR

- Honeysuckle leaves appear in woodlands
- First shoots of lesser celandine push through the soil
- Tufted duck numbers peak on lakes about now

WEEK THREE The Antics of Robins

It is Christmas week, and unless you deliberately escape the festivities, you won't be doing very much wildlife watching. Realistically, therefore, any natural encounters will be close to home. And what more appropriate home encounters could you have than with the bird of a thousand Christmas cards, the robin?

It so happens that robins are more active than most other small birds in December. One of their curious quirks is that, while many of their peer species are relatively quiet, robins are singing with gusto at this time of the year. And not only that, they will also sing during meek and mild nights, even on Christmas Eve! It seems that street lights, and by extension Christmas lights, stimulate them to sing, so the truth is that you are highly likely to hear a robin during the month. By the way, many of the general public are completely unused to the idea of any small birds singing at night, so they often assume that they are listening to nightingales. However, nightingales are long-distance migrants that are currently sitting out the winter in tropical Africa, so they won't be serenading us for many months yet (see page 77).

Another quirk of robin behaviour is that it sometimes seeks the indoors, especially if there is readily available food. A favourite such habitat is the garden centre, which provides shelter and warmth, and often insects and seeds as well. More often than not, a robin will be welcome to shoppers and staff in a festive mood. And now that garden centres are major sites for Christmas retail, it is likely that more and more people will come face to face with the birds on their cards.

Even if you cannot find an indoor robin, you can still feed it in your garden. It will come to all kinds of foods, especially **mealworms**. If the weather is cold and food is short, the local robin can easily be encouraged to take food from the hand. And, of course, it will do the usual robin things, such as sitting on spades, having spats with other robins and generally looking perky.

However, December can also be a time of significance for this popular character. For, while you might think that the only thing on any small bird's mind would be bare survival on the long winter nights, this isn't quite the case. It seems that cold weather, if anything, seems to defrost relations between some individuals. While robins remain vehemently territorial, some neighbours – if male and female – broker a truce. They not only tolerate each other, but actually spend more time together and, strange as it may seem, they form a pair bond. Such birds, if they survive, will go on to start breeding in the spring.

Why some robins should pair up at such a time, when survival is so tenuous, is something of a mystery. But it does give an extra dimension to their Christmas season.

Robins are famously at ease with people. Originally a forest bird, it is thought robins always had a habit of following large animals to feed on the insects that they disturbed as they grazed. So it isn't such a large step to follow the activities of the gardener.

WEEK FOUR Mosses and Lichens

It's the last week of the year, and you might find yourself at a loose end, particularly as a wildlife watcher. There isn't anything spectacular going on that won't be around in January, and the idea of starting the year off with a bang is an attractive one. On the other hand, now could be a good time to do something off the wall, something you simply wouldn't consider at any other time.

So here's a left-field suggestion – why not find a way to sample the diversity of Britain's mosses and lichens? Go on a field trip, perhaps, with some experts, and spend some time on your knees. I have personally found that bryologists (mosses) and lichenologists are among the best general naturalists you can meet anywhere. A day in their company wouldn't be wasted.

There is another reason to go now. December is an excellent month, if not the best, for both sets of organisms. Mosses, for example, revel in the dampness, and there is a star-studded cast in the north and west of Britain. Mosses also become more obvious when there is less vegetation cluttering them. They cling to trees, paths, earth, rocks ... there are even some that live underwater. All in all Britain has 763 species, along with nearly 300 species of their cousins the **liverworts**. You could easily find fifty species in a single December day, a day full of Latin names and the discussion of microclimates. Many mosses are handsome and a few stunning, especially under a good hand lens (20x at least). Moss clumps are like mini-forests and their forms can be weirdly fascinating, the sort of plants dreamed up by movie-makers to look alien. They are in fact quite primitive, reproducing by spores rather than seeds, and their ancestors were the first plants to colonize land 400 million years ago. They have capsules in place of flowers, and rather than roots they have rhizoids. There is a world of mosses out there, albeit an underworld.

Lichens are another of the wildlife enthusiast's quiet corners, with a small but erudite following. There are 1,800 species of lichen in Britain, found in all kinds of habitats, including well-known places such as tree trunks and rock faces, where they famously act as indicators of air pollution (and also general ecological quality and continuity of a habitat). Churchyards are also a favourite haunt of lichenologists. Lichens are what are known as dual organisms, an unbreakable symbiotic association between a fungus and an alga, and with just the single official name. Lichens grow in a variety of forms – crusty, scaly, leaf-like, hair-like and cup-like – and also many different colours, so there's plenty to see under the hand lens. On a good day you could see several hundred species.

If you do decide to push the boat out, there are two relevant societies that run field trips and are always delighted to attract new interest:

- British Bryological Society (www.britishbryologicalsociety.org.uk)

- British Lichen Society (www.thebls.org.uk)

Here at Corfe Castle, Dorset, you can find over 100 species of lichen, including four nationally rare varieties.

Lichens are often most obvious in winter, when the leaves of trees and other plants have died back.

ADDITIONAL USEFUL CONTACTS

British Ecological Society
www.britishecologicalsociety.org

Freshwater Habitats Trust
www.freshwaterhabitats.org.uk

National Biodiversity Network
www.nbn.org.uk

National Trust
www.nationaltrust.org.uk

Natural History Museum
www.nhm.ac.uk/nature-online

Naturenet (UK Nature and Wildlife
    Organizations)
naturenet.net

People's Trust for Endangered Species
    (PTES)
ptes.org

UK Agriculture
www.ukagriculture.com

Wild About Britain
www.wildaboutbritain.co.uk

Wildlife Britain
wildlifebritain.com

The Wildlife Trusts
www.wildlifetrusts.org

Wild Scotland
wild-scotland.org.uk

Woodland Trust
www.woodlandtrust.org.uk

BIRDS

British Trust for Ornithology (BTO)
bto.org

Royal Society for the Protection of Birds
    (RSPB)
www.rspb.org.uk

Wildfowl and Wetlands Trust
www.wwt.org.uk

MAMMALS

Badger Trust
badgertrust.org.uk

Bat Conservation Trust
www.bats.org.uk

The British Deer Society
www.bds.org.uk

The Mammal Society
www.mammal.org.uk

Whale and Dolphin Conservation
uk.whales.org

REPTILES AND AMPHIBIANS

Amphibian and Reptile Conservation
    Trust
www.arc-trust.org

Froglife
www.froglife.org

INSECTS

Amateur Entomologists' Society
www.amentsoc.org

British Dragonfly Society
www.british-dragonflies.org.uk

Buglife (mainly insects and spiders)
www.buglife.org.uk

Bumblebee Conservation Trust
bumblebeeconservation.org

Butterfly Conservation
butterfly-conservation.org

Royal Entomological Society
www.royensoc.co.uk

INVERTEBRATES

British Arachnological Society
www.britishspiders.org.uk

The Conchological Society of Great Britain
    (molluscs)
www.conchsoc.org

SEALIFE

Marine Conservation Society
www.mcsuk.org

British Marine Life Society
www.glaucus.org.uk

PLANTS

Botanical Society of the British Isles
bsbi.org.uk

British Bryological Society
www.britishbryologicalsociety.org.uk

British Lichen Society
www.thebls.org.uk

Plantlife
plantlife.org.uk

Wild Flower Society
thewildflowersociety.com

FURTHER READING

Asher, J, et al., *The Millennium Atlas of Butterflies in Britain and Ireland* (Oxford University Press, 2001)

Babbs, H. & The Royal Society of Wildlife Trusts, *152 Wild Things to Do* (Elliott and Thompson, 2010)

Barnard, P.C., *The Royal Entomological Society Book of British Insects* (Wiley-Blackwell, 2011)

Beebee, T., *Frogs and Toads* (Whittet Books, 1985)

Brooks, S., *Field Guide to the Dragonflies and Damselflies of Great Britain and Ireland* (British Wildlife Publishing, 1997)

Brown, R.W., Lawrence, M.J. & Pope, J., *Hamlyn Guide: Animals Tracks, Trails and Signs* (Octopus, 2002)

Chinery, M., *Spiders* (Whittet Books, 1993)

Clark, M., *Badgers* (Whittet Books, 1994)

Dietz, C., von Helversen, O. & Nill, D., *Bats of Britain, Europe & Northwest Africa* (A&C Black, 2007)

Dilger, M., *Britain's Best Wildlife: The Top 40 Sights to See* (HarperCollins, 1996)

Dunn, J., Still, R. & Harrop, H., *Britain's Sea Mammals* (WildGuides/Princeton University Press, 2012)

Everard, M., *Britain's Freshwater Fishes* (WildGuides/Princeton University Press, 2013)

Gurnell, J. & Flowerdew, J.R., *Live Trapping Small Mammals: A Practical Guide* (The Mammal Society, 2006)

Harrap, S., *Harrap's Wild Flowers* (Bloomsbury, 2013)

Harris, S., *Urban Foxes, second edition* (Whittet Books, 2000)

Harris, S. & Yalden, D.W. (eds.), *Mammals of the British Isles: Handbook, 4th edition* (The Mammal Society, 2008)

BBC Nature's Calendar (HarperCollins Publishers, 2007)

Holden, P. & Cleeves, T., *RSPB Handbook of British Birds* (Christopher Helm, 2002)

Inns, H., *Britain's Reptiles and Amphibians* (WildGuides, 2009)

Lang, D., *Britain's Orchids* (WildGuides, 2004)

Lewington, R., *Guide to Garden Wildlife* (British Wildlife Publishing, 2008)

Lowen, J., *52 Wildlife Weekends: A Year of British Wildlife Watching Breaks* (Bradt, 2013)

Mabey, R., *Flora Britannica*. Sinclair-Stevenson (Reed International, 1996)

Mabey, R., *Collins Gem: Food for Free* (HarperCollins Publishers, 2012)

Marren, P., *Britain's Rare Flowers* (T & AD Poyser, 1999)

Marren, P., *Mushrooms* (British Wildlife Publishing, 2012)

Naylor, P., *Great British Marine Animals, third edition* (Sound Diving Productions, 2011)

Newland, D. et al., *Britain's Butterflies* (WildGuides/Princeton University Press, 2010)

Plass, M., *RSPB Handbook of the Seashore* (Bloomsbury, 2013)

Press, J.R. et al., *Field Guide to the Wild Flowers of Britain* (Reader's Digest, 1981)

Richardson, P., *Bats* (Whittet Books, 2000)

Smallshire, D. & Swash, A., *Britain's Dragonflies* (WildGuides/Princeton University Press, 2014)

Sterry, P. & Cleave, A., *Collins Complete Guide to British Trees* (HarperCollins, 2007)

Sterry, P. & Cleave, A., *Collins Complete Guide to British Coastal Wildlife* (HarperCollins, 2012)

Waring, P & Townsend, M., *Field Guide to Moths of Great Britain and Ireland* (British Wildlife Publishing, 2003)

Wright, J., *Edible Seashore: River Cottage Handbook No. 5* (Bloomsbury, 2009)

Wright, J., *Hedgerow. River Cottage Handbook No. 7* (Bloomsbury, 2010)

PICTURE CREDITS

Lorne Bissell: 32, 37, 60, 66, 82 (*right*), 103 (*left*), 112, 115, 117, 119, 154, 168, 181, 183, 195, 197 (*top and bottom*), 206, 210 (*bottom*), 212, 215, 221, 229, 233 (*bottom*)

Aidan Brown: 22, 42, 43, 45, 53, 70, 74, 93, 94, 97, 109 (*left*), 111, 116, 127, 132, 137, 149, 155, 158, 186, 188, 205, 210 (*top*), 222, 224, 233 (*top*)

Carolyn Couzens: 80, 84, 146, 151, 153, 180

David Kjaer: 18, 20, 48, 50, 56, 61, 62, 64, 73, 78, 85, 107, 138, 172, 193, 198, 203, 226

Sara McMahon: 14, 28, 67, 82 (*left*), 103 (*right*), 126, 147, 167, 184, 201

Ralph Todd: 44, 88, 109 (*right*)

Trevor Wilkinson: 15

The following images were hand-drawn by Dave Nurney: 11, 26, 40, 57, 79, 101, 123, 145, 165, 182, 200, 217

All other images were provided by the author

INDEX

Page numbers in **bold** indicate illustration

aconite, winter, 25
acorn, 147, 168, 173, 183, 184, 185
adder, 39, 46, 64, 152, 156, 207
admiral, red, 28, 138, 161, 162, 167, 190, 202, 207, 220
  white, 115, 128
agaric, fly, 196, **197**
agrimony, 130
  hemp, 128
alder, 27, 31, 50, 52
alexanders, 32, 68
algae, 10, 232
amplexus, 42
anemone (water-dwelling animal), 143, 144
  snakelocks, 144
anemone (plant), 41, **44**, 48
Anglesey, 36
apple, 25, **59**, 63, 167, 168, 173
  crab, 30, 186
angle shades, 14, **220**
ant, 80, 98, 109, 131, 133, 142
  black garden, 125
  wood, 148
ants, flying, 125, 142, 154
antlers, 52, 56, 74, 160, 193, 194, 207, 212, 224
aphid, 133, 147, 148, 166
  plum-reed, 152, 153
archangel, yellow, 83
argus, brown, 90, 108, 140, 162
  northern brown, 113, 131
  Scotch, 132, 142, 152
ash, 44, 50, 72, 83, 173, 175, 184, 202, 222
aspen, 27, 38
asphodel, bog, 171
autumn colour, 157
auk, great, 134

backswimmer, 71
badger, 27, 41, 58, 81, 102, 124, 146, 162, 163–4, 166, 175, 183, 201, 214, 219, 225
bales, 85, 105, 128
balsam, Indian, 171
barbel, 88
barley, 30, 44, 128, 149, 168, 186, 202
barnacle, 143
bat, 12, 59, 102, 104, 148, 166, 175–6, 202, 220, 228
  boxes for, 176
  brown long-eared, 176
  Daubenton's, 176
  detector for, 175, 176
  noctule, 176
beaches, 33, **112**, 143, 206, 227–8
  beachcombing, 227–8
beans (crop), 168

bedstraw, lady's, 108
beech, 52, 147, 157, 174, 175, 183, 184, 185
bee, 63, 80, 139–40,
  honey, **138**, 139
beet, sea, 154, 174
beetles, 71, 80, 98, 119, 120, 146, 188
  great diving, 72
  larvae, 11
  lesser stag, 141
  stag, 141
berries, 109, 123, 124, 125, 150, 168, 169, 170, 173, 174, 183, 185, 186, 202, 203, 219, 220, 222
Big Garden Birdwatch, 25
Big Schools Birdwatch, 25
bilberry, 110, 132, 152, 154, 174
bindweed, field, 130
  hedge, 129
  sea, 134
birch, 15, 52, 63, 159, 188
  downy, 64
  silver, 48, 64, 72, 177, 218
bird-feeding, 24–25, 28, 210–12, 219
birds of prey, 69–70, 168
bird song, 11, 13, 27, 28, 29, 58, 59, 77, 91–93, 101, 128, 219, 223, 230
bistort, amphibious, 133
bittercress, hairy, 174
bittern, 18, 224
blackberries, 146, 166, 170, 173, 179
  (see also bramble)
blackbird, 9, 28, 34, 38, 56, 81, 92, 115, 125, 138, 186, 203
blackcap, 25, 56, 63, **93**, 94, 128, 177, 191
blackthorn, 10, 38, 41, **45**, 63, 77, 86, 152, 175, 186, 203
bleak, 65
blenny, 144
blossom underwing, 43
blue, Adonis, 90, 108–9, **109**, 159
  chalkhill, 131, 138
  common, 94, 140, 151, 162
  holly, 52, 59, 135, 148, 162
  silver-studded, 121, 131
  small, 94, 108, 109
bluebell, 41, 53, 61, 68, **74**, 77
boar, wild, 12, 62, 202, 221
bog, 65, 87, 110, 116, 131, 132, 136, 204
bordered straw, 202
bracken, 104, 188
bramble, 24, 45, 86, 128, 129, 170, 174, 185
  (see also blackberries)
bream, 89
brimstone (butterfly), 14, **43**, 59, 82, 90, 142, 161, 162
brimstone (moth), 104, **167**
brindled beauty, 43

pale, 14
  small, 29
brooklime, 172
brown, meadow, 115, 130, 131, 162, 171
bryony, white, 107, 222
buckthorn, 161, 186
  sea, 47, 68, 173
buddleia, 160–2
bug, 71
bugle, 83
bullfinch, 28, 96
bullhead, 65
bulrush, 224
bumblebee, 27, 41, 43, 139
  red-tailed, 50
bunting, 221
  corn, 39, **101**, 154
  reed, 56
  snow, 88, **109**, **217**
burdock, 108
burnet (flower), great, 130
  salad, 107, 130
burnet (moth), five-spot, 109
  five-spot, 130
bur-reed, 224
butterbur, 47
buttercup, 86
butterflies, 9, 12, 27, 28, 41, 43, 59, 72, 122, 123, 129, 131, 143, 148, 160–2, 166, 167, 171, 185, 202
butterfly migration, 162, 190
butterwort, 87
buzzard, common, 69, **70**, 210, 211

cabbage, 161
  red (crop), 221
  wild, 48, 68
campion, bladder, 150
  red, 86
  sea, 112
  white, 150
canals, 136
carp, common, 111
carpet, autumn green, 14, 220
  common, 104
  garden, 104
  red-green, 14, 185, 220
carrot (crop), 221
carrot, sea, 154
caterpillar, 72, 81, 82, 103, 109, 131, 146, 147, 148, 151, 161, 207
catkins, 10, 15, 22, 31, 47, 64, 82, 87
catshark, 228
cattle/cows, 15, 63, 84, 85, 105, 128, 168, 186, 221
cauliflower (crop), 203
celandine, lesser, 29, 37, 41, 44, 229
centaury, seaside, 112
centipedes, 11
cereal crops, 16, 30, 44, 63, 85, 128, 149, 203

cetaceans, 157-159, 227
chaffinch, 28, 37, 76, 115, 185, 195
chantarelle, 196
chaser, broad-bodied, 136
  four-spotted, **137**
cherry, 63, 128
  bird, 129
  wild, 60, 68, 116
chestnut (moth), 14, 167, 220
  beaded, 185
  dark, 14, 220
  dotted, 14, 220
  red, 43
chestnut (tree), horse, 50, 72, 86, 159, 170, 177
  sweet, 127, **172**, 174, 185
chicken, 98
chicory, 150
chickweed, common, 14, 43, 174
chiffchaff, 41, 50, 90, 92, 128, 160
chlorophyll, 207, 208
chrysalis, 161
chub, 133, 224
churchyards, 25, 61, 98, 202, 232
cicely, sweet, 86
cinnabar, 151
cliffs, 20, 31, 33, 75, 113, 155, 158, 190
cloudberry, 131
clouded yellow, 34, 212
clover, 112
  red, 170
  suffocated, 68
  white, 170
coast, 18, 32-33, 47–8, 68, 89–90, 112, 134, 153–154, 172–173, 190, 205, 206, 217, 226
cockle, 68, 142, 206, 215, 226
cocksfoot, 131
coltsfoot, 37, 46
comma, 34, 161, 162, 191
conifer forests, 36
coot, 18, 52, 66, 67, 133
copper, small, 90, 140, 162, 171, 195
coppice, 61, 77
cormorant, 20, 56, 114, 206
cornel, dwarf, 131
cotton-grass, 87
cowberry, 109, 131
cow parsley, 32, 63, 86, 131
cowslip, 63, **85**, 108
crab, 143, 215
  hermit, 144
  shore, 144
cranberry, 109, 131
cranefly, 167
cranesbill, meadow, 170
crescent, green-brindled, 185
crimson speckled, 202
cricket, bush-, 130
crocus, 13, 26, 28, 171
crossbill, 29, 36

crow, carrion, 68, 202, 211
crowberry, 131
cuckoo, 38, 58, 74, **79**, 90, **94**, 95, 115, 123, 135
cuckoo-flower, 52, 83
curlew, 25, 90, 216
cuttlefish, 228

dace, 31
daddy-long-legs, 167
daffodils, 9, 13, **53**, 53–4, 123
    wild, 53, 54
daisy, 14, 184
    oxeye, 72
damselfly, 72, 111, 136–7
    azure, 111, 136
    common blue, 111, 136
    emerald, 111, 115, 142
    large red, 136
    northern, 132
    scarce emerald, 115, 140
    small red, 132
    white-legged, 111
dandelion, 14, 43, 174
darter, banded, 172
    common, 136
    Highland, 132
    yellow-winged, 172
dawn chorus, 11, 58, 91–3
dead-nettle, red, 184
    white, 220
deathcap, 196
deer, 166, 213
    Chinese water, 96, 214, 224
    fallow, 17, **73**, 74, 109, 113, 177, 187, 191
    red, 52, 99, 160, 175, 188, 193, 193–4, 199
    roe, 17, 38, 96, 109, 140, 192, 207, 212
    sika, 56, 96, 191, **204**, 214
demoiselle, banded, 96, 140
    beautiful, 96, 113
dipper, 18, 191, 223
diver, red-throated, 34, 50, 65, 111, 154
dock, 123
    broad-leaved, 170
dodder, 131
dogfish, 228
dogwood, 106, 170, 222
dolphin, 145, 157–8, 175, 191, 227
    bottlenose, 157, **158**, 159
    common, 158
    white-beaked, 158
dormouse, 12, 183
    edible, 94, 207
    hazel, 73, 140, 191, 207
dotted border, 29
dotterel, 87–8
dove, collared, 59, 149
    turtle, 74, 115, 129
drab, clouded, 43
    lead-coloured, 43
dragonfly, 72, 96, 110, 111, 123, 136–7, 172, 188
drey, 58, 81, 102, 214
droppings, 55, 213–14
drought, 125

dry-stone wall(ing), 21, 65
duck, 47, 48, 152, 189, 206, 226
    tufted, 39, 229
Duke of Burgundy, 83, 94, 109, 116
dun, 100
dunes, sand, 116, 152, 155
dunlin, 65, 117, 142, 206, 216
dunnock, 14, 25, 76, 92, 140, 219

eagle, golden, 35, 70
    white-tailed, 70
early moth, 14
earthworms, 39, 98, 124, 125, 146, 163, 202, 219
earth star, 196
eel, European, 65, 188
eel-grass, 20
eggar, small, 29
egret, little, 160
eider, 32
elder, 22, 73, 154, 159, 170, 174, 177
elm, 121, 130
    wych, 27, 30
emerald, brilliant, 132
    downy, 132
    northern, 132
emperor (dragonfly), 172
    lesser, 172
emperor moth, **87**,
emperor, purple, 121, 124, 128
engrailed, 43
escape movements, 16
estuary, 18, 19, 20, 32–3, 47–48, 68, 89–90, 112, 134, 153–4, 172–3, 190, 191, 206, 215–16, **224**, 226
evening primrose, 150

farmland, 15–16, 27, 29–30, 44–5, 62–3, 84–5, 99, 105, 128–9, 149, 168–9, 186, 202–3, 221
fat hen, 173
fawns, 96, 99, 109, 113, 193
feeding signs, 213–14
fen, 136
fennel, 187
fescue, sheep's, 151
fieldfare, 16, 25, 73, 184, 186, 221
figure-of-eight, 185
figwort, common, 171
    marsh, 171
finches, 24, 221
fish, 10, 17, 31, 41, 47, 65, 68, 71, 72, 88, 89, 99–100, 102, 111, 133, 134, 143, 152, 159, 218, 228
    migration, 65, 134, 145, 166, 172, 190–2
    (see also under individual fish)
flax, purging, 107
flies, 10, 62, 80, 170, 218
floods, 27
fly, kelp, 228
flycatcher, 166
    pied, 74, 84, **145**, 150
    spotted, 76, 94, 104, 113, 160, 175
fly-fishing, 99
fog, Yorkshire, 131
footman, rosy, **103**

foraging, 170, 173–4, 185
forget-me-not, field, 63
forsythia, 28
fox, 12, 22, 24, 50, 76, **97**, 97–8, 102, 154, 213, 214, 221, 227, 228
foxglove, 123, 126, **127**
fritillary (butterfly), dark green, 115
    Glanville, 96
    heath, 115
    high brown, 121
    marsh, 99
    pearl-bordered, 94, 104
    silver-washed, 128, 138
    small pearl-bordered, 96, 104, 110
fritillary (flower), snake's-head, 63
frog, common, 13, 27, 40, 42, 47, 51, 59, 66, 71, 81, 102, 125, 147, 166–7, 184, 201, 219
    marsh, 89
frost, 16, 18, 19, 24, 33, 57, 183, 200
fulmar, northern, 20, 89, 114
fungi, 117, 118, 195–7, 218, 232
    bracket, 196, **197**
fungus foray, 195–7

gadwall, 206
galls, 218
gannet, northern, 20, 113, 114, **115**, 173, 190
gardens, 13–14, 24–5, 28–9, 43, 51, 59–60, 81–2, 92, 97–8, 103–4, 105, 109, 125–6, 131, 147–8, 160–2, 163, 167, 184–5, 202, 219–20
garlic, wild, **61**, 174
gatekeeper, 129, 130, 140, 154, 162, 171, 173
gem, 202
gentian, autumn, 171
glasswort, 154
globeflower, 108
gnat, winter, 220
goat, wild, 46, 188
goby, 144
godwit, 216
    bar-tailed, 48, 76, 142, 154, 216
    black-tailed, 142, 154
goldcrest, 48, 184
goldeneye, 47
goldenrod, Canadian, 187
goldfinch, 25, 50, 99, 140, 169, 171
golf courses, 116
goosander, 47, 111
goose, 19, 48
    barnacle, 74, 177, 190
    brent, 19, 39, 48, 179, 189, 190
    Canada, 52, 133, 135
    greylag, **20**, 52, 179, 207
    pink-footed, 19, 74, 173, 195
    white-fronted, 19, 25, 48, 72, 179, 195, 206
goosefoot, red, 154, 190
    saltmarsh, 154
gorse, 17, 86, 223
goshawk, 69, 70
gothic, beautiful, 185
grass, 17, 19, 30, 34, 107, **108**, 203
    quaking, 107
grasshopper, 130, 165

grassland 17, 30, 46, 63–4, 86, 107–9, 120, 130–1, 133, 150–1, 170–1, 187, 200, 203–4, 222
    acid, 87, 152
    chalk (calcareous), 17, 61, 63, 64, 86, 87, 106, 107–9, 116, 131, 150, 151, 152, 186
gravel pits, 117, 136
grayling (butterfly), 140, 152
grayling (fish), 65
grebe, great crested, 18, 38, 66, 67, 142, 154, 172, 224
greenfinch, 24, 50, 81, 94, 135
grey, early, 43
    mottled, 43
groundsel, 17, 184, 220
grouse, red, 17, 157
gudgeon, 111
guelder rose, 129, 203
guillemot, 18, 114
    black, 114
gull, 30, 113, 114, 158, 173, 206, 226
    black-headed, 30, 226
    common, 30, 48, 226
    Iceland, 226
    glaucous, 226
    great black-backed, 226
    herring, 72, 114, 226
    lesser black-backed, 30, 38, 73, 226
    Mediterranean, 226
gurnard, grey, 134
    red, 134
gypsywort, 152

hair-grass, tufted, 107
hairstreak, black, 121
    brown, 150, 152
    green, 76, 87, 94, 115
    purple, 138, 148
    white-letter, 121, 130
hare, brown, 17, 25, 34, **48**, 49, 52, 68, 90, 214
    mountain, 25, 34–5, 38, 96, 192
harebell, 203
harem, 193, 194
harrier, marsh, 70, 113
harvest, 149, 168
hawker, 136, 172
    azure, 132
    brown, 172
    common, 172
    migrant, 172
hawk-moth, convolvulus, 202
    hummingbird, 166
    lime, 122
hawthorn, 30, 34, 52, 68, **85**, 160, 173, 174, 177, 203
    Midland, 85
hay-making, 105
hazel, **15**, 22, 147, 159, 167, 173, 174, 213
heart and dart, 104
heath (butterfly), large, 117, 132
    small, 94, 162, 171, 192
heath (plant), cross-leaved, 151, 188
heather, 17, 34, 35, 131, 146, **151**, 174, 188, 223
    bell, 151

heath(land), 17, 21, 30–1, 46, 64–5, 86, 87–8, 109–10, 120, 123, 131–2, 146, 151–2, 155, 156, 171, 188, **188**, 204–5, 222–3, **223**
hebrew character, **28**, 43
    setaceous, 122, **147**
hedgehog, 9, 12, 27, 41, 58, 80–1, 98, 102, 124, 146, 166, 183, 201, 214, 219
hedgerow, 29, 59, 85, 86, 105, 129, 130, 133, 173, 183, 222
heliotrope, winter, 223
hellebore, stinking, 15
helleborine, broad-leaved, 115
    dark red, 115
    dune, 113
    green-flowered, 121
    marsh, 135
    narrow-leaved, 90
    narrow-lipped, 112
    red, 121
    violet, 154
    white, 90
hemlock, 111, 196
herald, 220
herb robert, 168
heron, grey, 18, 31, 37, 50
hibernaculum, 102, 183
hibernation, 12, 27, 28, 41, 50, 55, 56, 73, 94, 133, 142, 161, 166, 173, 175, 176, 179, 184, 190, 199, 201, 202, 207, 217, 219
hobby, 74, 110, **111**, 115, 132, 157
hogweed, 107
    giant, 131
holly, 104, 148, 175, 220
    sea, 33, 112, 134
hollyhock, 170
honesty, 63
honey, 139, 140
honeydew, 126, 131, 148
honeysuckle, 104, 159, 185, 229
hop, 174
horehound, black, 187
hornbeam, 184, 185
hornet, 148
hornwrack, 228
hoverflies, 63, 165, 167, 202

incubation, 39
invertebrates, tree-boring, 11
iris, yellow, 133
ivy, 148, 159, 168, 202, 220

jack-by-the-hedge, 174
jackdaw, 72, 202, 211
jay, 56, 183, 185
jelly ear, **195**
jellyfish, 145, 191
juniper, 174, 205

kale, sea, 48
kelp, 33
kestrel, 30, 90, **168**
kingfisher, 18, 46–7, 76, 140
kite, red, 70, **210**, 210–12
kittiwake, 114, 173, 226
knapweed, black, 131, 171

knot, 52, 216
knotgrass, sea, 154
knotweed, Japanese, 170

ladybird, 11
lady's mantle, alpine, 131
lady's tresses, autumn, 159
    creeping, 135
    Irish, 154
lake, 18, 19, 31, **32**, 47, 65, **66**, 66–7, 89, 111, 133–4, 152–3, 172, 189, 206, 224
lambs, 30, 44, 63, 84, 168
lapwing, **16**, 30, 45, 72, 99, 179, 221
larch, 52, 222
lark, 90, 111, 132 (see also skylark, woodlark)
leaf-fall, 10, 177, 182, 191, 200, 207–9
leaf colour, 207, **208**, **209**
leatherjacket, 146, 167
leveret, 68, 90
lichen, 231–2, **233**
lily-of-the-valley, 83
lime, 30
    common, 126, 127
    large-leaved, 127
    small-leaved, 127
limpet, 143
    blue-rayed, 144
ling, 151
linnet, 68, 85, 86, 94
liverworts, 232
lizard, common, 39, 50, 138, **154**, 156, 192
    green, 156
    sand, 87, 109, 140, 156
    wall, 156
loach, stone, 65
loosestrife, purple, **132**, 133
lords-and-ladies, 29, 62, 127
lousewort, 171
lugworm, 215, 226

machair, 112
magnolia, 28, 41
magpie (bird), 17, 76, 81, 211, 214
magpie (moth), small, 104
maize (crop), 149, 166
mallard, 39, 206
mallow, common, 170, 174, 187
    tree, 154
mammals, small, 30, 102, 168, 179, 180–1, 188, 204
mammal-trapping, 180–1
maple, 30, 184
    field, 52, 168, 173, 179, 191
marigold, marsh, 47
marjoram, 107
marshes, freshwater, 18, 19, 31–2, 47, 66–7, 89, 111, 117, 133–4, 136, 152–3, 172, 189, 206, 224
    salt-, 90
marten, pine, 52, 159, 212
martin, house, 72, 76, 82, 133, 212
    sand, 41, 48, 56
mayfly, 72, 99–100
mayweed, sea, 68
meadowsweet, 111
mealworms, 230

medick, black, 170
melilot, 150
mercury, annual, 184
    dog's, 14, 29
merganser, red-breasted, 32
merlin, 90
mermaid's purse, 227
merveille-du-jour, 185
Michaelmas daisy, 187, 204
midges, 101, 103, 205
milkwort, common, 170
    chalk, 108
mimicry, 105
mink, American, 17, 55, 89
minnow, 50, 96
mint, water, 152
mist-netting, 176
mistletoe, 30, 220, 221
mole, 34, 115, 213, 214
molehill, 213, 214
molluscs, 10, 215
monkeyflower, 153
moorhen, 18, 52, 67
moor(land), 17, 27, 30–1, 34, 46, 58, 64–5, 87–8, 109–10, 111, 117, 120, 131–2, 146, **151**, 151–2, 155, 171, 188, 204–5, 222–3
    maritime, 89
moor-grass, purple, 17
moss, 17, 218, 231–2
moth, 9, 14, 27, 29, 104, 119, 120, 121–2, 123, 126, 166, 202, 220
    December, 218, 220
    March, 43
    northern winter, 220
    winter, 14, 220
moth migrants, 202, 220
moth-trapping, 121–2, 185, 220
mother-of-pearl, 104
moulting, 20, 25, 35, 58, 73, 74, 88, 96, 125, 132, 134, 135, 147, 152, 177, 188, 191, 192, 201, 206, 229
mountains, 34, 58, 188, 217
mouse, 213
    harvest, 142
    house, 180
    wood, 30, 52, 180, 181, 183, 185, 213
    yellow-necked, 185
muck-spreading, 85, 149
mugwort, 204
mullein, great, 150
mullet, grey, 134
muntjac, Reeves', 90, 140, 221
mushroom, 174, 195–7
    oyster, 15
    St George's, 87
muslin moth, **82**
mussel, 33, 68, 142, 206, 215
mustard, black, 174
    garlic, 50, 63, 82, 83
myrtle, bog, 64, 87

navelwort, 130
nestbox, 42, 82, 84
nest-building, 17, 31, 38, 45, 82
nettle, stinging, 86, 105, 161, 174

newt, 71, 111
    great crested, 47, 89, 117, 140, 199
    palmate, 47, 89, 117, 135, 207
    smooth, 47, 89, 117, 135, 207
nightingale, 18, 28, 72, 77, **78**, 94, 121, 145, 230
nightjar, 65, 96, **119**, 119–20, 121, **123**, 142
nightshade, deadly, 196
    enchanter's, 148
    woody, 106
nuthatch, 22, 24, 76, 185
nycteoline, oak, 14, 220
nymph, 100

oak, 52, 72, 82, **83**, 84, 148, 159, 168, 173, 183, 191, 222
    sessile, 84
oak beauty, 43
oats (crop), 128, 166, 202
ochre, brindled, 14, 185, 220
onions (crop), 149
orange, frosted, **184**
orange-tip, 9, 59, **60**, 68, 72, 76, **82**, 90, 115
orange underwing, 43
    light, 43
orange upperwing, 14
orca, 9
orchard, 59
orchid, 80, 107, 112, 116–18
    bee, 115, **117**, 118, 218
    bird's-nest, 76
    bog, 138
    burnt, 94, **116**, 117
    chalk fragrant, 96
    common spotted, 96
    coralroot, 96
    early marsh, 96
    early purple, 61, 117
    early spider, 76, 118
    fen, 116
    fly, 90, 118
    frog, 121
    ghost, 118
    greater butterfly-, 94, 117, 118
    green-winged, 76
    heath fragrant, 96
    heath spotted, 99
    lady, 76
    lady's slipper, 99, 118
    late spider, 121
    lesser butterfly-, 96
    lizard, 121
    man, 96
    marsh fragrant, 96
    military, 96
    monkey, 99
    musk, 118
    narrow-leaved marsh, 96
    northern marsh, 99
    pyramidal, 118, 124
    small white, 113
    southern marsh, 113
osier, 38
osprey, 68, 134
otter, 89, 90, 175, **205**, 206, 212, 213, 218, 228

ouzel, ring, 56, 65, 90, 132
owl, 92, 198–9
  barn, 30, **186**
  little, 76
  short-eared, 30, **200**
  tawny, 56, **198**, 198–9
oyster, 33
oystercatcher, 96
oyster-plant, 154

painted lady, 96, 161, 162, 195
pansy, dune, 68
parakeet, (rose-ringed), 24
parkland, 187
parr, 65, 191
parsnips (crop), 203
parsley, milk, 111
pasque flower, 63
pea, sea, 112
peach blossom, **126**
peacock (butterfly), 28, 34, 161, 162,
      173, 202, 218
pear, 168, 183
peas (crop), 45, 63, 85, 149
pennywort, wall, 130
perch, 47, 68, 172
peregrine, 24, 68, 69, 70, **206**
periwinkle, **142**, 215
pheasant, 221
phenology, 10
pilchard, 134
pine beauty, 43
pigs, 128
pigeon, 24, 59, 69, 98
  wood, 37, 39, 59, 76, 92, 127, 154,
      159, 220
pike, **18**, 31
pineapple weed, 128
pinion, brown-spot, 185
  pale, 14, **67**, 172
  tawny, 14, 220
pipistrelle, common, 60, 176
  Nathusius', 229
  soprano, 176
pipit, 111
  meadow, 52, 90, 132
  tree, 68
plankton, 153
plantain, sea, 112
plover, golden, 16, 39, 46, 76, 221
  grey, 216
  little ringed, 41, 50
  ringed, 32, 94
plum, 152
polecat, 17, 99, 160
pollination, 118
pond, 18, 31–2, 47, 51, 66–7,
      71–2, 89, 111, 125, 133–4, 136,
      152–3, 172, 189, 206, 224
pond-dipping, 71–2
pond skater, 71
poplar, 30,
  black, 47
  grey, 47
poppy, common, 90, **91**, 105, **106**,
      128, 174
  Welsh, 104
  yellow horned-, 112
porpoise, harbour, 157

potato (crop), 44, 63, 85, 128, 168, 186
primrose, 46, 73, 222
  bird's-eye, 86
  Scottish, 86
privet, wild, 222
ptarmigan, **88**, 110, 132, 188
puffball, 296,
  giant, 196
puffin, 113, 114
purslane, sea, 154, 190
pursuit-flights, 39

quaker, common, 43
  red-line, 185
  small, 43
  twin-spotted, 43
  yellow-line, 185
quail, 120
quarry, 116

ragworm, 215, 226
ragwort, 150
rabbit, 17, 24, 25, 34, 38, 49, 52,
      166, 212
ragged robin, 89
railway embankments, 150, 155, 187
ramsons, 61
rape, oilseed, 44, 63, 85, 128, 149, 168
raptors, 69–70
raspberry, wild, 129, 174
rat, common, 55, 98, 180
  'water', 55
rattle, yellow, 107
raven, 37, 46, 48, **210**, 211
ray, 228
razorbill, 114
redpoll, 24, 28
redshank, 90, 216
redstart, common, 68, 84, 94, 150,
      159, 166
redwing, 16, 25, 72, **182**, 184, 186,
      191, 221
reed, common, 89, 189, 224
reed beds, 13, 18, 23, 89, 152, 153,
      189, 201
reptiles, 10, 109, 155–6, 166
reservoir, 18
ringlet, 121, 130, 142
  mountain, 116, 132
rivers, 17, 31, 46–7, 55, 56, 65, 88–9,
      111, 132–3, 136, 152, 171,
      188–9, 190, 191, 192, 205–6,
      215, 218, 223–4
roach, 88
roadsides, 17, 25, 30, 46, 63–4, 86,
      107–9, 130–1, 150–1, 168,
      170–1, 174, 187, 195, 203–4,
      222
robin, 52, 73, 78, 81, 92, **103**, 117,
      154, 222, 230, **231**
rocket, sea, 112
rock-pools, 20, 143–4, 145
rock-rose, common, 131
rook, **26**, 38–9, 50, 202, 211
rookery, 38–9
roost(ing), 19, 22, 23, 104, 175, 176,
      202, 211, 215–16, 219
rose, 106, 174, 201, 204
  burnet, 106

dog, 94, 106, **107**, 157
rowan, 50, 52, 68, 132, 142, 152,
      159, 177
rudd, 68
rustic, autumnal, 167
  black, 167, 185
rut, 140, 166, 175, 187, 188, 191,
      193–4, 199, 202, 214, 221, 224

saffron, meadow, 171
sage, wood, 168
sallow, 185
  barred, 185
  dusky-lemon, 185
  pale-lemon, 185
  pink-barred, 185
salmon, (Atlantic), 47, 65, 90, 190–2,
      205, 223–24
saltwort, prickly, 190
samphire, rock, 33
sandbank, 112
sanderling, **215**, **229**
sandhopper, 228
sandpiper, common, 76, 88, 117
  curlew, 138, 154, 173
  green, 117, 133
satellite, 14, 220
saxifrage, purple, 31
scabious, field, 150
scoter, common, 32
  velvet, 32
scrub and thicket, 17, 30, 45, 63, 72,
      85–6, 106–7, 129–30, 150,
      169–70, 186, 203, 221–2
scurvy-grass, common, 68, 190
sea bean, 228
seabirds, 18, 20, 89, 113–14, 190
sea-blite, 154
  shrubby, 190
seaducks, 32
sea fan, 228
seal, common, 112, 117, 121, 134
  grey, 112, 225, **226**
sea lavender, 172
sea-spurrey, 112
sea-turtle, 155, 191
sea wash ball, 228
seaweed, 33, 143, 144, 218, 227,
      228
service tree, wild, 174
sett, 58, 102, **162**, 163–4, 201, 214,
      219
  see also badgers
shag, 20, 50, 114, 190
shank, velvet, 15
shanny, 144
shark, 191
  basking, 9, 145, 153, 173
  blue, 173
shearing, 84
shearwater, Manx, 90, 175
sheep, 16, 30, 44, 84, 105, 186,
      213, 221
shelduck, 134, 138
shell(fish), 68, 144, 228
  razor, 68, 142
  spire, 226
shoulder-knot, Blair's, 185, **201**
  grey, 14, 167, 185, 220

shoveler, 189
shrew, 12, 180, 181, 228
  common, 52, 96, 115, 181, 212
  shrike, great grey, 188
shrimp, 143, 215
silage, 85
silverweed, 17
silver Y, 14, 220
siskin, 28
skate, 228
skimmer, keeled, 132
skipper, chequered, 94
  dingy, 86, 94, 108, 157
  Essex, 116, 131, 138, 159
  grizzled, 63, 72
  large, 99, 108, 113, 135, 151
  Lulworth, 121, 138
  silver-spotted, 142, 151, 154, 157
  small, 115, 131, 135, 160
skua, 113, 172
  Arctic, **165**, 173
  great, 89, 90, 112, 113, 154, 173
skylark, 16, 34, 92, 96, 105, 135,
      138, 221
sloes, 175, 203
slow worm, 50, 109, 155, 156, 157,
      179
slug, 125, 146
smolt, 65, 90, 191
snail, 10, 12, 58, 71, 125, 126, 146
  great pond, 72
snipe, 87, 120
snake, Aesculapian, 156
  grass, 50, 74, 111, 156, 160, 192
  smooth, 87, **155**, 156
Sorbus whiteana, 86
sorrel, sheep's, 171
  wood, 29, 60
sow-thistle, **169**
snout, Bloxworth, 14, 220
  buttoned, 14, 220
snow, 10, 12, 16, 18, 26, 33, 35, 40,
      57, 183, 216, **218**, 222
snowberry, 222
snowdrop, 13, 14, 26, 28, 29, 33,
      53, 123
sparrow, house, 94, 138, 149
sparrowhawk, 24, 70, 94
spawning, 31, 42, 59, 6, 66, 68, 89, 96,
      111, 133, 152, 190, 191
speedwell, common field, 17
  germander, 46
  grey field, 17
sphagnum moss, 17, 110, 138
spindle, 221, **222**
spider, 125, 133, 177–8, 179
  garden, 178
  jumping, 178
  money, 178
  water, 72
  wolf, 178
spiders' webs, 177, 178, **179**
spinner, 100
spraint (otter), **212**
sprat, 134
sprawler, 220
spraying, 44
spring usher, 14, 28
sprouts, Brussels (crop), 221

spurge, petty, 14, 184
  Portland, 48, 68
  sea, 154, 190
squill, autumn, 154
  spring, 68
squinancywort, 108
squirrels, 12, 98, 102, 175, 213, 214
  grey, 9, 12, 27, 36, 41, **42**, 58, 81,
    102, 125, 147, 166, 183–4, **183**,
    185, 201, 219, 221
  red, 22, 36–7, **37**, 73, 94, 135, 184,
    191, 212
starfish, 144
starling, **22**, 23, 43, 73, 81, 94, 103,
  160, 170, 203, 216
stickleback, three-spined, 65, 71, 172
stitchwort, greater, 63
stoat, 24, 64, 73, 142, 229
stock, sea, 112
stonechat, 17, 76, 223
storm petrel, European, 90
strandline, 227, 228
strawberry, wild, 126, 146, 174
  cultivated, 126, 128
sugar beet, 16, 45, 85, 168, 186
sundew, common, 204
summer visitors/migrants, 35, 40,
  41, 58
swallow, 48, 56, **57**, 58, **62**, 63, 68,
  111, 113, 120, 132, 142, 160,
  166, 168–9, 177, 214
swallowtail, 96, 111
swan, Bewick's, 32, 195
  mute, 66–7, 188
  whooper, 179
swarming, 99–100, 125
swedes (crop), 221
swift, 72, 76, 82, 103–4, 111, 132,
  133–4, 140, 145, 154
sword-grass, 14, 220
  dark, 202
  red, 14, 220
sycamore, 50, 52, 60, 159, 168, 177

tadpole, 59, 71, 81, 102, 125, 166
tamarisk, 134
teal, 39, 206
teasel, 17, 150
Tegenaria domestica, 178
tellin, 142, 215, 226
tench, 89
tern, 158, 173
  Sandwich, 48

terrapin, red-eared, 156
thistle, 109, 128, 169, 170, 171
  carline, 17, 107
thorn, August, 167
  canary-shouldered, 167
  dusky, 167
  early, 167
  September, 167
thrift, 48, 68, 89, **135**, 190
thrush, 16, 186, 221
  mistle, 10, 22, 30, 68, 96, 103
  song, 13, 52, 65, 73, 92, 125, 126,
    135, 170, 186, 103, 227
thunder(storm), 79, 122, 123
thyme, wild, 86
tide, 143, 144, 158, 215–16, 227
tiger, scarlet, **130**
tissue, 14, 220
tit, 24, 59, 81, 185
  bearded, 189
  blue, 9, **11**, 12, 24, 27, 41–2, 56, 76,
    81, 82, 96, 102, 125, 147, 166,
    184, 201, 219, 224
  coal, 13, 24, 219
  great, 13, 24, 25, 76, 82, 96, 219
  long-tailed, 45, 72
  marsh, 39
toad, 37
  common, 47, **50**, 51–2, 66, 68,
    133
  natterjack, 56, 64, 66, 179
toadflax, common, 170
toadlet, 111, 133
toadstools, 196–7
tooth-striped, barred, 43
tortoiseshell, small, 28, 34, 135, 142,
  179, 202
tracks, 212–14
traveller's joy, 17, 129
treecreeper, 50, 76
trefoil, bird's-foot, 151
trout, brown, 99–100, 224
  sea, 205
twayblade, common, 76, 118
  lesser, 96

umbel(lifer)s, 63, 167
umber, mottled, 220
underwing, copper, 167
  lunar, 167, 185
upland, 17, 30–1, 46, 56, 63, 64–5,
  87–8, 109–10, 131–32, 151–2,
  171, 188, 204–5, 222–3

velvet, 38, 160, 193
vestal, 202
vetch, bush, 150
  common, 170
  horseshoe, 86, 109
  kidney, 107, 108
  tufted, 150
vetchling, yellow, 150
violet, 29, 104,128
  common dog, 29, 61, 104, 110
  marsh, 110
  sweet, 29, 61
vole, 24, 200
  bank, 30, **31**, 74, 180, **181**, 185,
    192, 213
  field, 30, **180**, 181, 214, 227
  water, 25, 55–6, **56**, 68, 113

waders, 27, 48, 206, 215–16, 226
wagtail, grey, 18, 76
  pied, 96, 135, 219
  yellow, 68
wall (butterfly), 94
warbler, 128, 166
  Cetti's, 18
  Dartford, 222
  garden, 74, 96, 160
  grasshopper, 72, 160
  reed, 73, 89, 94, 115, 142, 153, 160
  sedge, 74, 89, 99, 153
  willow, **45**, 56, 63, 94, 140, 150, 154
  wood, 84
warren, 49, 213
wasp, 34, 146, 170, 202
  common, 147
wayfaring tree, 150
weasel, 12, 73, 121
watercress, 173
water crowfoot, 111, 152
water-dropwort, hemlock, 111
waterfall, 190
water flea, 71
water-lily, white, 133
  yellow, 111
water plantain, 111
water scorpion, 72
water stick insect, 72
waxwing, 219
whale, 157–9, 227
  minke, 134, 157
  northern bottlenose, 157
wheat, 30, 44, 149, 166, 168, 186,
  202, 203

wheatear, northern, 35, **40**, 41, 65,
  94
whelk, common, 228
whinchat, 74, 99, 150, 160, 199
white, green-veined, 86, 90, 135, 159,
  161, 162, 202
  large, 59, 74, 82, 94, 138, 161, 162,
    191, 202
  marbled, 116, 131
  small, 50, 59, 82, 85, 90, 135, 161,
    162, 167
  wood, 83, 94
whitebeam, 86
whitethroat, common, 63, 73, 86, 94,
  99, 140, 157, 195
  lesser, 76, 96, 140, 160, 192
wigeon, 20, 191
wildcat, 73, 207
willow, 30, 222
  crack, 65
  goat, 25, 47
  grey, 47
  'pussy', 25, 65
willowherb, great, 133
  rosebay, 123, 150
winkles, 33
wintergreen, 131
wood (butterfly), speckled, 68, 104,
  115, 161, 162, 192
woodcock, 120, 202
woodland, 14—15, 24, 29, 44, 75,
  82–4, 92, 104–5, 116, 123,
  126–8, 133, 148, 167–8, 185,
  202, 207–9, 220–1, **221**
  ancient, 29, 44, 83
woodland floor flowers, 41, 44
woodlark, 39, 72
woodpecker, great spotted, 29, 35,
  73, 90
  green, 22
  lesser spotted, 39, 73
worms, 10, 11, 16, 71, 215
woundwort, hedge, 123, 150
  marsh, 172
wren, 18, 34, 90, 92, 117

yarrow, 174, 187
yellowhammer, 48, 99, 105, 142, 160
yew, 142, 202